ELECTORAL DYNAMISM OF INDIAN POLITICS

ELECTORAL DYNAMISM OF INDIAN POLITICS

Deciphering *the* Enigma

Bidyut Chakrabarty
Rajendra K. Pandey

Los Angeles | London | New Delhi
Singapore | Washington DC | Melbourne

First published in 2021 by

SAGE Publications India Pvt Ltd
B1/I-1 Mohan Cooperative Industrial Area
Mathura Road, New Delhi 110 044, India
www.sagepub.in

SAGE Publications Inc
2455 Teller Road
Thousand Oaks, California 91320, USA

SAGE Publications Ltd
1 Oliver's Yard, 55 City Road
London EC1Y 1SP, United Kingdom

SAGE Publications Asia-Pacific Pte Ltd
18 Cross Street #10-10/11/12
China Square Central
Singapore 048423

Published by Vivek Mehra for SAGE Publications India Pvt Ltd and typeset in 10/12.5 pt ITC Stone Serif by AG Infographics, Delhi.

Library of Congress Control Number: 2021944301

ISBN: 978-93-5479-050-8 (HB)

SAGE Team: Rajesh Dey, Syed Husain Naqvi, Sonam Rana and Rajinder Kaur

Dedicated to the colleagues at Visva-Bharati who, in adverse circumstances, stand for fairness, justice and fair play.

Thank you for choosing a SAGE product!
If you have any comment, observation or feedback,
I would like to personally hear from you.

Please write to me at **contactceo@sagepub.in**

Vivek Mehra, Managing Director and CEO, SAGE India.

Bulk Sales

SAGE India offers special discounts
for purchase of books in bulk.
We also make available special imprints
and excerpts from our books on demand.

For orders and enquiries, write to us at

Marketing Department
SAGE Publications India Pvt Ltd
B1/I-1, Mohan Cooperative Industrial Area
Mathura Road, Post Bag 7
New Delhi 110044, India

E-mail us at **marketing@sagepub.in**

Subscribe to our mailing list
Write to **marketing@sagepub.in**

This book is also available as an e-book.

Contents

List of Tables

List of Abbreviations

AIADMK	All India Anna Dravida Munnetra Kazhagam
AITC	All Indian Trinamool Congress
AJGAR	Ahir, Jats, Gujjars and Rajputs
BJD	Biju Janata Dal
BJP	Bharatiya Janata Party
BJS	Bharatiya Jana Sangh
BSP	Bahujan Samaj Party
CPI(M)	Communist Party of India (Marxist)
CPI	Communist Party of India
DMK	Dravida Munnetra Kazhagam
ISF	Indian Secular Front
JMM	Jharkhand Mukti Morcha
JP	Jayaprakash Narayan
NCP	Nationalist Congress Party
NDA	National Democratic Alliance
OBCs	Other Backward Classes/Castes
RJD	Rashtriya Janata Dal
RLD	Rashtriya Lok Dal
RSS	Rashtriya Swayamsevak Sangh
SAD	Shiromani Akali Dal
SCs	Scheduled Castes
SP	Samajwadi Party

Preface

A preface is just like a preamble to the book. Here, the author puts forward the major arguments that are distinctive of the book. The purpose here is twofold: on the one hand, by drawing attention to the arguments, the preface defends the point that the book is unique in the field of study, and on the other, it highlights the contention that the book is a stepping stone for further research on the theme that the book concentrates. *Electoral Dynamism of Indian Politics: Deciphering the Enigma* is a sequel to many of our books on changing texture of Indian democracy and governance. With the publication of *Indian Politics and Society since Independence: Events, Processes and Ideology* (2008) and *Indian Government and Politics* (SAGE, 2008) by Bidyut Chakrabarty and Rajendra K. Pandey, the journey had started. Immediately before the current publication, we had published a book entitled *Reconceptualizing Indian Democracy* (SAGE, 2020). While being involved in analysing the complex nature of the evolution and consolidation of democracy in India, we are guided by the consideration that this effort will lead others to undertake serious studies on this phenomenon. That democracy is just 'top-dressing', as B. R. Ambedkar apprehended, does not seem to be appropriate since regularly held elections confirm that for the Indian citizens, concern for constitutional democracy can never be undermined. With this assumption in place, one is persuaded to make two conceptually valid points: on the one hand, democracy has developed organic roots which are far more well entrenched than they appear on the surface, and one may also tweak, on the other, the system of governance but the attack on the foundational values on which democracy rests shall never be allowed. The 1975–1977 Emergency is an example: despite having adopted 'constitutional authoritarianism', the ruling party readily accepted the 1977 electoral verdict and transferred the baton to the victorious Janata Party.

Electoral Dynamism of Indian Politics is not just a study of the national elections held so far. On the basis of a thorough analysis of the voting behaviour, the text draws our attention to the fact that there is hardly a well-defined conceptual framework to comprehend how voters vote; there are many factors which one must take into account to arrive at a plausible explanation. Fundamental here is the point that since voting behaviour is also context dependent, one has to pay special attention to the contextual peculiarities in which elections take place. For instance, the defeat of the United Progressive Alliance in 2014 is attributed to its failure to weed out corruption in the government. Anti-incumbency sentiments decisively shaped the electoral responses in favour of the Bharatiya Janata Party led National Democratic Alliance in the 16th general elections.

A book is author's own articulation of a theme, though s/he is supported by many in this venture. We are grateful to have caring teachers who always supported us whenever we undertook challenging academic works. Our colleagues always stood by either as supporters or as opponents. The role of our family always remains critical to our academic pursuits. We will be failing in our duties if we do not recognize the importance of our students in putting our views in a perspective. Without them, it would not have been possible for us to sustain our academic search in circumstances which were not always conducive for creative works.

The preface shall remain incomplete without underlining the fact that this is one of the rarest ones in our repository of books because the book was incomplete when one of the authors was down with COVID-19 attack. In view of the uncertainty following the revelation that the COVID-19 virus attacked one of us, it was apprehended that the deadline for the submission of the manuscript was likely to be dishonoured. The apprehension did not appear to be unfounded since once the test result was announced, it affected everybody and all of a sudden, the world became a place of uncertainty and gloom. It caused irritation and was a source of agony because COVID-19 victims are also expected to remain socially isolated to avoid the spread of the virus. So it was a double punishment for the affected persons: being a victim, one undergoes the physical–mental trauma which no one is able to share; furthermore, forcible home isolation is also a deterrent to enjoy life in its full glory. Nonetheless, it was also a new experience to see life in the so-called neo-normal format. This was an occasion too to conceptualize human existence in a uniquely textured manner. Many of our behavioural patterns which were almost inconceivable in the recent past appear possible. COVID-19 has replaced most of the available conventional platforms for interactive dialogues with the new ones and they are now happily acceptable.

Isolated human existence of the COVID-19 victims does lay the foundation of collectivity based on care, compassion and concern for others. Although it does not happen in a vacuum, it is required to be articulated by human endeavour. At Visva-Bharati, we have an extremely compassionate human being, Sri Anirban Sircar, who has the only mission of serving his colleagues and those in dire needs. His job profile, as Visva-Bharati's public relations officer, does not adequately explain his domain of work since he knows no bounds when it comes to serving humanity. As soon as 16 of our colleagues were found COVID positive, it was Arindam who immediately arranged for them safe stay in one of the University guest houses and arranged food and medicine as instantaneously as possible. The authors also acknowledge the selfless effort of those who are associated with Anirban in his mission to serve the COVID-19 patients even in circumstances when there is a constant threat of being affected due to contamination. We, on behalf of Visva-Bharati, salute their courage and admire the steadfast commitment to serve humanity regardless of adversarial consequences.

In this battle against COVID-19, the fact that medical staff are absolutely essential is reinforced beyond doubt. Once the test results were made available, our doctors at PM Hospital undertook all medically required protocols in an electrifying speed. With Dr S. Debnath at the helm of affairs, his team of well-qualified doctors, paramedical staff and other sisters extended whatever help was required for relief. Visva-Bharati is proud and compliments these colleagues for being devoted to the cause.

The authors would like to mention Dr Partha Pal of Durgapur Mission Hospital who was a saviour to us when the symptoms appeared to be little disturbing. To give us immediate relief and also to suggest proper medication, Dr Pal suggested a series of tests which were of help to gradually weed out the symptoms. Along with an efficient team of doctors, paramedical staff and other supportive staff, Dr Pal is continuously engaged in serving the COVID-19 victims notwithstanding the possible threat of being contaminated. This is exemplary to all of us who tend to avoid social responsibility by one pretext or another in this neoliberal existence of humanity. Although the present viral attack is most debilitating for the globe, it has, thus, taught us again that UNITED WE WIN AND DIVIDED WE FALL.

Introduction

I

Elections are significant milestones in liberal democracies; they are also the first formal point of contact between the electorates and those seeking to win elections as their representatives. Elections are, therefore, a battle-deciding phenomenon that has gained near universal acceptance presumably because there is hardly a better alternative than this. That elections are also a mode of communication governed by individual/collective interests is very candidly described by James Mill in his 1820 text entitled 'Essay on Government' in which he admitted that 'it is indisputable that the acts of men follow their will, that their will follows their desires, and their desires are generated ... by their interests'.[1] Based on this assumption, he further argued that the Legislative Assembly 'must have an identity of interests with the community, otherwise it will make a mischievous use of its power'.[2] Representatives truly represent the collective interests. Acting as trustees of the nation, they constitute, in themselves, 'a microcosm of the nation [seeking to] maximize the happiness

---

[1] James Mill, *Essay on Government, Jurisprudence, Liberty of the Press and Law of Nations*, reprint (New York, NY: Bobbs-Merrill, 1955), 84.

[2] Ibid., 67.

of the whole community'.[3] Viewed in this perspective, representation is a complex relational idea because representation always entails one entity that represents and another entity that is represented.[4] Implicit here are two points: on the one hand, it is clear that representation is a two-way traffic in the sense that both the representatives and those who are represented are dialectically interconnected. Despite clearly being a relational phenomenon, representation is, on the other hand, perhaps the most effective means of interlinkages between the representatives and the represented. The argument highlighting the critical importance of representation is directed to suggest that elections that are meant to choose representatives remain an important device. In other words, elections and representation seem to follow each other since the latter is the outcome of the former. Whether it is liberal democracy or otherwise, elections are difficult to do away with presumably because they appear to be fair means of selection of representatives. In other words, notwithstanding some of the obvious limitations of the system of representation in liberal democracies, there is no doubt that election is perhaps the only time-tested design in which the *demos* get a chance to participate, though indirectly, in the decision-making.

In view of an interplay of a complex set of factors, India, after Independence, had adopted constitutional democracy of the Western variety drawn, to a significant extent, on the Westminster model of governance. Due to historical reasons, it had emerged as a logical corollary of the system of governance that seems to have evolved organically with the consolidation of democratic zeal of the people at the behest of the nationalist forces. Opposition notwithstanding, liberal democracy ultimately triumphed and created a space in which the idea that the *demos* remained a significant player in the formation of the government gained ground. The idea that liberal democracy

[3] A. H. Birch, *Representation* (London: Macmillan, 1971), 55.
[4] Jane Mansbridge pursues this point in her 'Clarifying the Concept of Representation', *American Political Science Review* 105, no. 3 (2011), 621–630.

was the best form of political system in which people reigned supreme gradually seeped in popular psyche which finally culminated in a series of nationalist campaigns in its favour. The seed was sown in 1882 when Lord Ripon adopted the famous Local Self Government Resolution of 1882 to introduce election for the formation of municipal councils in three presidency towns of Madras, Calcutta and Bombay. Regarded as the Magna Carta of local self-government, the Ripon Resolution ushered in a new era in India's journey towards democracy. As per the Resolution, the actual municipal administration was to be transferred to the elected representatives of the people working under a government-nominated chairperson who held the authority. It was a new beginning because the system of election to the municipal councils was introduced for the first time in India with a limited franchise. The aim was to involve the people in local governance which now figured prominently in the overall administration of the Raj. What was initiated in 1882 was further institutionalized in a number of governmental decrees and constitutional designs, such as the 1909 Morley–Minto and 1919 Montagu–Chelmsford reforms, which also confirmed the government's commitment to establish constitutional democracy in India. A sequel to the entire process of democratizing India, the 1935 Government of India Act was also a significant step in institutionalizing election as a mode of choosing the representatives who were to be bestowed with the responsibility of constituting the government. It did not come all of a sudden; there were series of nationalist campaigns which finally led to the acceptance by the Raj of democratic election in colonized India. By zealously participating in the 1937 election, Indians seem to have responded positively to the new set of democratic rights that, so far, remained distant. This election is also important because it moulded India in the liberal democratic matrix in which election was accepted as a legitimate means of electing the representatives. The 1937 election stands out because besides the two major contenders, the Indian National Congress and the Muslim League, there were some major regional players, such as the Unionist Party in Punjab and the Krishak Praja Party in Bengal, that also had won significant number of seats in the provincial legislative assemblies of Punjab and Bengal, respectively, as the following table shows.

Electoral Outcome of the 1937 Election in India

Province	Total Seats	Number of Seats for the Congress	Number of Seats for the Muslim League
Madras	215	159 (65%)	11 (28%)
Bihar	152	98 (75%)	20 (21%)
Bengal	250	54 (25%)	37 (33%)
Central Provinces and Berar	112	70 (61%)	27 (23%)
Bombay	175	86 (56%)	1 (11%)
United Provinces	228	134 (65%)	9 (21%)
Punjab	175	18 (13%)	
North-West Frontier Province	50	19 (42%)	
Sind	60	7 (12%)	
Assam	108	33 (42%)	
Orissa	60	36 (49%)	

Source: John Linlithgow, 'India Office Records, R/3/2/2' (8 February 1937).
Note: Figures in the parenthesis show the proportion of popular votes that had gone in favour of the Congress and Muslim League, respectively.

On a surface reading of the results, the 1937 outcome does not seem to be critical now though it was indicative of decisive changes in India's electoral behaviour. By being an important player in the nationalist politics, the Muslim League established its claim that it represented the Indian Muslims as well which was contrary to what the Congress had, so far, been maintaining. As the available literature demonstrates, the 1937 election had brought to the fore, in clear terms, what the Muslim League had espoused so far. In conceptualizing the 1940 Lahore Resolution which formally demanded partition on the basis of M. A. Jinnah's two-nation theory, the 1937 poll results had a critical role to play; the 1947 vivisection of India into two sovereign nations, India and Pakistan, was a continuity with what was conceptualized in the Lahore Resolution. As history has shown, electoral democracy has struck deep roots in India while it is not so in the case of Pakistan though elections were held on various occasions to legitimize the army rule there. A perusal of the history of electoral democracy in India confirms that it has become part and parcel of India's existence as a democracy except during the 1975–1977 Emergency when, with the suspension of the Constitution, it was feared that India was likely to deviate from democratic governance. The 1977 national poll, however, proved otherwise and journey of India as a democratic country had resumed. Basic here is the point that electoral democracy is integral to India's existence as a democratic country.

For representative democracy to succeed, elections remain paramount because *first*, by putting the voters on the centre stage in voting, it provides them with an opportunity to evaluate the incumbent political authority during its reign in power. In this sense, it is also an occasion for auditing the performances of the ruling parties in governance. *Second*, elections are an index of the importance of the issues that gain prominence during the campaign for votes. In view of the breakdown of 'the vote banks', elections have largely become issue based. It is true that there always remain some major issues which tend to galvanize the voters regardless of age and social locations. But the crucial shift in voting is generally attributed to area-specific issues or issues that sway specific sections of population than the rest. *Third*, elections are also commentaries on the electoral viability of the political parties and their leadership. It is obvious that the electoral outcome is critical for the future of the political parties that participate in the elections; it is equally significant for the leadership that, if failed to capture popular imagination, is likely to fade away. In other words, political leadership is a crucial component in electoral battle, just like the party organization which by projecting a specific type of leadership, seeks to gain politically in competitive situations.

Fourth, the electoral outcomes are also indicative of the changing nature of the political parties involved in elections. Just like the leadership, parties cannot survive if they are not amenable to change in terms of the ideological preferences that they prefer to project both during the election campaign and in its aftermath. In other words, unless political parties are organic to the system in which they are located, the chances of their survival are low, if not bleak. What it suggests is the fact that political parties need to reinvent themselves in tune with the surrounding social, political and economic milieu simply because they, in a liberal democracy, are the most time-tested vehicle for articulating new values, ideas and perspectives. The British Conservative Party is known for clinging to 'orthodox' values and yet its nature has undergone radical changes in contrast with what it was in the past. Similarly, the Congress Party in India that was so enthusiastic about 'socialist values' in the past began appreciating 'the neoliberal' values since the 1990s. Even in the past national elections, the importance that the Congress Party gave to 'economic liberalization' clearly suggests that the Party is seeking to shake off its earlier ideological mould.

Fifth, elections are important 'moments' for the country in two specific ways: one, in a diverse 'Third-World' situation, it is impossible, if not difficult, to identify issues that will gain political salience in elections. In the 2004 Lok Sabha poll, both the pan-Indian political parties in India, the Congress and the Bharatiya Janata Party (BJP), raised more or less similar issues packaged in a calibrated response to economic liberalization. The outcome was not dramatic in the sense that both the parties were more or less evenly poised in terms of Lok Sabha seats. In extraordinary circumstances, however, the election results are most likely not to conform to what is projected. The outcomes of the 1977, 1984 and 1991 Lok Sabha polls in India are illustrative here because of the peculiar circumstances that arose in the aftermath of the 1975–1977 Emergency, or the assassination of Indira Gandhi in 1984 and Rajeev Gandhi in 1991, and radically altered the electoral behaviour that manifested in the results. These elections, characterized as 'plebiscites', though exceptional, reflect a particular moment of the national mood that was translated into votes. Two, elections are also moments when the organizational strength of the political parties is tested and assessed.

It is true that 'swing' is a critical factor in elections in the first-past-the-post system though organization is what sustains the party regardless of whether it wins or not. Organization is 'the life wire' of political parties in any ideological set-up. One of the reasons for the growing decline of the Congress Party is certainly 'the weakening' of its organization since the breakdown of the Congress system of the earlier days. A contrasting example of the Left Front that ruled West Bengal for almost three decades will suffice here to show the importance of organization in con-solidating its position in the state. The continuity of the Left Front government in West Bengal for more than three decades is attributed to the organizational grip that its leading partners, the Communist Party of India (Marxist); (CPI(M)) had over the voters in the state. It was possible for the CPI(M) to remain politi-cally viable, if not invincible, largely because the party leadership did not seem to be averse to reinvent its strategies by taking into account the changing social, economic and political circum-stances. Furthermore, it would not have been possible for the Front to translate its near acceptance by the majority of the West Bengal voters into votes without a well-entrenched organization that gradually evolved in state. What is, thus, significant, as the West Bengal example demonstrates, is the fact that an appropri-ate strategy leads to successful electoral mobilization provided there exists a strong organization with tentacles at the grassroots.

Sixth, the poll results also indicate the growing importance of new segments of society that hardly mattered in politics. In this sense, election provides a mechanism for social mobility. As evident in most of the recently conducted elections in India, the decline of the upper/forward-caste dominance follows the ascendancy of the Other Backward Classes/Castes (OBCs) in political decision-making. The emergence of these hitherto peripheral segments of Indian society has brought about radical changes at the grassroots. The increasing importance of OBCs and the Scheduled Castes (SCs) in contemporary Indian politics redefined the political discourse that remains largely unidimensional presumably because of the centrality of the dominant castes in its articulation. Indian elections—whether at the national or provincial levels—seem to be symptomatic of social transformations in the sense of 'the rise and fall' of caste groups in various forms. *Seventh*, elections seem to articulate a process of interaction between civil society and state. The so-called anti-incumbency wave can, for instance, be conceptualized as civil society's backlash against the state. Similarly, following Gramsci, the Italian Marxist, one can also argue that civil society also acts as a buffer for the party holding state power. Election results are illustrative of whether the civil society is a buffer for or against the prevalent political authority. The outcome of the 2011 West Bengal Assembly elections that replaced the incumbent Left Front government after an uninterrupted rule of more than three decades demonstrates how the civil society activists acted in shaping the poll outcome.

Finally, elections are also an occasion when the federal balance of the Indian polity is clearly tilted in favour of the union government in various ways. The growing importance of the Election Commission in elections in India reduces the role of state-centred governmental agencies, including the police. With its non-controversial image, the Election Commission is readily accepted by the voters and its role in conducting free and fair election is highly acclaimed. Whether the intervention of a supra-state agency is conducive for federal practices is debatable though this is indicative of processes contributing to the refashioning of India's federal texture. But there is no doubt that the revamped Election Commission has changed the complexion of election in India in recent times by being proactive. While the poll outcome in the 2005 Bihar election is largely attributed to the role played by the Election Commission in containing the poll malpractices, in West Bengal, the Commission's intervention in 2011 assembly elections was condemned as 'unwarranted' for indulging in 'practices' that provoked mass consternation in both urban and rural West Bengal. Nonetheless, in view of the well-entrenched malpractices in elections, the Election Commission is perhaps one of the most significant constitutional machineries that, by being true to its constitutional obligation, can be said to have visibly refashioned elections in India.

II

Election is not merely a process of expressing one's politico-ideological choice, it is also a specific voice at a particular juncture of history. For instance, the contribution of the Indian National Congress was critical to its massive victory in the first national election, held in 1952; the nationalist zeal of the voters was reflected by their electoral choice. As history of election shows, the scene did not remain the same later. Voters' preference was determined by other politico-ideological priorities, as the book demonstrates. This is conceptualized at two levels: at the level of theory, it can be articulated merely as voters' choice based on what they deem appropriate at a particular historical juncture; at another level, the electoral decision, being a contextual response, is an outcome of how the prevalent milieu shapes how the electorates choose their candidates. The moot point is about the changing nature of the elections and the politico-ideological voices that gain pre-eminence at a particular period of history. What governs the electoral choice is, thus, a complex set of factors which are required to be taken into account to provide a persuasive description how elections are fought and how the voters choose their representatives.

Given the peculiar texture of Indian democracy, one should also remember that Indian elections cannot be meaningfully understood within the derivative framework of analysis. It is a matter of common knowledge that none of the classical theorists was sure whether the electoral democracy of the Western variety will survive in India in view of her sociocultural diversity. Yet democracy has flourished in India which confirms that its growth is linked with the consolidation of a mindset. In other words, the unfolding of democracy in India draws on and contributes to the mindset that was favourably disposed towards the increasing importance of democratic ethos in course of time. In order to understand the exact nature of democracy and elections in India, what is critical is to comprehend the dialectics between the mindset and the context in which democracy and a concomitant electoral system evolve as integral to her rise as a polity. Hence, it is fair to describe India as 'a liberally oriented multi-communal democracy [in which] both individuals and ethnic and religious communities lie at its basis, making it both an association of individuals and a community of communities'.[5] Implicit in the argument are two fundamental points that deserve attention: on the one hand, to win election, the candidates have to be sensitive to India's sociocultural texture. An appeal, directed in communal or ethnic terms, may not always work presumably because of the prevalence of multiple communities with multiple politico-ideological priorities. That India continues to be liberal is based, on the other, on the claim that elections are the only acceptable design to express the voters' choice when they are asked to do so. Taken together, these two points direct our attention to a wider argument suggesting that democracy and elections go in tandem. That it hardly requires further elaboration can easily be established by a careful scan of the elections that India witnessed since the first national poll, held in 1952. As the available studies on polls show, elections are an occasion when individual leadership of the contending political parties is as critical as the politico-ideological agenda that it seeks to pursue once elected to power. Here too, what is emphasized is the critical role that leadership plays while championing a specific political agenda. Hence, the leadership such as Jawaharlal Nehru, Indira Gandhi and later Narendra Modi stand out presumably because they shaped, to a significant extent, the electoral behaviour in their favour which does not however preclude the critical importance of the ideological priorities that they represented. For instance, Nehru's initial electoral success was largely the outcome of the role that he had in

[5] Peter Ronald deSouza, Hilal Ahmed, and Mohd. Sanjeer Alam, 'Foreword' by Bhikhu Parekh, in *Democratic Accommodations: Minorities in Contemporary India'* (New Delhi: Bloomsbury, 2019), xviii.

wresting power from the colonial authority. In other words, the nationalist sentiments acted critically in his favour. Indira Gandhi's socialistic governance was one of the major factors that ensured her successive poll victories, especially in 1977 and 1980, while Narendra Modi's electoral win in 2014 and 2019 was largely an endorsement of Hindutva and the Right-wing-tilted economic agenda. Illustrative here is the point that there is hardly a set method of electoral victory; one needs to comprehend the phenomenon by taking into account the critical roles that the leaders uphold while campaigning for votes in support of specific ideological priorities.

There are three important points that need attention here. First, the competitive elections provide many conceptual ideas which help us understand how democratic voice is articulated at the grassroots in response to the political agenda that leaders uphold. The idea is simple because it seeks to capture the theoretical claim that the voters' choice is governed, to a great extent, by how they view the ideas that the leaders represent during campaign for the party to which they belong to. Second, a careful scan of the election campaign and how it unfolds are illustrative of the contextual influences shaping the voting behaviour. There are, of course, contrasting politico-ideological claims that the contending parties represent. Nonetheless, the poll outcome shows which claims play critical roles in determining the way the voters vote. On occasion, there are triggering factors which decisively affect the voters while casting their votes. The assassination of the incumbent prime minister, Indira Gandhi, in 1984 and the opposition leader Rajiv Gandhi in 1991 were such examples showing how the dastardly killing of these two leaders of the Congress ensured victory in Lok Sabha with a massive majority. Similarly, the 2019 surgical strike in Balakot in Pakistan by the Indian Air Force acted decisively in generating support for the ruling National Democratic Alliance (NDA). Finally, the regular holding of elections in India since 1952 confirms that liberal democracy is no longer peripheral to the Indian mindset but has organically evolved with India's growth as a polity with firm commitment to the fundamental precepts of the philosophy of Enlightenment. The fact that elections have been accepted as the only constitutionally legitimate mode of electing rulers reinforces the argument that political democracy has survived surmounting great odds though B. R. Ambedkar expressed his doubts about this in his final speech on 25 November 1949 in the Constituent Assembly. This is a matter of great satisfaction for the nationalists who not only removed the alien rule but also laid a solid foundation for liberal democracy that has flourished in the course of time.

III

Elections are integral to the growth of democracy in India for the following reasons. *First*, elections provide an opportunity to the voters for evaluating the incumbent political authority. In this sense, it is also an occasion for auditing the performances of the ruling parties in governance. *Second*, elections are an index of the importance of the issues that gain prominence during the campaign for votes. In view of the breakdown of 'the vote banks', elections have largely become issue based. It is true that there always remain some major issues which tend to galvanize the voters regardless of age and social locations. But the crucial shift in voting is generally attributed to area-specific issues or issues that sway specific sections of population than the rest. *Third*, elections are also commentaries on the electoral viability of the political parties and their leadership. It is obvious that the electoral outcome is critical for the future of the political parties that participate in the elections; it is equally significant for the leadership that, if failed to capture popular imagination, is likely to fade away. In other words, political leadership is a crucial component in electoral battle, just like the party organization which by projecting a specific type of leadership, seeks to gain politically in competitive situations. *Fourth*, the electoral outcomes are also indicative of the changing nature of the political parties involved in elections. Just like the leadership, parties cannot survive if they are not amenable to change in terms of ideology which they prefer to project both during the election campaign and otherwise. In other words, unless political parties are organic to the system in which they are located, the chances of their survival are low, if not bleak. What it suggests is the fact that political parties need to reinvent themselves in tune with the surrounding social, political and economic milieu simply because they, in a liberal democracy, are the most time-tested vehicle for articulating new values, ideas and perspectives. The British Conservative Party is known for clinging to 'orthodox' values and yet its nature has undergone radical changes in contrast with what it was in the past. Similarly, the Congress Party in India that was so enthusiastic about 'socialist values', especially so long as Indira Gandhi held power, began appreciating 'the neoliberal' values since the 1990s. Even in the 2004 national elections, the importance that the Congress Party gave to 'economic liberalization' clearly suggests that the Party is seeking to shake off its earlier ideological mould. *Fifth*, elections are important 'moments' for the country in two specific ways: *first*, in a diverse 'Third-World' situation, it is impossible, if not difficult, to identify issues that will gain political salience in elections. In the 2004 Lok Sabha poll, both the pan-Indian political parties in India, the Congress and the BJP, raised more or less similar issues packaged in a calibrated response to economic liberalization. The outcome was not dramatic in the sense that both the parties were more or less evenly poised in terms of Lok Sabha seats. In extraordinary circumstances, however, the election results are most likely not to conform to what is projected. The outcomes of the 1977, 1984 and 1991 Lok Sabha polls in India are illustrative here because of the peculiar circumstances that arose in the aftermath of the 1975–1977 Emergency, or the assassination of Indira Gandhi in 1984 and Rajeev Gandhi in 1991 radically altered the electoral behaviour that manifested in the results. These elections, characterized as 'plebiscites', though exceptional, reflect a particular moment of the national mood that was translated into votes. *Second*, elections are also moments when the organizational strength of the political parties is tested and assessed. It is true that 'swing' is a critical factor in elections in the first-past-the-post system though organization is what sustains the party regardless of whether it wins or not. Organization is 'the life wire' of political parties in any ideological set-up. One of the reasons for the growing decline of the Congress Party is certainly 'the weakening' of its organization since the breakdown of the Congress system of the earlier days. A contrasting example of the Left Front that ruled West Bengal for almost three decades will suffice here to show the importance of organization in consolidating its position in the state. There is no doubt that the leading partner of the Left Front, CPI(M), is perhaps the most organized party in India that remains politically viable, if not invincible, by regularly reinventing its ideology by taking into account the changing social, economic and political circumstances. It would not have been possible for the Front to translate its redefined ideology into votes without a well-entrenched organization that gradually evolved in West Bengal. What is, thus, significant, as the West Bengal example demonstrates, is the fact that ideology becomes a powerful vehicle for electoral mobilization provided there exists a strong organization with tentacles at the grassroots. *Sixth*, the poll results also indicate the growing importance of new segments of society that hardly mattered in politics. In this sense, election provides a mechanism for social mobility. As evident in most of the recently conducted elections in India, the decline of the upper/forward-caste dominance follows the ascendancy of OBCs in political decision-making. The emergence of these hitherto peripheral segments of Indian society has brought about radical changes at the grassroots. The increasing importance of OBCs and SCs in contemporary Indian politics redefined the political discourse that remains largely unidimensional presumably because of the centrality of the dominant castes in its articulation. Indian elections—whether at the national or provincial levels—seem to be symptomatic of social transformations in the sense of 'the rise and fall' of caste groups in various forms. *Seventh*, elections seem to articulate a process of interaction between civil society and state. The so-called anti-incumbency wave can, for instance, be conceptualized as civil society's backlash against the state. Similarly, following Gramsci, the Italian Marxist, one can also argue that civil society also acts as a buffer for the party holding state power. Election results are illustrative of whether the civil society is a buffer for or against the prevalent political authority. The successive poll victories of the Left Front in West Bengal between 1977 and 2006 are a testimony here. *Eighth*, elections are also an occasion when the federal balance of the Indian polity is clearly tilted in favour of the union government in various ways. The growing importance of the Election Commission in elections in India reduces the role of state-centred governmental agencies, including the police. With its non-controversial image, the Election Commission is readily accepted by the voters and its role in conducting free and fair election is highly acclaimed. Whether the intervention of a supra-state agency is conducive for federal practices that are being refashioned in a newly emerged coalitional context is debatable. But there is no doubt that the revamped Election Commission has changed the complexion of election in India in recent times by its proactive role. While the poll outcome in the 2005 Bihar election is largely attributed to the role played by the Election Commission in containing the poll malpractices, in West Bengal, the Commission's intervention in 2011 assembly poll was condemned by the ruling Left Front as 'unwarranted' for indulging in 'practices' that provoked mass consternation in both urban and rural West Bengal. Nonetheless, in view of the well-entrenched malpractices in elections, the Election Commission is perhaps the most significant constitutional machinery that has meaningfully redefined elections in India. In contemporary polls, as the evidence shows, the proactive role of the Election Commission is hailed since it contributes to the holding of free and fair elections in India, a phenomenon that appears to have disappeared with the increasing criminalization of the electoral battles in recent years. Constitutionally empowered (Articles 324–329 of Part XV of India's Constitution), the Election

Commission can be said to have created an environment which should have been the case to sustain Indian democracy in its true spirit. *Finally*, whatever may have been the nature of elections in India, a careful scan of the 17 national elections, held so far, reveals that the zealous participation of the voters in elections strengthens participatory democracy in India. It is true that voters' choice may not always be ideology driven, yet it gives adequate inputs to suggest that their enthusiastic involvement demonstrates that, for them, election is an occasion to establish the claim that they continue to remain an important player in Indian democracy. There are two aspects here: on the one hand, by being stringent in fulfilling its role, the Election Commission discharges its constitutional role as efficiently as expected. The critics, however, characterize the role as 'excessive' because 'a robust and [seemingly] impartial Election Commission of India', instead of serving as a constitutional wing is reduced to be a wing of the incumbent government which is 'ultimately harmful for Indian democracy'.[6] By drawing attention to the way the Election Commission functions during an election, it is further argued that the excessive bureaucratic surveillance creates an milieu which is actually deterrent to the expressing of voters' preferences without fear.[7] Whether the argument has substance is debatable. Nonetheless, there is no denying that the proactive role of the Election Commission has ushered in a new era in India's democratic history which defends the claim that 'the ECI [Election Commission of India] is a trusted body [in comparison] with other institutions of the state, both political and bureaucratic'.[8] In view of its success in largely combatting electoral malpractices and helping create an environment where voters are free to cast their without intimidation.

[6] Partha Chatterjee, 'Cleaning Up Democracy', *The Telegraph*, Kolkata, 16 March 2006.
[7] Ujjwal Kumar Singh and Anupama Roy have highlighted this point in their *Election Commission of India: Institutionalizing Democratic Uncertainties* (New Delhi: Oxford University Press, 2019).
[8] Ibid., 221.

No study of election becomes complete without discussion of the nature of campaign for soliciting votes. Here too, one notices striking changes over time. The 1952 election was held at the backdrop of the success that the nationalist leadership had attained in wresting power from the British. The election campaign was couched accordingly. Given the popularity of the Congress leadership, the task of winning a majority appeared to be easier. It was also less difficult since the Congress Party was able to accommodate the dissenters, to a significant extent, in view of the fact that it was largely an umbrella organization that was not, at all, ideologically rigid. In other words, as the euphoria over independence continued, the Congress candidates drew the voters rather easily to them. As days passed on, the scene became complicated and it was not possible for the Congress to retain its popularity presumably because of the failure of the government to fulfil most of the major election pledges. As a result, there had emerged a chasm between the Congress and the voters. What was, so far, effective in garnering votes did not appear to work in the elections that followed, especially the second Lok Sabha poll in 1957. A careful analysis of the election campaign demonstrates that there were three major features which the party leadership usually deployed to seek votes. First, it was a common feature that the top and popular leaders were invited to address the voters in selective places. In their speeches, as the contemporary evidence shows, they remained confined to the poll manifestos that were generally released before the campaign took off. The speeches were also ideologically coached. For instance, while Jawaharlal Nehru in his electoral speeches always hammered on his heartfelt belief in socialistic pattern of society, his bête noir, Chakravarti Rajagopalachari, by highlighting the shackle-free economy, always expressed his difference, though in a very civilized manner. In other words, a scan of the campaign speeches reveals that it was primarily an ideological battle, waged by reference to their respective preferences. Second, the nature of the poll campaign began changing with the 1967 State Assembly poll between those within the Congress and the dissenters who left the Congress and formed new political outfits. For the first time, in India's political history, the election campaign started in an environment of distrust. Both the Congress and its opposition lost no opportunity to expose the weaknesses of the contending political parties; nonetheless, it remained a battle that was more or less governed by the failure of the incumbent government and the hype of hope for the voters if the opposition was voted to power. From the 1971 Lok Sabha poll, one notices a radical shift in the election campaign. Instead of focusing on plethora of issues, the outcome of elections was determined by one major slogan or issue. Parliamentary elections became, in effect, a single-issue referenda'.[9] Describing this phenomenon as 'plebiscitary politics', Rudolphs attributed its rise to the de-institutionalization of the Congress.[10] The Congress victory was attributed to its strategic resort to populist or plebiscitary politics in terms of electoral and mobilizational strategies. The Lok Sabha elections, held so far since 1971, were decided not by plethora of promises, made in election pledges, but by a single slogan which appeared decisive at a particular point of time because of peculiar historical circumstances,[11] as evident in parliamentary elections: in 1971, it was *garibi hatao* (remove poverty) which helped the Congress gain power; in 1977, *Emergency hatao* (remove politicians responsible for 1975–1977 Emergency) generated mass support for the Janata Party; in 1980, *Janata hatao* (replace the Janata Party government for its chronic instability) helped the Congress return to power; in 1984, *desh bachao* (save the country) acquired a new majoritarian connotation following the assassination of Indira

[9] Achin Vanaik, *The Painful Transition: Bourgeois Democracy in India* (London: Verso, 1990), 93.
[10] L. I. Rudolph and S. H. Rudolph, The Congress Party: Deinstitutionalization and the Rise of Plebiscitary Politics, in *In Pursuit of Laxmi: The Political Economy of the Indian State* (New Delhi: Orient Longman, 1987).
[11] Vanaik, *The Painful Transition*, 93–97.

Gandhi in 1984 which created a conducive environment for the Congress in contrast with the opposition parties; in 1989, *corruption hatao* (remove the Congress government for its involvement in the Bofors scandal) made the task easier for the Janata Dal to dislodge the Congress from power. The scene continued: in 2014, the Congress lost to the BJP given the alleged involvement of the former in corruption; the 2019 Lok Sabha poll determined the outcome largely due to the popularity of the BJP star campaigner and the incumbent prime minister, Narendra Modi, who, along with his agenda for development, was easily acceptable by the voters presumably because of the popularity of Hindutva as a persuasive ideological preference. The rise of plebiscitary politics led to the decline of the party system. In order to obtain votes, individual leadership appeal became far more important than the party which appeared insignificant in elections.

As argued, the decline of the party offsets the rise of the leadership: the party maverick is the mascot for electoral campaigns. The trend was visible once Indira Gandhi rose to prominence; it is being continued now as the last two Lok Sabha polls show. In both the 2014 and 2019 national elections, it was Narendra Modi who was always projected even in the State Assembly elections which confirms that his charisma was enough to bring voters in BJP's favour. That leadership is very crucial in winning elections is a noticeable transformation in India's polls. While this is an important development which one should not ignore, there are also radical changes in the nature of election campaign in which political parties participate to create a constituency of supporters for them in elections. This is an inescapable feature that neither the party activists nor its leaders pay attention to the way the campaign is caried forward. The language of political speeches by the leaders and their disciples while attacking and counter-attacking their opponents to show their capability of augmenting the votes for them has clearly lost the limits of civility. Despite scathing criticisms in the public domain, the quality of the language has hardly changed. There is scarcely any dearth of example as evidence from recent election campaigns underline. It is true that to garner votes, the leaders often resort to smear campaign which actually generates support for the party that they represent. As it appears to be effective in gaining votes, there are hardly attempts to stop this, which, despite being severely criticized by a section of the voters, remains integrally connected with the election campaign. Here, a detailed exposition of how the election campaign is coached in West Bengal just on the eve of 2021 State Assembly election shall be helpful in illustrating the above point.

There is a similarity between the 2021 and 2011 West Bengal State Assembly elections. The main objective of the parties opposed to the incumbent ruling authority is to bring about *badal* or change. The Trinamool Congress (TMC) came to power initially with the slogan, *badal chai badla noi* (we want change, not revenge). What was strikingly dissimilar this time was that the main contender for power in West Bengal was a pan-Indian party, the BJP, which was operating within a strategy to dislodge the present government. The 2021 election stands out also because the erstwhile archenemies, the Congress and the Left parties, had already formed a coalition to fulfil their electoral goals. It is also worthwhile to note that although the election was to be held in the months of April–May, political parties appeared to have brought out the big guns much ahead of schedule. By bringing out star campaigners, including the prime minister and other important office-bearers from Delhi, the BJP had implemented its plan of action well in advance. The ruling party had similarly revved up, by organizing meetings in those areas where the BJP bigwigs had held meetings in the immediate past. The Congress–Left conglomeration had already reached an agreement over the share of seats in the election.

At the preparatory stage, the 2021 election looked very different from the earlier polls in Bengal. The following features stand out: *first*, the recrudescence of violence was unprecedented. Voters were threatened with dire consequences, including even death. By being not adequately active, the state police expressed how helpless were their members, largely due to the politicization of the forces. Before the actual battle, the major contending parties seemed to have gathered weapons to demoralize the opposition: cases of disproportionate income were being investigated and innumerable criminal cases were being lodged against even the union ministers and those who were identified by the state as supporters of the BJP. *Second*, the coarse language that was being used by those holding high offices in West Bengal was a source of bewilderment, if not humiliation, to the Bengalis, who, as people, take great pride in the cultural values and social ethos. This was not, however, a one-off because even in the past, the current chief minister of West Bengal Mamata Bannerjee had been abused, often just as filthily, by the so-called Left, particularly during electoral campaigns. Tragically, what was vehemently opposed by the then opposition leader, Ms Mamata Banerjee, was being encouraged by her now since she was not free from this charge of unseemly language. *Third*, West Bengal was a witness of the *Aya Ram Gaya Ram* tradition which first appeared in Haryana in the aftermath of the 1967 State Assembly election. The TMC was constituted in 1998 by its supremo, who aligned with her colleagues in opposition to the Congress which meant that those who joined her back then were ideologically identical to her. With the shifting of allegiances among many of her most reliable comrades towards the BJP, it was also clear that those who were disillusioned with the TMC leadership seemed to have been inspired by *Hindutva*, which had hardly any admirers in West Bengal, not so long ago. *Fourth*, with the increasing importance of the BJP as a strong contender for power in West Bengal, the slogan *Jai Shri Ram* appeared to have gained tremendous salience. It had emerged as a powerful voice of protest against TMC's misdeeds. By characterizing the slogan as an abuse during the 2019 campaign for the Lok Sabha poll, not only did Mamata Banerjee take cognizance of it, but she also helped build its emotional base among those who resented TMC's excesses. On January 23, 2021, when the chief minister lost her cool during a formal event at Kolkata's Victoria Memorial Hall as soon as some of the participants raised the slogan, it further proved how effective and irritant it was, and, therefore, the slogan automatically became a rallying instrument for mobilizing support against the incumbent ruling authority. *Fifth*, the campaign strategy also involved concerted attempts by the political parties to persuade voters by appropriating the views and ideas of the nationalist icons. It was a battle to prove which of them was a genuine flag bearer of the traditions that these iconic ideologues bequeathed. It was, therefore, unsurprising that social reformers like Vidyasagar, revolutionary nationalists like Aurobindo, the ascetics Ramakrishna and Vivekananda, the hardcore nationalist Netaji Subhas Chandra Bose, the Nobel laureate Rabindranath Tagore, *inter alia*, had become integrally connected with the election campaign of the BJP, the TMC and other contending players. This conscious effort to draw on their legacies reveals that their lives and ideas remain integral to the Bengali psyche. This explains why specific Bengali stalwarts had suddenly received great amounts of attention from the state government or the BJP star campaigners, including the prime minister and his colleagues, who never finished their address without reciting in Bangla a few lines from the known texts of Rabindranath Tagore, or some inspiring lines by Netaji Bose. *Sixth*, this was also a period when Bengalis were inundated with promises from both the state government and its union counterpart, since foundation stones for many developmental projects had been laid in a very short period of time. The reason is not difficult to find, for with the application of the code of conduct following the formal announcement of election, the inauguration of any new project should be forbidden. Whether these projects would come to fruition is a million-dollar question, though Bengalis should have reasons to be happy given the importance that West Bengal had received, thanks to the 2021 assembly election. *Finally*, with the recognition of their worth in polls, the voters had suddenly become critical to the political leaders, and this had generated a sense of importance and electoral zeal. Despite being unfortunately transient, it gave them certain resources, both worldly, that is, in terms of material benefits, and emotional, that is, by bringing those who were seen on TV to their doorsteps.

V

Why are elections in India becoming enigmatic day by day? Reasons are not difficult to find. Since it is getting difficult to understand election within the established conceptual framework, the analysts seem to be baffled. Here also lies defence for the argument that in a vibrant democracy, as India, it is perfectly understandable which is an aid to revisit some of the so-called axiomatic theoretical paradigms. In other words, elections in India can never be conceptualized in derivative formats; it is incumbent on those seeking to grasp the distinctive character of Indian polls to take into account the contextual peculiarities to arrive at a persuasive conclusion. The argument is crystal clear here and can easily be defended. Given the sociocultural diversity of the voters, the contestants need to approach them with reference to what will bring them in the favour of specific candidates. In the national elections, some triggering emotional issues (namely the 2013 Muzaffarnagar riots or 2019 Balakot surgical strike) played critical roles; but the fact that the opposition parties had also won in many constituencies show that there were other factors which made their victory possible. Here, one should also keep in mind the system of election on the basis of the first-past-the-poll which also allows electoral victory with minority votes. As the past has shown, no pan-Indian party has ever won the majority votes; the Rajiv Gandhi led Congress had won 44 per cent of votes which still remains a record for a party winning maximum number of votes and Lok Sabha seats though one should not forget that the 1984 election took place following the brutal assassination of the incumbent prime minister, Indira Gandhi, who belonged to the Congress Party. One can say that the triggering factor was the dastardly killing of the leader of the Congress which created sympathy for the Party leader who was Indira Gandhi's son as well. Besides the 1984 national poll, the contending political parties, both the pan-Indian and their regional counterparts, never touched the 40 per cent mark.

The days of election are critical in democracy because the voters express their preferences or otherwise of a candidate.

What is, however, more interesting is the nature of the election campaign for candidates in the fray. It is true that the parties publish manifestos of assurances to the voters, besides stating what they had accomplished in the past. Many studies have shown that the election manifestos do not seem to be always effective in garnering votes to the extent it is visible in Western democracies. There are other critical factors which, on many occasions, decisively shape the voters' choice. Here, J. S. Mill's assumption that education and economic equality remain significant in comprehending how voters vote the way they vote. Implicit here is the argument that these are factors which create a sense of togetherness in support of democracy and the method of choosing the rulers. In India, Mill's basic argument appears to be valid: his claim that democracy survives and flourishes because of the support of the multitude in its favour though they are drawn to the election booth to cast votes for their chosen candidates on the basis of factors that the Utilitarian Mill failed to conceive presumably because his ideas were exclusive to the Western socio-economic context.

A careful analysis of the factors that act as a determinant to voters' choice shows that democracy as a process has different trajectories presumably because it is organic to the prevalent socio-economic circumstances. Despite having deviated from the derivative conceptual parameters, the Indian example provides newer ideas and viewpoints which are useful to grasp the nature of democracy and election in general. In other words, democracy as it unfolded in India will help us build newer theoretical models to persuasively explain the distinctive nature of democracy in non-Western milieu. W. H. Morris Jones's argument endorsing that there are three idioms—traditional, modern and saintly—which are critical to the shaping of Indian politics appears plausible.[12] One should add a caveat here: these idioms may not work in isolation on most occasions, they are

[12] W. H. Morris-Jones, 'India's Political Idioms', in *Politics and Society in India*, ed. C. H. Philips (New York, NY: Frederick A Praeger, 1962), 133–154.

dialectically interconnected. A careful look at how election campaigns are organized and pursued will be of help here. If one goes through the election manifestos, released by any political party, one witnesses the effort of the parties to draw voters by all modern idioms, such as secularism, equality and fraternity, among others. They seem to show that on the surface, the party manifestos represent an urge to articulate their thoughts in exclusive modern idioms. As soon as election campaign starts, the parties do not feel hesitant to conveniently bypass, on many occasions, the publicized politico-ideological priorities and cling to the primordial social identities since they are an easy way to bring the voters in their fold. The past electoral campaigns suggest that the caste appeal creates an emotional affinity with the candidate/political parties and their voters. The assumption that victory to a candidate with specific caste identities will help their brethren have access to resources and opportunities prevails over other considerations. This is what provoked the Rudolphs to place their argument in favour of the modernity of tradition which actually means the unfolding of complex sociopolitical processes connecting 'congenial elements of the old society to the needs of the new [creating a context of] a dialogue between the two'.[13] The argument emphasizing the importance of 'saintly idioms' may not be as effective as it is in the first two national polls, held in 1952 and 1957, when the nationalist euphoria remained an important source of the Congress popularity which was based on the selfless devotion of the leaders to the cause of political freedom from colonialism. Not only did they sacrifice their worldly comfort, they were also accepted by the voters at large for their commitment to the nation and its people. These characteristics do have an appeal even in contemporary elections, especially in the days when even the top functionaries of the government, ministers etc., are indulged in corrupt practices to augment their personal wealth. In many cases, the charges were proved

[13] Lloyd I. Rudolph and Susanne Hoeber Rudolph, *The Modernity of Tradition: Political Development in India* (Chicago, IL: The University of Chicago Press, 1967), 14.

which made the voters more suspicious of the politicians seeking votes. Under these circumstances, honesty and genuine commitment of the candidates to the nation seem to put them ahead of those embroiled in controversies.

Elections in India are also governed by primordial clinging to caste and religion. There are instances to substantiate the claim that the caste identity of the candidates works favourably in polls barring a few exceptions where ideological appeal persuades the voters to a contesting candidate. It is, therefore, not odd to see that the party functionaries take ample care while selecting candidates for the electoral fray. For example, that Mulayam Singh Yadav of Uttar Pradesh (UP) or Lalu Prasad Yadav of Bihar draw maximum of their supporters from the Yadavas illustrates the point.[14] Caste identity is so ingrained that it is simply inconceivable to understand polls in North India without reference to this aspect of political mobilization.[15] Similarly, Muslims form a critical part of the vote bank and political parties nurture them carefully to gain their support in elections. West Bengal is a good example. One of the factors for the victory of the TMC in 2011 and 2016 State Assembly elections is attributed to the support that Muslims (constituting 23% of West Bengal's demography) extended to the party. In fact, the Congress victory at the national polls till 1969 was also largely possible since the Muslims voted in its favour given its commitment not to disturb their socio-religious values at any cost. Now, there have been competitions for the contending political parties to woo the Muslim support presumably because of the well-entrenched belief that they always vote in a group which justifies the claim that they constituted a solid vote bank. It is, thus, not surprising that political parties prefer to field a Muslim candidate if the Muslims form a significant part of the demography.

[14] Rajni Kothari, *Caste in Indian Politics* (Hyderabad: Orient BlackSwan, 2010).
[15] Mamta Chitnis Sen, *Realpolitik: Exposing India's Political System* (New Delhi: SAGE Publications, 2020), 116–120.

Recent elections in India also demonstrate the growing importance of women in shaping the poll outcome. In other words, it is evident that women play a critical role in determining the fate of the political parties. With the adoption of the Seventy-Third Constitutional Amendment Act in 1992, 33 per cent seats are reserved for women candidates in local level polls. The demand has also been made to implement it at the State Assembly and national elections which, however, has not been conceded so far. Nonetheless, that women constitute a critical part of the voters is firmly established. A careful scan of the candidates who fought the elections shows that the number of women candidates has increased over the years. A new era has ushered in with the official endorsement of reservation of seats for women in the panchayats which is likely to have a spiralling effect in urban India. The issue of 33 per cent reservation has been raised in the Indian Parliament several times and was deliberated upon threadbare though it did not, so far, result in legalizing the demand. There are two critical points that deserve attention here: on the one hand, the growing demand of reservation of seats in both assembly and Parliament reveals that it is a powerful voice that cannot be muzzled so easily, especially when there are supporters for reservation among those who matter in the decision-making. This is also, on the other, a strong step to abandon the so-called gender cloak to become integral to the battle for ensuring gender equality in its real connotation. We must add a caution here: mere victory in elections shall not make women independent of the socially justified gender discrimination; what is required is to launch an organized campaign against the mindset detrimental to the idea and the appreciation of gender parity.

An understanding of elections shall remain incomplete unless one looks at the distribution of tickets to the candidates in the electoral fray. This is a tight rope walk for the party on most occasions. Political parties agree to field one candidate rejecting claims of many on the basis of their calculation of their winnability. Here, all the possible factors are taken into account before the name of the candidate is announced.

Nowadays, the political parties also depend on the experts who prepare a list of the candidates by applying their distinctive methods though there is no guarantee that it is going to work under all circumstances since electoral choice by the voters does not always follow a set pattern. The defeat of Indira Gandhi in 1977 or the Left Front in 2011 after having ruled West Bengal continuously for more than three decades are revealing instances. Implicit here are two major claims: on the one hand, although ticket distribution is an important step for ascertaining electoral victory, this cannot be a guarantee for successfully winning an assembly or a parliamentary seat in elections. The voters' mindset cannot, thus, be captured in a neatly done conceptual format; they vote in accordance with their preferences. This also suggests, on the other, that *vox populi* is based on those factors which the electorates privilege when they cast votes in the polling booths. Hence, there is hardly a reliable formula which is likely to ensure victory for candidates with reference to the suggestions made by the poll pundits. Here is a wider point: the calculation by devising specific yardsticks which are certain to bring voters in favour of specific political party or candidates may work in the Western context presumably because voters being generally well-informed make their decision on the basis of their assessment of the nature and quality of governance of the party in power. In India, it is partly true because elections are fought mainly on the basis of emotional issues and concerns for development and other politico-ideological considerations do not seem to be generally critical in voters' electoral choice. It is, therefore, not surprising that the 2019 Balakot surgical strike by the Indian Air Force in Pakistan instantaneously created a support base for the BJP-led NDA seeking power for the second time.

There is one final point here: unless one pays attention to importance of those who become significant because of their accident of birth, our understanding shall remain vitiated. The point being made here is about the excessive significance of the dynasts in Indian politics; the unconditional support to the heirs of Indira Gandhi as they are generally accepted by the people at large presumably because they belong to a dynasty. Apart from fame and fortune and connections and accessibility, 'leaders belonging to dynastic political families have the advantage and the experience of being there and [worked] for the country and people'.[16] Nonetheless, the claim that by belonging to a politically well-entrenched dynasty is an easy step to poll victory appears to be little overstretched because examples abound to show that it is not so. That does not mean, however, that dynasts with affiliation by birth to a dynasty have no advantages; they also undergo the litmus test which other candidates have to pass to win an assembly or a parliamentary seat. Scholars, thus, argue that India's dynastic politics is a creative blending of both modern and traditional aspects: modern because the dynasts do not gain votes by virtue of their dynastic identity; they are required to win the voters' support by approaching them on certain politico-ideological agenda. In other words, their winnability is not guaranteed by being born in a politically important dynasty. This is also traditional because, unlike the general political activists, the dynasts easily gain acceptance by virtue of their family pride or its contribution to India's political cause. As per one analyst, the primary objection to dynastic politics in modern democracy is that 'it introduces a form of exclusion among elected representatives that is antithetical to democracy'.[17] This is reinforced by the argument that 'a ruling class for which birth is itself a qualification … is a prima facie illegitimate basis for democratic representation'.[18] The argument has substance though not adequate to understand the complex nature of elections in India which represent an equally complex interface of many factors, of which the dynastic connections may appear to be one. It is, thus, fair to argue that 'if dynasts are

[16] Ibid., 198.
[17] Kanchan Chandra, 'Democratic Dynasties: State, Party, and Family in Contemporary Indian Politics', *Democratic Dynasties: state, party and family in contemporary Indian politics*, ed. Kanchan Chandra (Cambridge: Cambridge University Press, 2016), 47.
[18] Ibid.

wealthier and have stronger local organizational capacity than other politicians ... the dynasts would continue to be a feature of the Indian political landscape' in democratic elections.[19] The defeat of Rahul Gandhi as a Congress candidate in Amethi (UP) in the 2019 Lok Sabha poll is illustrative here. There are many examples to support the contention. Given the nature of democratic elections in India, just by belonging to a powerful political dynasty does not automatically ensure victory in elections. What is required is the backup of an organization which works hard to champion the claim of the dynastic candidate not with reference to the dynasty but with reference to the politico-ideological preference that s/he represents. Hence, the conventional argument that dynasts automatically create a space in India's political milieu does not seem to be absolutely correct since they need to prepare themselves to be adequately equipped to democratically appreciate the importance of the vox populi in elections.

VI

Apart from an introduction and a conclusion, *Electoral Dynamism of Indian Politics: Deciphering the Enigma* has 10 interrelated chapters. Chapter 1 is an elaboration of the Indians welcoming elections immediately after Independence since it allowed them to contribute to the formation of government; it was a mode of empowerment as far as the voters were concerned. By concentrating on the role of personalities, Chapter 2 is an analytical account of how leadership remained critical in general elections. In other words, leaders stood out and shaped the voting behaviour in accordance with their priorities. Unlike elections in Western democracies, elections in India are also characterized as plebiscites which means that the outcome of

[19] Anjali Thomas Bohlken, 'Dynasty and "Paths to Power"', in *Democratic Dynasties: State, Party and Family in Contemporary Indian Politics*, ed. Kanchan Chandra (Cambridge: Cambridge University Press, 2016), 264.

elections is governed by a general issue which appears to have swayed the voters. Indira Gandhi's *garabi hatao* (remove poverty) was one of those electoral agendas that became critical to ensure her victory in the 1971 general election. Chapter 3 deals with this. Ideology continues to remain significant in Indian elections. By dwelling on how ideological preferences play an important role in garnering votes, Chapter 4 highlights how they worked in elections held so far in India. Caste is critical to shaping voting behaviour which is the principal theme of Chapter 5. The objective of the chapter is to show that caste is both divisive and integrating: divisive because it compartmentalizes caste groups on the basis of caste identity; it is integrating since it brings people together since they have identical caste identities. The victory of the Rashtriya Janata Dal (RJD) in Bihar is attributed to the success of the leadership in cementing a bond among those who belonged to OBCs. Chapter 6 argues that cultural bonhomie forms a solid support base for the parties upholding specific cultural priorities. The Ram Janmabhoomi campaign is an example showing how cultural unity could be an effective mobilizing tool. Chapter 7 is about regional electoral divergences which means that there is hardly one-size-fits-all formula insofar as Indian elections are concerned. Till the 1967 State Assembly election, it was the Congress Party that held power at both the state and union levels; the anti-Congressism created a wave challenging the Congress hegemony in the states. While seeking to analyse the poll outcome in the post-1967 election, Chapter 7 enforces the argument that ideology matters in shaping the voting behaviour. As a follow-up of this argument, Chapter 8 identifies those critical factors which establish the point that voters follow different criteria while casting vote for the national elections and do not generally hold them while making electoral choice for the State Assembly elections. Chapter 9 is an in-depth analysis of how identity politics remains critical in determining voters' choice. The outcomes of 2014 and 2019 Lok Sabha polls are illustrative of how identity is critical to voters' electoral choice. The final chapter, Chapter 10, dwells on nature of voting behaviour amidst anti-incumbency sentiments/preferences. The electoral victory of the BJP-led

NDA in 2014 is attributed to the anti-incumbency passion that evolved presumably because of the scams in which the ruling party was involved. Voters replaced the Congress Party by the BJP and its constituents since the former was reported to have completely failed to combat corruption in governance.

VII

Instead of providing a descriptive account of the elections, held so far, the monograph provides an argument that elections in India are multidimensional which cannot be meaningfully comprehended monochromatically. Voters vote in accordance with their preferences in the shaping of which the role of the leadership cannot be ignored. In other words, leaders prepare the milieu in which voters exercise their choice. It is also emphasized here that there are triggering factors which also act decisively in generating a wave in favour of a party or a conglomeration of parties. For instance, the 2013 Muzaffarnagar riots acted critically in building a strong support base for the BJP in the 2014 Lok Sabha poll; similarly, the 2019 Balakot surgical strike created a momentum for the incumbent ruling party. On the whole, the study makes two fundamental points: on the one hand, it is about the study of national elections with reference to how voters exercise their franchise; on the other, in view of the peculiar unfolding of electoral processes in India, the text underlines the view that voting behaviour cannot be conceptualized in derivative theoretical format since it is context dependent. On the whole, the book, in contrast with what is usually shown in election studies, forcefully makes the point that the universal adult suffrage is critical to India's democracy with reference to the successful conduct of elections since the first general election in 1952. Contrary to the apprehension that democracy had no future in India, the enthusiastic participation of voters in one election after another, India's political history has firmly established that it is completely unfounded. In the first general election, the voter turnout was less than 46 per cent, while it reached 65 per cent in the seventeenth Lok Sabha poll, held in 2019. In assembly elections, the voting percentage is usually much higher. What it reveals is a steady deepening of democracy in India despite noticeable economic disparities and social schism. The regular elections also reinforce 'the faith in universal adult franchise placed by the framers of the Indian Constitution'.[20] While appreciating the willingness of the voters to enthusiastically participate in elections, an analyst thus wrote, 'the general elections are a very great event, greater than I had anticipated. Adult franchise has had a wonderful start. It has meant an awakening and education which could not have been achieved by any other means'.[21]

There is hardly an exaggeration here. Elections are being held regularly and newer voters zealously take part since they seem to have been emotionally linked with the process of democracy as it unfolded following the 1947 transfer of power. The rise of political democracy and its consolidation since Independence offer a new conceptual trajectory of India's journey as a democratic polity. In this respect, elections play a critical role. With elections being held at regular intervals, it can be persuasively argued that the phenomenon has successfully been indigenized which, in turn, means that it has developed organic roots in India. Fundamental to the book is this argument which is critical to understand elections in India in a novel and intellectually challenging perspective.

[20] Ramchandra Guha, *India after Gandhi: The History of the World's Largest Democracy* (New Delhi: Picador India, 2017), 769.
[21] Devdas Gandhi's statement cited in ibid.

1

Voting for a Dream

Holding of the first general election in India during 1951–1952 was fulfilling of a promise that nationalist leadership had made to Indian masses in calling for their active participation in the freedom struggle. Such a promise seemed significant in view of the fact that the liberal political ideas such as democratic rights, constitutional polity and representative government based on free and fair elections appeared quite utopian to the Indian masses in the face of the repressive and authoritarian colonial rule. In a way, the genesis of the national movement, in fact, could be traced to the strong desire of Indians to have a modern democratic life underpinned by basic rights and constitutional polity. The freedom struggle, thus, progressed with the twin objectives of throwing out the yoke of colonial rule from India, on the one hand, and establishment of a modern democratic polity, on the other.

Remarkably, however, as long as the socio-economic character of national movement remained elitist and exclusionary, the mass support for it was abjectly absent. The national movement acquired a mass character only after shedding of its elitist character to a large extent and consequent exhortation to common people to become its critical stakeholder. Constitution of India into a democratic polity where free and fair elections would be a cardinal principle of political life of the people was, thus, a foregone conclusion when one looked at the proceedings of the Indian National Congress in its annual conventions. In other words, during the course of the national movement, apart from initiating several powerful mass agitations, the national-ist leadership was also putting forward a vision of India that it wanted the colonial rulers to grant or establish after attaining independence. Afterwards, when the independence was eventu-ally won and the Constitution was adopted, democratic spirit underpinning all walks of life became a foregone conclusion whose concrete articulation in part was to be through the hold-ing of free and fair elections.

With an in-depth analysis of the first three national elec-tions, the chapter has two aims. Besides seeking to understand the ideological perspective, it is also a reinforcement of an argument that these elections were reflective neither of voters' choice nor an attempt to explore other possibilities. The reason is obvious because the voters uncritically accepted the heroes of the nationalist struggle who sacrificed everything while being engaged in the battle for freedom. The outcome of the election is, thus, said to have been anticipated since voters themselves, as the contemporary media report underlines, campaigned for the Congress candidates and their leader, Jawaharlal Nehru.

Preparation for the Election

The organization of the first general election on the basis of universal adult suffrage obviously generated a lot of anxieties among the important stakeholders.[1] For instance, the common people took these elections as the fruition of a vision in which their rulers would be elected by them unlike the authoritarian colonial rulers. So it was a vital movement for them to celebrate

[1] Navin Chawla, *Every Vote Counts: The Story of India's Election* (New Delhi: HarperCollins India, 2019), 49.

and relish with a sense of responsibility as their vote was going to determine the future of the nation. But for the Election Commission, anxieties lied in arranging for mammoth logistical and managerial preparedness critical in organizing the elections at such a large scale in the highest possible professional manner. The task of the Commission seemed more gigantic given the introduction of universal adult suffrage on such a large scale for the first time anywhere in the world. In other words, there was not much previous experience or practice for the Commission to fall back upon and, therefore, it had to creatively set up the entire machinery, procedures and logistics in the conduct of the first general election. Notwithstanding the daunting nature of the task in hand, the Commission did not seem to have any other choice than to take the challenge head on in a constructive manner and lay down the standard operating procedures for conduct of free and fair elections.

The most disquieting anxiety was, however, on part of the political parties, their leaders and prospective candidates for the upcoming elections. This anxiety was apparently rooted in the long-held apprehension of a section of Indians in granting right to vote to the entire mass of people living in a condition of widespread illiteracy and social and economic backwardness.[2] Although this issue was discussed in detail in the Constituent Assembly as well as other relevant forums, there still remained doubts in certain quarters about the electoral behaviour of the people and its impact on the political class in both short and long terms. Nevertheless, the decision to hold the general election to constitute the first Lok Sabha was already taken in accordance with the constitutional provisions and there was no question of going back on that. The first general election was, thus, organized amidst great hope and disquiet among different stakeholders, each weighing their respective losses and gains out of it. But the general voter

---

[2] Ornit Shani, *How India Became Democratic: Citizenship and the Making of the Universal Franchise* (Cambridge: Cambridge University Press, 2017), 13.

appeared quite determined and joyous to avail the golden opportunity thrown by the general election and express their desire of voting for a dream.

What to Vote for?

The aspirational frame of mind that had set on among electorates during the last phase of the national movement had got crystallized into a vision of nation-building accompanied with the desire of a life of dignity and contentment which was distinctively epitomized by the Congress Party, in general, and Jawaharlal Nehru, in particular. This is definitely not to discount the significant contributions of other political formations as well as leaders, both from within and outside the Congress, in waging tireless struggle against the colonial rule and winning independence for the country. What is being argued here is that on account of its leadership role in the national movement, the Congress came to become synonym of freedom struggle to the comparative marginalization of other political groups. Similarly, while there was a galaxy of prominent leaders in the Congress and outside as well, most of them either passed away or got confined to ceremonial and electorally inconsequential positions before the beginning of electoral battles in the country. So in terms of exemplifying the legacies of national movement, representing the governmental resolve to redeem the pledges made to the common people and embarking upon the ambitious path of social and economic reconstruction of post-colonial India, neither the Congress nor Nehru seemed to have any parallel at that point of time.

More significantly, thus, when voting rights were granted to the people with the constitutional stipulation that their elected representative would now form the government, the public perception of elections appeared to be more as a tool of nation-building than an instrument of fighting for their personal, communal and sectarian group interests. Furthermore, elections were apparently construed by the masses as not just an exercise to elect a government for a term of five years but a prelude to the fruition of a dream held by them for a long time. Logically, therefore, in the early years of inauguration of democracy in India, general masses seemed to carry two parallel visions of life for them—mundane and sacred. Insofar as the mundane affairs were concerned, people did not appear to link that with their sacred idea of building a sovereign, democratic republic as per the dreams of their national leaders. Such a state of affairs existed despite the people suffering from all sorts of denials and deprivations so much so that it was quite difficult for them to meet even the basic needs of their life. But in no case did they seem to take elections as bargaining time with the contending parties and individuals to get favour towards smoothening the mundane affairs of their life.

In other words, despite all the odds of life, the people kept their spirit high in the hope of seeing India emerging as an independent and democratic country on the basis of the support they extended to their leaders. Amidst such fervour for creation of a nation of their dream, the masses did not mind any other aspect of either their private life or the political alternatives offered by other political players.[3] Taking the Congress as the conscience keeper of the nation, they did not appear to waver even an inch in their unflinching support and vote to the party in the hope that it would translate the vision of a nation as articulated during the national movement into reality. Their dream of India as an independent nation was a sacred objective, voting for which would require no rethink among the teeming millions. They probably appeared conscious of the fact that the prevailing social and economic conditions would not permit the leadership to wave magic wand and get the issues of livelihood resolved soon after the transfer of power from the colonial rulers. On the contrary, it was the time for rapid social and economic development in accordance with the vision agreed upon by national leaders and executed under the leadership of Nehru. This was in fact a sacred project whose implementation would

[3] R. K. Tiwari, *Political Parties, Party Manifestos and Elections in India, 1909–2014* (Oxon: Routledge, 2019), 11.

have required a longer period of time. The context of first three general elections in India, therefore, appeared to be characteristically different from what it turned out in the post-Nehru period.

The nationalistic fervour as the basis for voting in India arguably remained the most significant marker of Indian elections as long as Nehru was at the helm of affairs. In the persona of Nehru, the common people used to see the embodiment of the shape of the nation of their dream cherishing which they had participated in the national movement and helped in making their motherland free from the shackles of British colonialism.[4] Hence, the first three general elections saw mammoth support for the Congress party through which Nehru promised to steer the country and its people towards realization of their cherished goals. Although after sometimes, signs of people's dissatisfaction from the policies and programmes of the government in ameliorating the pathetic conditions of life for the mass of the people were clearly visible, their continued support for the Nehru government distinctively demonstrated their prioritization of sacred over mundane insofar as the general elections were concerned. Thus, Indian elections in their early phases used to be understood by common people as a medium of voting for a dream than changing the embedded power equations. Such character of elections came to close with the disappearance of Nehru from the political scene. Later, though at times, certain stakeholders did try to rake up emotive issues in order to win hearts of the people, the voting in general was not in accordance with the same logic as had been the case with the early years of Indian independence.

Political Landscape

The political configuration on the eve of first general election was as diverse and multi-polar as it is today. The ideological divide among the major political parties was almost complete

[4] Ornit Shani, 'Origins Trust in India's Electoral Process', in *The Great March of Democracy: Seven Decades of India's Democracy*, ed. S. Y. Quraishi (New Delhi: Penguin, 2019), 221.

with further divisions within both Left and Right parties.[5] Moreover, simultaneous holding of the general as well as State Assembly elections had presumably motivated a large number of political parties to join the electoral bandwagon of Lok Sabha or State Assemblies. Further, in the absence of clear-cut guidelines on the recognition and status of a political party, as many as 14 parties were recognized as national parties on the basis of their claims of having presence across states. What had, however, been more perplexing was the exceptionally large number of state parties joining the electoral fray with focus on contesting assembly elections. The political landscape was, thus, extremely complex that did not make the task of Election Commission any easier in conducting the maiden election on the basis of universal adult franchise in the country.

Amidst the ideological straight jacketing among various political parties, the party that stood apart in terms of both its ideological flexibility and representation of diverse social and economic interests was undoubtedly the Congress.[6] During the course of its stewardship of the national movement, the party had acquired the widest possible reach among the common people in terms of both representing different shades of ideology and incorporating all possible class and caste interests. Emerging as the sole spokesperson of Indians, the party, thus, not only was successful in articulating the public angst against the colonial rule, towards which it initiated a number of formidable agitations, it also kept expressing the demands and desires of common Indians. Although the growing strength of certain religion- and caste-based parties on the clandestine support of the British did lead to dwindling of the Congress support among those religious and caste groups, the party nonetheless

[5] S. V. Kogekar and R. L. Park, eds, *Reports on the Indian General Elections, 1951–52* (Bombay: Popular Prakashan, 1956), 5.
[6] Gopal Krishna, 'One Party Dominance: Development, Trends and Perspectives', *Indian Journal of Public Administration* 12, no. 1 (January–March 1966): 84.

remained the most powerful political organization through which Indians could voice their concerns and aspirations.

While the Congress was occupying the pole position in the electoral landscape, there did exist a number of other parties drawing their inspiration from Left or Right ideologies and claiming to represent certain sections of society. Majority of such parties were of Leftist orientation and claimed pan-Indian presence in standing for the interests of exploited classes. Prominent among these were the Bolshevik Party of India, the Communist Party of India (CPI), the Forward Bloc (Marxist Group), the Forward Bloc (Ruikar Group), the Kisan Mazdoor Praja Party, the Revolutionary Communist Party of India, the Revolutionary Socialist Party and the Socialist Party. These parties came into existence on the ground that the Congress Party was able to represent the interests of exploited classes as their domination by landed gentry and capitalists rob them of their class consciousness. So these parties came up at different points of time to articulate the class interests of peasants and workers. What was, however, quite astonishing about these parties was wide difference of opinions among themselves to such an extent that they could not put up a joint platform from which the interests of exploited sections could have been articulated in a concerted and forceful manner. The entry of these parties, many of which were able to put up good fight against the nominees of the Congress or other parties, really went to make the electoral fight multi-cornered.[7]

As against the large number of Leftist parties, the Rightist bloc appeared quite meek and consisting of just a few political formations only. The overwhelming sweep of the communist ideology over majority of Indian leaders did, in fact, leave much scope for other parties particularly those espousing the cause of propertied classes or the Hindus. Nevertheless, three important political groups appeared very active and powerful

[7] Margret W. Fisher, Joan D. Bondurant, and Hugh Tinker, eds, *Indian Experiences with Democratic Elections*, Monograph Series No. 3 (Berkeley, CA: Indian Press Digests, 1956), 19.

in representing the interests of Rightist forces in the country: the All India Bharatiya Jana Sangh, the Akhil Bharatiya Hindu Mahasabha and the Akhil Bharatiya Ram Rajya Parishad. All these three parties derived their inspirations from the Hindu cultural traditions and sought to reconstruct the social, economic and political order in the post-Independence period in accordance with the traditions and postulates existing in the country since ages.[8] In terms of their support groups and class representation, all the three political formations appeared pretty distinct from each other. Hence, when they entered the electoral fray in 1951, their social and economic perspectives on post-Independence India were clearly at variance with each other.

To further complicate the political landscape on the eve of first general election, a few other parties rooted in caste or representing the interests of peasantry also joined the electoral bandwagon. Prominent among these were the Krishikar Lok Party and the All India Scheduled Castes Federation. Although these parties did not appear to have powerful presence in any part of the country, what they tried to demonstrate was the fact that the mainstream parties such as the Congress and other Left parties could not represent the interests of these castes or sections of people. The entry of these parties in the electoral arena appeared more symbolic than making any significant impact on the outcomes of the polls. Further, apart from the national parties, there existed a very large number of state parties staking claims on the vote of the people of their states. While a number of these parties put up candidates for the Lok Sabha polls as well, their focus was majorly on the elections for respective State Assemblies. What the political landscape, therefore, demonstrated was the plurality of political opinions despite the overbearing presence of the Congress as the hegemonic party relying on its historic role in Indian national movement.

[8] Richard D. Lambert, 'Hindu Communal Groups in Indian Politics', in *Leadership in Political Institutions in India*, eds Richard L. Park and Irene Tinker (Princeton, NJ: Princeton University Press, 1959), 113.

Electoral Promises

As the first general election was the occasion for different political parties to put forward their considered views and opinions on different aspects of social, economic and political life of the people in terms of concrete electoral promises, all the national as well as state parties came up with policy announcements and declarations that later crystallized into their manifestos before the elections. Given the wide rift and variance among these parties on vital aspects of Indian society, economy and polity, it became mandatory for the parties to articulate their points of view in greater detail before the people in order to make them understand their respective perspectives and make informed choices at the time of casting their votes. In this context, remarkably, while the Congress carried forward its avowed declarations and promises made during the course of national movement, other political parties grabbed the opportunity to locate their perspectives on the future shape of India strictly within the ideological frameworks espoused by them since long. That way the promises that these parties made to the electorate appeared nothing more than presenting their loaded views and finer programmes of actions before the people to consider while casting their vote to choose the dawn of a new life for them.

Congress's promises during the first general election were clearly a vision of nation-building rooted in socialist mould along with providing adequate space for other ideological persuasions to also exist within the fold of the party. After Independence, the party asserted through a resolution that '[P]olitical independence having been achieved, the Congress must address itself to the next great task, namely, the establishment of real democracy in the country and a society based on social justice and equality'.[9] Accordingly, it set up the Economic Programme Committee to be headed by Jawaharlal Nehru to suggest a comprehensive framework of social and economic development. The Committee after extensive deliberations

---

[9] Tiwari, *Political Parties*, 198.

came up with a detailed outline of development in core sectors of economy such as agriculture, industry, rural industries, planning, industrial relations and cooperation, among others. The recommendations of the Committee later formed the basis of drafting the party manifesto for the election in 1951 in which it offered a holistic vision of social and economic development under the stewardship of the state. The party promised to carry out the visions articulated during the national movement and ensure rapid social and economic development.

As if finding the Congress commitment towards establishing democracy and socio-economic order based on social justice and equality inadequate, the Left parties came up with more radical policy statements and programmes of action. The Socialist Party, for instance, stated,

> the present economy must be brought under state control and subordinated to an overall plan of development; certain sectors of its must be socialised immediately; investments must be rigidly controlled and directed by the State; taxation must tone down vast income disparities; such property relationships as zamindari must be abolished forthwith and a living wage, a decent shelter must be guaranteed to the worker.[10]

Taking the path of revolutionary transformation of Indian society a step ahead, the CPI asserted,

> the new state of revolution in India was not socialist and that the urgent task was the completion of the anti-imperialist and anti-feudal revolution ... in order to achieve this task, it is necessary to build a united front of the working class, kisans, petty bourgeoisie and the national bourgeoisie interested in freedom and national advance ... (there is) need for India evolving its own path of revolution, taking into considerations the concrete features of our country and its specific conditions.[11]

[10] Ibid., 201.
[11] Ibid., 200.

In contrast to the radical measures for social and economic reconstruction promised by the Congress and Left parties, the electoral promise of Jana Sangh was more in consonance with its avowed objective of restoring the ancient glory of India. The party declared that its object

> is the rebuilding of Bharat on the basis of Bharatiya sanskriti and maryada as a political, social, and economic democracy granting equality of opportunity and liberty to individuals so as to make her a prosperous, powerful and united nation, progressive, modern and enlightened, able to withstand the aggressive designs of others and to pull her weight in the council of nations for the establishment of world peace.[12]

Almost similar, if not identical, announcements were also made by other Rightist parties such as Hindu Mahasabha and Ram Rajya Parishad. What was unique in the electoral promises of the Rightist political organizations was their distinct focus on chartering the course of new India in accordance with the indigenous inputs and systems drawn from the ancient Indian history, culture and traditions as against the Congress and Left's focus on socialism as the mainstay of social and economic transformations in the life of the nation.

The electoral pronouncements of different political parties through their declarations and party resolutions clearly presented three distinct visions of making the nation tread the path of its post-colonial journey. The two extreme views presented by the Leftist and Rightist mainstream political parties reflected the prioritization of their ideological predilections over practical imperatives through which incremental changes could have been brought about in the social and economic fabric of India. They also marked fundamental departures from a vision of India presented in the newly adopted constitution. Above all, these perspectives did apparently not gel well with the ideals and goals with which the national movement succeeded in driving the colonial rulers out of India. Amidst these

[12] Ibid., 201.

political extremities, the vision of social and economic development presented by the Congress seemed to reflect the broad consensus among different stakeholders. At the state levels, though the Congress remained the major player in the electoral arena, presence of a number of smaller parties actually created a propitious ambience for democracy to get ingrained in the psyche of the Indian masses. The voters were, thus, provided a wide spectrum of political choices to go for when weighing the immeasurable value of their votes.

First Three General Elections

Organization of first general election in India was truly a pioneering exercise in seeding the representative democracy as per the vision of the Constitution makers. For both the organizational and the substantive work of voting by the common people for their representatives, the election was really 'first'. The sheer scale and nature of this election made it altogether different from the electoral exercises carried out in India in the past. Further, apart from electing members of the Lok Sabha, Indian electorate was also required to vote for members of State Legislative Assemblies. Given the mass illiteracy and socio-economic backwardness of the people, the task in hand for the Election Commission was stupendous indeed. In other words, the Commission was not only needed to stretch its resources to reach all the nooks and corners of the country by arranging massive logistics, what involved ingenuity of the Commission was devising the ways and means of ensuring that the unlettered people were able to vote for candidates of their choice for both national and state legislatures through some infallibly identifiable visual marks. The indefatigable spirit and creative genius of the first chief election commissioner, Sukumar Sen, must be credited with meeting all the challenges efficiently and leading the first general election to its logical conclusion.[13]

[13] Ramchandra Guha, 'A Forgotten Bengali Hero', *The Telegraph* (Kolkata), 27 September 2018.

Given the geographical expanse of India and logistical challenges, the first general election was conducted over a period of four months, beginning in November 1951 and completing in March 1952. While much of the polling in large parts of the country took place during the winter months of February and March 1952, the process of election was set rolling in November 1951 in order to secure voting in hilly and mountainous regions of North before the heavy snowfall made them inaccessible for polling parties. The preparation for the polls had clearly begun much before the scheduling of elections given the mammoth task of enumerating and enrolling all the eligible voters in electoral roll. Enormous efforts on this front were made by the Election Commission with praiseworthy support from the staff of Constituent Assembly Secretariat. In the meantime, passage of the Representation of the People Act in 1950 which was amended in 1951, the legal framework of elections in India was already in place. With untiring efforts of all the stakeholders, India finally appeared ready for holding its maiden general election taking the most significant step towards its rise as the largest democracy in the world.[14]

While the administrative machinery for conducting the polls was working overtime to make sure that the elections were held in a flawless manner, the political parties and their leaders busied themselves in raising the electoral bar. Although all the parties and candidates drew upon their role in the national movement to strike an emotional chord with the general masses, the appeal of the Congress Party and its leaders undoubtedly appeared more impressive and meaningful in comparison to others. Given the stewardship of the national movement, the Congress also was the only party with pan-Indian presence fielding its candidates in highest number of seats. This, however, did not deter its opponents from joining the electoral fray with exceptional vigour and aspiration. For instance, the ideological mobilization of people in certain parts of the country by the CPI had placed

[14] S. Y. Quraishi, *An Undocumented Wonder: The Making of the Great Indian Elections* (New Delhi: Rupa, 2014), 69.

it in formidable position to win the seat. Similarly, the support gained by the Right-wing parties from a number of erstwhile royalties helped them gain foothold in the areas over which the writ of royal families ran large. The political atmosphere in the country had clearly turned festive with the common people taking the elections as concrete reflection of their holding the baton of power, and political class joining the fray with the hope of asserting their influence among the masses.[15]

Ever since the plan for holding the first general election was announced, different political parties were announcing their vision of social and economic development of the nation. Many of these parties also came up with their manifestos at the time of election to put forward their perspectives of future of India before the people. What, however, appeared striking in these circumstances was the fact that unlettered mass of people would surely not had gone for the election manifestos to assess the vision of different political parties before casting their vote. The thumb rule for the people to assess the candidates and political parties was the sacrifices they had made in the course of national movement. In other words, barring the Congress Party, the personal character and integrity of individual candidates seemed to have played a decisive role in securing the support and vote of the people. Insofar as State Assembly polls were concerned, local issues also played a critical role apart from the legacies of the national movement.[16]

The political configuration on the eve of the first general election appeared very much dominated by the stalwarts of the national movement mainly belonging to the Congress Party.[17] Although important leaders of the major parties did

[15] Ramchandra Guha, 'Democracy's Biggest Gamble: India's First Free Elections in 1952', *World Policy Journal* 19, no. 1 (Spring 2002): 56.

[16] Irene Tinker and Mil Walker, 'The First General Elections in India and Indonesia', *Far Eastern Survey* 25, no. 7 (July 1956): 21.

[17] E. Sridharan, 'The Origins of the Electoral System Rules, Representation and Power Sharing System in India's Democracy', in *India's Living Constitution*, eds Zoya Hasan, E. Sridharan, and R. Sudarshan (New Delhi: Permanent Black, 2011), 284.

	First General Election		Second General Election		Third General Election	
Political Parties	**% of Votes**	**Seats**	**% of Votes**	**Seats**	**% of Votes**	**Seats**
Indian National Congress	44.99	364	47.78	371	44.72	361
Communist Party of India	3.29	16	8.92	27	9.94	29
Bharatiya Jana Sangh	3.06	03	5.97	04	6.44	14

TABLE 1.1 *Performance of Select Parties in First Three General Elections*

Source: Computed from the *Statistical Report on First, Second and Third General Elections* (New Delhi: Election Commission of India, 1952, 1957, and 1962), available at https://eci.gov.in/statistical-report/statistical-reports/ (accessed on 31 July 2020).

visit different parts of the country to campaign in favour of their party candidates, the major determinant of voting behaviour of the electorate was the legacy of the national movement with which the Congress had entered the poll arena. The other parties and their leaders did not bank too much on their nationalist legacies and instead emphasized upon their ideological standpoint as the major poll plank to woo the voters. Spanning over the different phases, out of a total of 176 million registered voters, 45.7 per cent cast their votes to elect 489 members of the Lok Sabha.[18] Barring a few cases of electoral malpractices, the voting was by and large peaceful so as to make it the biggest electoral exercise of the time. The results of the first three general elections are presented in Table 1.1.

The figures presented in Table 1.1 speak of clear-cut domination of the Congress Party in this election that eventually

[18] Election Commission of India, *Report of the First General Elections in India, 1954*, vol. 1 (Delhi: Manager of Publications, Government of India), 5.

culminated into the formation of the 'Congress' system in India.[19]

> The Congress victory was natural because the opposition parties were groping in the dark. They had yet not matured to be able to formulate any acceptable principles. The electorate probably was not prepared mentally to take their manifestos at their face value and was therefore inclined to tilt towards the freedom fighters and the Constitution givers among whom were Jawaharlal Nehru, Sardar Vallabhbhai Patel, Dr. Rajendra Prasad, Maulana Abul Kalam Azad and many stalwarts in the galaxy of the hallowed leadership which wielded tremendous influence.[20]

The party was, therefore, able to win 44 per cent of votes converting into 364 seats.[21]

Thus, barring a few minuscule challenges visible in certain parts of the country, this election was in fact a validation of the transformation of the Congress Party from being the shepherd of the national movement to that of the ruling party of free India. The leaders who had made great sacrifices during the freedom struggle were rewarded handsomely by the people by getting them elected to the Lok Sabha with good margins. It also acted as the popular approval for the Nehruvian vision of India that apparently drew upon the ideation of India through the course of the national movement. Apart from the adoption of the Constitution in which the major aspects of future Indian polity were already outlined, the Nehruvian perspectives of social and economic reconstruction of the newly independent country were further articulated through his concrete steps in the form of planned economic development. This election,

[19] See Rajni Kothari, 'The Congress System in India', *Asian Survey* 4 (1964): 72.

[20] Shiv Lal, *Indian Elections since Independence* (New Delhi: The Election Archives, 1972), 52.

[21] David Butler, Ashok Lahiri, and Pranoy Roy, *India Decides, Elections 1952–1995* (New Delhi: Books and Things, 1995), 14.

thus, appeared to be vote for the dream that the common people of India sought to realize through the personality and endeavours of Nehru.

Apart from the Congress, the other political formations that could show their sizeable hold over the electorate in certain pockets of India were the CPI and the Socialist Party. The sweep of the CPI was clearly visible in the southern state of Kerala where the hard work of leaders such as A. K. Gopalan and E. M. S. Namboodiripad had helped in creating a distinct sphere of influence for the party that paid it rich dividend in good number of seats despite the Congress wave sweeping other parts of the country. Similar was the condition of the Socialist Party that had been able to create a strong foothold among the backward castes of UP and Bihar under the leadership of redoubtable Ram Manohar Lohia and Jayaprakash Narayan (JP). As a matter of fact, the parties that could show their sustenance in the face of the Congress wave were none other than these two parties that could secure double digit seats in the Lok Sabha and emerged as the real opposition at a time when numerical preponderance of the ruling party was scarring.

Another major gainer in the first general election was the Kisan Mazdoor Praja Parishad spearheaded by Acharya Kripalani. Although this party was also cast in the mould of the Leftist framework, it could not adjust either within the Congress or along with other Leftist parties. Left, therefore, with no other option than joining the electoral fray on its own, the party joined the electoral bandwagon on a relatively subdued note; its remarkable performance in the elections came as a pleasant surprise to its leaders, many of whom had won the elections on the basis of their personal rapport with the voters of their constituencies. Interestingly, when one looks at the combined performance of the Left parties in the first general election, it is quite evident that these parties had indeed struck deep roots among the poor and marginalized sections on the basis of their agenda of land reforms and other economic measures. Moreover, when the Left elements within the Congress Party were also taken as representing left of the centrist ideology of the party, it demonstrated the depth to which the majority of the common populace in the country had been fascinated with the Left as the emancipatory ideology.

As against the notable performance of the Left parties, the Rightist parties such as the Hindu Mahasabha, the Ram Rajya Parishad and the Jana Sangh could not cut much ice with the electorate presumably for the reason of their ideological aberration amidst the domination of the Left forces both within and outside the Congress. In other words, given the respectability and overall acceptance of socialism as the underlining ideology of nation-building in the country, it was unmistakably a great gamble on the part of the Rightist parties to go to the electorate and seek their support and vote in the elections. Moreover, the ideological standpoint of the Rightist parties did not appear to match with the vision that lay at the root of an India dreamt by the national leaders and accepted by the masses as their destiny. It was probably for this reason that despite the hard labour put by the leaders of these parties, they could not secure even respectable number of seats. Whosoever won on the ticket of these parties had done so on the basis of his or her personal credit among the electorate. These winners would have won their seats irrespective of the party on whose symbol they contested. An interesting example in this regard can be seen in the case of Maharaja Hanwant Singh of Jodhpur. Fighting the election for Lok Sabha on the ticket of the Ram Rajya Parishad, he decisively trounced the Congress Party in his pocket borough in both the parliamentary and assembly elections.[22] That way, the first general election did not seem to bode well for the Rightist parties as they were considered by the masses more as spanners in the fructification of an India of their dream than as helpful partners in carrying forward the cherished legacies of the national movement.

The decisive outcome of the first general election did not probably come as a shocker for any of the major players in view

[22] L. S. Rathore, *Life and Times of Maharaja Hanwant Singh* (Jodhpur: Book Treasure, 2012), 183.

of the fact that the setting of the poll was already preordained by the proceedings and legacies of the national movement. For example, the party and leaders that had been in the forefront of the freedom struggle and whose perseverance and selfless sacrifices the people had seen on their own, this election would not have been anything else than rewarding them for their service to the cause of the nation. Even the parties and leaders who privileged social and economic reforms over and above the freedom struggle were also accepted by the people as their representatives though such cases were few and sparse. Rather, the electoral plank that was accepted by the people as the undercurrent of the first general election was the vision of nation-building presented by the Congress Party through the persona of Nehru. The idea that seemed to have reached the deepest corner of public consciousness was that this election was to be a vote for realization of the dream of India for which the Congress had waged such a long and excruciating national movement.

Riding on the decisive mandate the Congress Party was handed down in the first general election, the following five years were the time of hectic activities for the government both on the social and the economic fronts. In accordance with its electoral promises and rising aspirations of the people, the government initiated a number of path-breaking measures primarily with a view to ameliorate the pathetic economic conditions of people. Although the Planning Commission had already been established to epitomize the governmental resolve to concretize its economic promises through five-year plans, structural changes were also sought to be made in the economic system through radical measures such as land reforms and creation of public sector undertakings to meet the basic needs of the masses. The period following the first general election was, thus, presented as the phase of planting seedlings whose fruits in terms of fulfilling the needs and desires of the people would be bearing in the years to come. More importantly, the government was seen as doing its best to realize the promises it made to the people amidst the constraints of both finances and skilled manpower.

In such euphoric circumstances when the dates for second general election were announced, the political landscape did not seem to have changed much from what it was during the first general election. Not only were the major participants in the ensuing elections the same, the machinery and officials at the helm of affairs of the electoral system also more or less remained intact. This election, in a way, looked like a repeat of what has happened in 1952.[23] The results of the election vindicated the position of the Congress as the party seeking to fulfil the dreams of the national leaders. With the departure of many of the party stalwarts from electoral scene, the stage appeared perfectly set for Nehru to dominate the political scene by being seen as a synonym of the Party. Public faith in the avowed vision of the Congress Party as well as the leadership of Nehru was reflected in the massive votes the Party won in the second general election.[24]

Even the third general election, which was the last general election to be fought under the leadership of Nehru, also tended to continue the streak of winning mandate for the Congress. In the fast-changing political landscape while the Congress was indeed able to keep itself abreast with the pulse of the people, the opposition parties remained busy in sorting their internal ideological and programmatic issues. The context of the third general election was also poised in favour of the Congress as the social and economic reconstruction policies of the government were seen by people as illustrations of earnest efforts by the Party to fulfil the promises it made to the people. These elections reflected the political mind of the people of India.[25] An illiterate and backward electorate had proved its unparallel wisdom in welcoming and sustaining India's tryst with

[23] S. L. Poplai, ed. *National Politics and 1957 Elections in India* (New Delhi: Metropolitan Book Co., 1957), 7.

[24] Pranab Mukherjee, *Challenges before the Nation* (New Delhi: Vikas Publishing House, 1993), 184.

[25] Ashok Mehta, *The Political Mind of India: An Analysis of the Results of the General Elections* (Bombay: A Socialist Party Publication, 1952), 1.

democracy. The general masses seemed convinced that the best bet for them to vote for at the national level could have been none other than their time-tested Prime Minister Nehru. Although there existed sufficient space for political parties and organizations of other ideological persuasions than the Congress, none of them could ever think of coming remotely close to the ruling party. The results of the third general election indeed carried forward the unflinching faith of common people in the impeccable leadership of Nehru and accommodative character of the Congress within which all shades of opinions and interests could find a breathing space.

Concluding Observations

The first three general elections in India could arguably be termed as unconventional in view of the routine and conservative results that they threw up. Irrespective of the fact that the Constitution of India had provided for the introduction of universal adult franchise as one of the radical measures of political reforms in the country, the mindset of the masses bestowed with the constitutional right to vote did remain focused on looking for the commitment of the Congress and its leaders to fulfil the dream that they had promised to usher in once India became independent. The public perception of elections in India, therefore, drastically differed from the West where elections were considered as the means for changing the rulers and rotating the power holders in society from one group to another.[26] On the contrary, common people in India tended to take the elections as an opportunity for reaffirming their faith in the political leadership of the party and people who not only won independence but also provided them the dream with which they would live and vote for. That way, during the initial years of Indian democracy, it was the Congress all the way that held sway over the general electorate and remained

[26] Surinder Suri, 'Towards a Theory of Indian Politics: Some Implications of the Results of the General Elections', *The Economic Weekly* 14, no. 48 (December 1962): 69.

the ruling party under the leadership of Nehru as long as the people did not lose hope in its capacity of delivering on the dreams for which people had been voting for it all through.[27] For, the voting in the first three elections was not for choosing the leader or changing the government but was the voting for a dream with which the mass of Indians walked over from colonial shackles to dreamy independence.

Despite the initial uncertainty regarding the survival of democracy in India, the holding of regular election is a testimony to the argument that democracy has not only survived but also struck organic roots. It is also logically plausible to argue that although the claim that democracy was planted in India by the colonial rulers, it gradually became an important ingredient of India's public life; democracy was no longer an alien conceptual parameter but one that developed organic roots. There is also substance in the argument that it was easy for democracy to thrive in India presumably because of the avowed belief that India had experienced democracy in the distant past. So the argument that there existed a mindset in its favour even before the British arrived in India. The purpose here is not to verify the veracity of the claim but to point out that the argument that democracy was a British gift does not seem to be tenable in view of the evidence that the mechanism of involving people in governance was an age-old phenomenon in India. Nonetheless, it is also true that the electoral democracy that evolved in British India and later after the withdrawal of the colonial power in 1947 was a continuity in the sense that whatever came up in the wake of the alien governance became part and parcel of our public life once India became politically free.

As per the evidence available, the outcomes of the first three national elections, held in 1952, 1957 and 1962, respectively, were illustrative of the mass euphoria that the political freedom had generated. Although B. R. Ambedkar was not sure whether winning of political freedom was adequate to ensure

[27] Surjit S. Bhalla, *Citizen Raj: Indian Election, 1952–2019* (Chennai: Westland Publications, 2019), 192.

economic freedom,[28] it hardly deterred the voters from supporting the Congress presumably because in their perception, it was the Congress that fought hard to dislodge the foreign power. There was hardly a powerful ideological critique of the policy designs that the Congress ministry had adopted after electoral victory largely because of the emotional attachment of the voters with the Congress leaders. For the Congress, it was easier to accommodate the dissenting elements presumably because it, by being an umbrella organization, did not seem to be so catholic in its ideological persuasions. The challenge to the leadership was, in other words, resolved before it caused any harm to the Congress which also means that the prevalent Congress leadership was widely respected and, as a result, the opponents were never allowed to take the difference to a position of no return. The situation had, however, undergone a sea change later. But the available inputs regarding the first three general elections allow us to defend the point that the success of the Congress was not exactly a comment on its governance but was a voters' gift for its altruistic sacrifice for India's freedom from the British yoke.

[28] B. R. Ambedkar's speech in the Constituent Assembly on 25 November 1949, *Constituent Assembly Debates*, Book No. 5, 979.

2

Personalizing Elections

It is a matter of knowledge that leaders lead not in a vacuum but in a specific context which is both given and constructed: it is given since a specific socio-economic milieu always remains in which leaders evolve their ideas; it is constructed because the leaders shape history sometime merely by tweaking and sometime by radically altering the existent mode of thinking. This can be illustrated with reference to how issues metamorphose in elections that took place in India so far. For instance, in the first Lok Sabha poll in 1952, nationalist legacy remained perhaps the most effective instrument for creating a solid vote bank for the Congress Party. This means that the role that the nationalist leaders played in the struggle for freedom supported their claim for power. Election was, therefore, an occasion when those who fought for India's political liberation interacted with circumstances which they created in the wake of their struggle against an alien rule. The 1952 national poll, therefore, provided the participants in election with an opportunity to shape the future of India in accordance with their politico-ideological priorities. The aim of the nation builders to push India to accept the socialistic pattern of society was sought to be fulfilled and the election pledges were articulated accordingly in the first national election. So the process for transforming India in a particular fashion had begun with the initiatives of a collective of the nationalists under the care of Jawaharlal Nehru. What Nehru had set in motion reached its fruition in 1971 when his daughter, Indira Gandhi, constitutionalized the idea of socialistic pattern of society by amending the Constitution accordingly. For the country, it was a radical turn though it had its roots in the past. Similarly, the increasing importance of Ram Mandir as critical to voters' choice cannot be understood meaningfully unless one is aware of the radical socio-economic and political metamorphosis in response to the implementation of reservation for OBCs following the adoption of the Mandal Commission Report in 1990. It does not require any further elaboration that in contemporary India, the issues of Mandal and Mandir remain most significant in determining how the voters voted in the election since 1990. The demand for Ram Mandir did not appear to have been so critical as it became later, especially with the demolition of the controversial Babri Masjid in Ayodhya in UP. The BJP and its leaders seemed to have struck an emotional chord with the voters that was manifested in the 1999, 2014 and 2019 Lok Sabha polls.

With above detailed elaboration of how the text is reformulated in the specific socio-economic and political contexts, the chapter argues the point that leaders become important in election since they interact with the voters with pledges which are both context driven and about a blueprint for future India. What is being reiterated here is the contention that though the aim of the chapter is to understand how leaders personalize elections, it also takes into account the importance of the context in which specific ideological belief gains precedence.

Conceptualizing the Issue

Personalizing election does not seem to be odd conceptually because the leaders put before the led what is required to be done to translate into reality what they feel as appropriate for the country or *demos*. As the history of democracy reveals, there are phases in which the leaders grow in importance. Broadly speaking, the 1648 Puritan Revolution in England led to the abolition of monarchy and the establishment of the Commonwealth under the aegis of the leader of the revolution, Oliver Cromwell. The Puritan Revolution can be said to have initiated a process whereby the *demos* attained a space in governance which was not conceivable in the past. The idea acted positively in preparing the ground for the Glorious Revolution in 1688 which created constitutional monarchy in England; this was a remarkable event because it set in motion the unfolding of democratic governance in which the importance of the *demos* and their leaders was firmly established. The 1779 American Revolution was also critical to the strengthening of the democratic zeal which was also supportive of the view that a true democracy evolved once the meaningful interaction between the leaders and their followers took place. The trend reappeared in the 1789 French Revolution which defended the ideas of liberty, equality and fraternity as essential for the consolidation of democratic governance.

The above historical account appears to be pertinent to dwell on the conceptual underpinning of how the leaders' personalization of political processes is complementary to the creation of a solid base for democracy. Here, the purpose is not to delve into the theoretical issues but to underline the importance of the context in which the leaders explore the possibilities of gaining what they stand for. The argument that Hobbes provided in his *Leviathan* (published in 1651) seems pertinent. In order to explain why an institutionalized authority needs to be created Hobbes says that, it helps build an organized life. In other words, without the existence of sovereignty, human life is miserable and, thus, not worth living. In the context of uncertainty, the role of authority, managed by competent leadership, is most critical for sustaining a stable and stress-free society. While seeking to justify his argument, Hobbes, thus, stated,

> the final cause, end or design of men (who love liberty, and dominion over others) is the introduction of that restraint upon themselves, in which we see them live in Commonwealth, is the foresight of their own preservation, and of a more

contented life thereby; that is to say, of getting themselves out from that miserable conditions of war which is necessarily consequent ... to be the natural passion of men when there is no visible power to keep them in awe, and tie them by fear of punishment to the performance of their covenants, and observation of those laws of nature fulfilling their collective mission.[1]

Implied here are two core points: on the one hand, Hobbes expressed his concern for the creation of a sovereign authority since it was capable of contributing to a peaceful social life and not a life which was constantly under threat. Who constituted the authority? Hobbes suggested, on the other, that those who were capable of managing most efficiently the interpersonal relationships and steered the members of the Commonwealth away from what caused harm to them and had the potential for creating a stress-free life for them constituted the authority.

As mentioned above, the purpose of drawing upon Hobbes is not to defend a strong state but to suggest that leaders remain important in the creation of a stable society. Uncritical acceptance of the leaders as infallible leads to, as Ambedkar apprehended, authoritarian leadership.[2] Nonetheless, there is hardly an effective substitute for leaders in any system of governance, more so, in the Westminster system of democracy that the British rule bequeathed once it came to an end in 1947. A perusal of the history of establishment and consolidation of democracy in India shows how leaders became relevant in governance in response to the decision of the colonial rulers to couch administration in the democratic mould.[3] What is striking is also the fact that despite not having the basic

[1] Thomas Hobbes, *Leviathan or the Matter, Forme, & Power of a Commonwealth Ecclesiastical and Civil* (London: Andrew Crooke, 1651), 103.

[2] B. R. Ambedkar's speech in the Constituent Assembly on 25 November 1949, *Constituent Assembly Debates*, Book No. 5, 980.

[3] Bidyut Chakrabarty has dealt with this aspect of the development of constitutional democracy in India in 'Constitutional Identity: The British Liberal Inputs', in *India's Constitutional Identity: Ideological Beliefs and Preference* (Oxford: Routledge, 2019), 21–46.

sociocultural characteristics for generating demands for democratic governance, India has emerged as a successful democracy. It has been possible presumably because of the consolidation of a favourable mindset and the rise of an appropriate leadership for its sustenance. Barring the 1975–1977 Emergency, there has hardly been an instance when democracy was effectively challenged, which also means that democracy has struck deep roots in India. In such an environment, the personalization of political processes by the leadership does not appear to be a deterrent so long as it is pursued by the leaders at the cost of the *demos*. It is, therefore, complementary to the sustenance, if not strengthening, of democratic governance that the Constitution of India upholds.

Unfolding of the Process

A persistent question before the theorists of democracy and elections has been how some people come to rise and dominate the political process at a particular juncture and gradually disappear from the scene after playing their innings in the political arena. This question gains particular salience in the parliamentary democracies where the pivot of political system, in general, and electoral politics, in particular, is considered to be the political parties rather than individual leaders, unlike the presidential democracies where general elections are fought on the basis of personality and vision of competing individuals for the top office. The primary reason for the salience of political parties in parliamentary democracies is the long-term perspective with which they come into being on the basis of distinct ideologies, policies, programmes and perspectives on vital issues facing the country. They reflect plurality of ideas and visions in society that vie for wider acceptance so as to become the dominant discourse of public life. The parties indeed set the terms of political process in parliamentary democracies and dominate the electoral process through fielding their candidates in different constituencies. In other words, the commonality of identity and purpose throughout the country is provided by none other than the political parties entering the electoral fray with their unique election symbols. The role of individuals, in these circumstances, normally gets subordinated to the overbearing sweep of political parties. As a result, leaders of political parties become the pall-bearer of their organizations rather than overshadowing the existence of the party by their towering personalities.

India, like other parliamentary democracies, has, by and large, begun its march towards becoming a vibrant democratic polity with the same kind of arrangements with parties of various hues such as Left, Right and left of the Centre like the Congress dotting the electoral arena right from the beginning. But what becomes curious in the case of India is the fact that many of the parties, despite remaining in the fray for quite longer times, or even freshly formed, could come at the centre stage of the political arena only with the arrival of a particular leader at the helm of affairs. The arrival of such leaders converts the electoral system of the particular geographical space into what Dhirubhai Sheth terms as 'wave elections'.[4] Even more interesting is the fact that in many, if not all, of the cases, the party's electoral buoyancy remained intact only as long as its charismatic leader continued to hold sway over the party. Once the person departed from the scene, the electoral fortunes of the party dwindled fast and became almost negligible afterwards. This results in what may be called personalization of elections. The obvious consequence of this process is the relative marginalization of political parties in the democratic process.

The practice of personalization of elections in India may be said to have begun right from the post-Independence period but gained prominence with the gradual weakening of the Congress and assiduous efforts of certain regional leaders to carve out a space for them at the local level. The earliest examples of

[4] D. L. Sheth, *At Home with Democracy: A Theory of Indian Politics*, edited with an Introduction by Peter Ronal deSouza (Singapore: Palgrave Macmillan, 2018), 205.

personalization of elections in the country could be seen in the persona of leaders such as E. M. S. Namboodiripad in Kerala and C. N. Annadurai in Tamil Nadu. Subsequently, this tendency gained momentum with a number of leaders emerging at both the regional and national levels who could sway the voters in such a way that they emerged as the sheet anchor of electoral fortunes in that particular election. Thus, the rise and fall of a number of political parties as formidable players in the electoral arena could be attributed to the tendency of personalization of elections as a result of which voters associate themselves with the leader rather than the ideology, programmes or policies of the party.

Genesis of Personalization of Elections

Personalization of elections apparently began in India soon after the first general elections with Jawaharlal Nehru's emergence as the face of the Congress Party as well as government within a short period of time. Although Nehru was an important leader of the party even before Independence, there was tremendous enhancement in his stature immediately after Gandhi's announcement of Nehru as his political heir. Thus, Nehru's prominent position within the party was formalized as the leader who would steer the party after Independence as representative of the party's supreme leader, Mahatma Gandhi. But Nehru, with his own vision of the future course of India's social and economic development, did not act as per the Gandhian ideas, and clearly chartered an independent course as far as the development strategy of India was concerned. Moreover, at the time of the first and successive general elections till his death in 1964, Nehru came to symbolize the party and government in an undisputable manner. This, in fact, laid the foundation for the rise and growth of personalization of elections in the country that has remained undiminished in Indian political processes since then.[5]

[5] Jaimini Bhagwati, *The Promise of India: How Prime Ministers Nehru to Modi Shaped the Nation* (New Delhi: Penguin, 2019), 61.

There can be no denying the fact that during its pre-Independence phase, the Congress was a very democratic party, having a galaxy of important leaders who existed in the party in their own weight and played significant role in the national movement by heading the party at different periods of time. The democratic character of the party, however, underwent subtle transformations after the arrival of Gandhi whose dramatic reinvention of the party from an elitist platform to a mass organization naturally made him its supreme leader. Since then, whether Gandhi held any formal position in the party or not, he clearly remained its sheet anchor and majority, if not all, of the leaders in the party accepted Gandhi's personality and ideas as their guiding principle. In such a scenario, when there were a number of powerful leaders within the Congress who wielded considerable influence among both the masses, in general, and party cadres, in particular, what appeared to have tilted the scale in favour of Nehru was Gandhi's declaration making Nehru his heir apparent. This unprecedented move on the part of Gandhi practically put aside the issue of leadership of the party as well as government both during and after Gandhi with Nehru emerging as the clear winner.

What, however, made Nehru further consolidate his position, both within the party and outside, was the gradual turn of events, particularly after Independence. Looked at as acting for and on behalf of Gandhi, though in reality implementing his own agenda of social and economic reconstruction of the country, Nehru started decisively having upper hand in the party vis-à-vis other senior leaders such as Patel and Rajendra Prasad from the time of formation of interim government. As the prime minister of India, Nehru's stature and operational dynamism within the party probably increased manifold though the other leaders could also hold their forte as the formidable leaders whom Nehru could ignore at his peril. Such a delicate balance in party structure as well as working of the democratic process was most visible during the formation of government after Independence and the way the Constituent Assembly functioned to draft and finalize the Constitution of

India. Moreover, in certain spheres of government activities such as the integration of princely states, leaders like Patel seemed as if acting in a very autonomous manner to discharge their given responsibilities without much, if any, interference by the prime minister.

Insofar as personalization of elections in India is concerned, the turn of events soon after Independence proved to be very crucial in making Nehru the supreme leader of both the party and the government. In this regard, death of Mahatma Gandhi on 30 January 1948 was a critical factor. Despite Nehru having his own vision of future of India and quite often acting in variance with the views and perspectives offered by Gandhi, he uncritically accepted Mahatma as the conscience keeper of the nation whose moral authority presumably acted as the foremost check on hegemonic designs and tendencies of any leader in India. So once Gandhi was out of scene, the biggest counterbalance to Nehru's emergence as the personification of the Congress Party had become nil. The resultant precarious political ambience was further given a definite push towards emergence of Nehru as the undisputed leader of both the party and the government with the passing away of Patel in 1950. As a matter of fact, Patel was the only other leader in the party who could match the charisma and charm of Nehru, and commanded considerable influence over the masses of India. His 'iron man' image through the integration of princely states had further made him a political figure matching, if not outgrowing, the personality of Nehru.[6] But his untimely passing away even before the first general election obviously left the political landscape widely open for Nehru to steer both the party and government as per his own volitions. Although there still existed a number of important leaders who had played a vital role in the national movement, none of them probably matched the personality and charisma of Nehru so as to offer even the slightest resistance to him and become a rallying

[6] Mukesh Kumar Singh, *Nehru, Gandhi and Patel* (New Delhi: Centrum Press, 2013), 195.

point for those opposed to Nehru both within the party and the government.

Amidst the scenario when Nehru was the public face of both the party and the government, the first general election appeared as the most opportune occasion for genesis of personalization of elections in India. While most of the prominent leaders of the party had already been out of the picture, the ones who held formal party positions or remained in the reckoning either fell out with Nehru or could simply not match the aura and operational dynamism of Nehru. For instance, Acharya J. B. Kripalani, who was the party president in 1947, could not hold on to the party and after falling out with Nehru, formed his own party to contest the first general election. Similarly, leaders like Rajendra Prasad who could have offered some check to the political dynamism of Nehru were offered ceremonial position in the government that made them virtually out of reckoning from the electoral frays. Further, leaders like P. D. Tandon who became party president could neither match Nehru's towering personality nor carry on with him. Resultantly, at the time of the first general election, Nehru not only continued to occupy the august office of prime minister of India but also became party president to steer the party through the thick of the election. The first general election was, therefore, not less than a referendum on the personality, vision, action plan and performance of Nehru both as head of the party and the government. The election results going overwhelmingly in favour of Nehru, that was very much anticipated given the nationalistic fervour amidst which this election was held, helped a great deal in the rise of personalization of elections.[7]

As if the pointers of the first general election were not enough to point the unconventional unfolding of electoral politics in the country, the second general election led to further consolidation of the tendency of personalization of

---

[7] David Gilmartin, 'The Paradox of Patronage and the People's Sovereignty', in *Patronage and Politics in South Asia*, ed. Anastasia Pivliavsky (Cambridge: Cambridge University Press, 2014), 152.

elections. Interestingly, by the time the second general election was organized, the political landscape had become quite monotonous with a large number of leaders having illustrious background of the national movement fading away from the electoral scene. Further, Nehru's vision of social and economic reconstruction of post-Independence India had been put to practice with bold measures in terms of adoption of 'socialistic pattern of society' as the avowed goal of the party and governmental resolve to materialize the goal through the instrument of five-year plans. Moreover, the aspirational sentiments among the masses still remained intact to a large extent with people looking at Nehru as the messiah who would not only steer India on the path of rapid social and economic development but would also fulfil both their mundane and sacred desires. Clearly, in the electoral hustling, it was no one else than Nehru all the way as the mascot of both the party and the government, though the formal reins of the party was in the hands of U. N. Dhebar. Throughout the electoral process, Nehru made whirlwind tour of all nooks and corners of the country explaining the people his achievements and plans for the future. The electorate indeed remained mesmerized with the charisma of Nehru even during this election and voted him for the second time to continue as the maker of their destiny.

What virtually ingrained personalization of elections as the characteristic feature of political process in India was the third general election held in 1962. Officially, the president of the Congress Party was Mr Neelam Sanjeeva Reddy, but the election was fought virtually on the basis of the personality of Nehru and the achievements of his government. The domineering influence of Nehru on these elections was reflected in two distinct areas of the entire process. One, within the Congress Party, though there were a number of prominent leaders who occupied the formal party positions including its president, the critical decisions with regard to the choice of candidates and electoral strategy of the party were primarily taken by Nehru albeit in consultation with his party office-bearers and ministerial colleagues. The party, in fact, appeared to be looking at the prime minister to guide it in taking vital decisions with regard to the election rather than vice versa. Two, in the electoral hustling also, it was Nehru who was visible all the way from finalizing the campaign strategy of the party to setting the discourse of election by raising favourable issues and crystallizing the electoral debates around those issues. The election, indeed, turned out to be a vote on the personality and performance of Nehru as the opposition also tried to undermine his personal standing and governmental performance by highlighting the corruption cases and inefficiency of his government in the course of its campaigning strategy. But the voters still seemed to be captivated with the charismatic personality of Nehru and held hope in the capabilities of his government to deliver on the promise of happy and dignified life for them. Unsurprisingly, therefore, when the election results were announced, the Congress Party remained the invincible force with the other opposition parties lying unimaginably behind the ruling party in both percentage of votes and number of seats won. Although there was a slight decline in the percentage of votes and seat share of the Congress, it did in no way undermine the persona of Nehru as the sole arbiter of electoral fortunes of his party.

The Nehruvian phase of electoral democracy produced a number of distinct characteristics of Indian political process of which personalization of politics could be seen as the lasting one. Although the theorists of Indian party system and electoral democracy sought to conceptually articulate this phase of electoral politics through the prism of 'Congress system', pivotal role of Nehru in transforming the nationalist legacy of the party into a vision for new India capable of not only emerging as a vibrant democratic society but also securing the basic needs of its people through the instrumentality of planning could never be undermined. While the umbrella nature of the Congress Party was undoubtedly a construct of the Gandhian politics, its consolidation and perpetuation over the three general elections was the seminal contribution of Nehru that also paid rich dividends to him by catapulting him to power throughout his life.[8] Steady onward march of Indian democracy further witnessed the reinforcement of Nehruvian personality and policies as the cardinal issue in the successive elections. This clearly helped in emergence of the phenomenon of personalization of elections as a distinct trait of Indian democracy that remains quite evident even today.

Congress during Indira and Rajiv Gandhi

After the departure of Nehru from the political scene, electoral fortunes of the Congress Party plunged into doldrums. Short span of Lal Bahadur Shastri's prime ministership did not allow him to gain control of either the party or the government. After his passing away under suspicious conditions, the leadership crisis within the Congress Party came out in open. While Indira Gandhi staked her claim to be the heir apparent of her father, the old guards of the party were not ready to oblige her and the party as her dynastic fief. The resultant bickering led to deep divide and eventually split in the grand old party of India. While Indira Gandhi walked away with the governmental faction of the party to save her government, the organizational structure of the party remained in the hands of the old guards whose organization was called the Congress (Organization). The split in the Congress had deep impact on the texture of party system as well as electoral politics of the country. Ripples arising out the split of the party at the national level were also felt at the level of states leading to tremendous weakening of the party in many states.

In the election for the fourth Lok Sabha, the Congress Party had to face tremendous losses. Absence of the charismatic personality of Nehru, on the one hand, and intense internal bickering within the party, on the other, had resulted in radically altered political scenario. Although Indira Gandhi was

[8] Shashi Tharoor, *Nehru: The Invention of India* (New Delhi: Penguin, 2018), 184.

able to form government with support of the Communist Party and some independents, her hold over the party and government was still not complete. After running the government for some time, she decided to take the calculated risk of advancing the fifth general election after taking certain radical economic decisions in terms of bank nationalization and abolition of privy purses. In a bid to outgrow the party organization, she took these elections as a personal pursuit by throwing the catchy slogan of *garibi hatao* and seeking votes of the poor masses on this plank. Her gamble unsurprisingly paid rich dividends to her and she emerged as the convincing victor of this election. The old party organization remained far behind her party and she came to symbolize the party that she spearheaded after breaking away from the parent organization. This election unquestionably re-established the phenomenon of personalization of elections as people voted for the personality and promises of Indira Gandhi rather than the party.

The turn of events after the fifth general election witnessed the rise and fall of Indira Gandhi as the reference point of political processes in India.[9] Her landslide victory in the fifth general election though further helped in the consolidation of her position as the supreme leader of her party, its ominous culmination in the imposition of Emergency and her decisive defeat in the sixth general election were significant landmarks in the political history of India. The failure of the Janata experiment, however, provided her another chance to bounce back and take pole position in the electoral politics. In the seventh Lok Sabha polls, she entered the fray playing the victim card against the Janata government which was already in shambles. However, her appeal to voters was more in the nature of seeking personal favour from them rather than banking upon the organizational structure of the party to win the election. Her win in this election resulted in

[9] Pranab Mukherjee, *The Dramatic Decades: The Indira Gandhi Years* (New Delhi: Rupa, 2014), 29.

further consolidation of her persona as the party in herself and reinforced the process of personalization of elections.[10]

The tragic death of Indira Gandhi in 1984 led to the arrival of Rajiv Gandhi on the political landscape. Soon after his assumption of office, election for the eighth Lok Sabha was announced. Riding on the sympathy wave in the wake of his mother's death, Rajiv Gandhi also came to contest the election more on the basis of his personal appeal than on the strength of the party organization. His appeal to the masses to vote for him in order to defeat the secessionist forces that had killed his mother was indeed able to cast deep impact on the psyche of voters who voted overwhelmingly for him. The electoral gains of Rajiv Gandhi even surpassed the percentage of votes and number of seats won by Nehru and Indira Gandhi. This clearly established Rajiv Gandhi as the boss of the party as well as the government. However, given the novice that he was in politics, the party structure continued to be dominated by the old guards who were previously Sanjay loyalists. Although he did control the lever of the party, his untimely death could not permit him the chance to personalize the party structure and win elections on the basis of his own personality.

The phenomenon of personalization of elections that had begun with the period of Nehru was deliberately sought to be institutionalized by Indira Gandhi through her move of splitting the party and establishing her as the unchallenged leader of the party. Her move somehow got massive support of the general electors as a result of which she succeeded into trammelling the autonomy of party in the electoral process. However, her personal electoral successes gave rise to inner coteries within both the party and the government that tended to blind her democratic credentials eventually resulting in the imposition of internal Emergency. Although in the later phase of her electoral

[10] Yogendra K. Malik, 'Indira Gandhi: Personality, Political Power and Party Politics', in *India: The Years of Indira Gandhi*, eds Yogendra K. Malik and Dhirendra K. Vajpeyi (Leiden: E. J. Brill, 1988), 19.

politics, she did realize the importance of party organization and tried to take her companions along, the distinct traits of personalizing the elections were clearly discernible from her personality. Later, riding on the dynastic lineages of his party, though Rajiv Gandhi could also secure a landslide victory in the eighth general election, his proclivities towards personalization of elections could not be fully fructified due to his untimely death. Moreover, the dwindling fortunes of the Congress Party in the later years increasingly reduced the probability of any of its leaders including Gandhi–Nehru scions attaining such a towering position through which they could have personalized the elections they fought.

Personalization at State Level

Personalization of elections did not remain an underlying feature of Indian democracy at the central level only. Its percolation to the level of states began soon after the erosion of the Congress hegemony once Nehru was no longer the rallying point for all the sections of society in the name of the party. In other words, Nehru's dominance over the electoral politics of the country was so expansive that during his stewardship of the Congress, it remained the nucleus of political process at both the central and state levels. But once Nehru was out of the picture, the Party witnessed gradual disintegration not only at the central level but also at the level of states. The decline of the party curiously was speedier and deeper in the states in comparison to its central organization. Naturally, the space vacated by the Congress at the level of states was occupied by different regional parties. While many of these parties were in existence from the pre-Independence days, a few of them emerged as formidable force in the states after electoral churnings over the years. Yet the personalization of elections was an inevitable phenomenon across many states.[11]

[11] Sadhna Sharma, *State Politics in India* (New Delhi: Mittal Publications, 1995), 157.

Rise of coalitional politics has produced varying patterns of personalization of elections in the country.[12] Further, emergence of powerful regional satraps in the aftermath of weakening of the Congress, thus, marked the penetration of personalization of elections at the state level as well. The beginning in this regard was made by the southern states, particularly Kerala and Tamil Nadu, where the social reform movements during the national movement had helped the regional parties to strike chord with the people and put up a great challenge to the Congress hegemony in these states. Although the Congress was indeed able to win handsomely in these states as well in the first general election, the bright prospects of the regional parties in these states started becoming visible by the second general election. For instance, during these elections, the CPI was able to carve out a formidable place for it in Kerala by putting up a brave fight against the Congress in the second general election. Ultimately, a number of parties in the state decided to join hands together under the leadership of E. M. S. Namboodiripad to oust the Congress from the state. Namboodiripad in the later years emerged as the most important leader of the Left front in the state and remained the epicentre of the non-Congress politics in the state. Likewise, in Tamil Nadu, the non-Congress forces joined hands under the leadership of C. N. Annadurai to emerge as the most significant political force in the state. Over the years, personalization of elections became a countrywide phenomenon with a number of Hindi heartland states witnessing the rise of grassroots leaders such as Lalu Prasad Yadav in Bihar, Mulayam Singh Yadav and Mayawati in UP, N. Chandrababu Naidu in Andhra Pradesh, Parkash Singh Badal in Punjab, K. Chandrashekar Rao in Telangana, among others who not only formed their own parties but also contested and won elections on the basis of sheer personal charisma and reach among the common voters of their respective states. These leaders have tended to make

[12] Bruce Bueno Mesquita, *Strategy, Risk and Personality in Coalition Politics: The Case of India* (Cambridge: Cambridge University Press, 1975), 211.

the politics of their respective states thoroughly rooted in their personalities as the parties formed by them have continued to rule the roost in the electoral politics by remaining either the ruling party or even as opposition.

Contemporary Scenario

In the contemporary times, rise of Narendra Modi as the undisputed leader of the ruling BJP has helped him perpetuate the long-term trend of personalization of elections in the country. Modi's charisma as the sole vote catcher became quite apparent during the proceedings of the 17th Lok Sabha polls. Right from the readying of the party for the polls through the choice of candidates to the campaign trail, the footprints of Modi were distinct in all nooks and corners of the country. In fact, the long-drawn period of polling spanning over seven phases provided the parties and their star campaigners sufficient time to hop different parts of the country to put forward their perspective before voters. In elections, campaigning happens to be the most important mechanism to reach out to the common voters and establish a personal rapport with them by highlighting their issues and concerns from public platform. At the same time, campaign also provides the parties and candidates an opportunity to enter into a public debate with their opponents on the contentious issues over which wider disagreements prevail among them. The campaign strategy for the 17th general elections, thus, presents a bird's-eye view of the issues raised by different parties and their leaders which reflected their vision and action plan for the country. While the campaign strategy of different parties more or less hovered around the conventional wisdom of fielding their star campaigners at strategic areas to reap maximum benefits out of that, a remarkable feature of these parliamentary elections was their special focus on certain key areas where they expected to make rich dividends. Such a strategy was most visible in the campaigns of the major national parties.

BJP's campaign strategy was overwhelmingly centred on the personality of its charismatic leader and Prime Minister Modi.

But apart from Modi, the party also banked upon the massive electoral tours of its President Amit Shah as well as other party heavyweights.[13] A remarkable aspect of the campaign strategy of the party was to focus on those areas where it could sense bright prospects of bettering its previous records of seats in addition to paying sufficient attention to its traditional strongholds lying mainly in the Hindi heartland and western part of the country. For instance, the party could very well visualize fair prospects for it to have a strong foothold in the hitherto unexplored territories in the eastern part of India with special stress on West Bengal.[14] It began with weaning away dissenter leaders of the TMC like Mukul Roy who acted to mobilize a number of TMC supporters in support of the BJP.[15] Moreover, the party stationed one its very seasoned strategist to be in charge of the state on a long-term basis so as to have the feel of ground realities of the state, issues and challenges faced by the people, governmental responses to their problems and how the party could convert the public disenchantment with the ruling party into its favour. Such a master stroke of the party really worked well in the state and the party was indeed able to emerge as a formidable force in the state in terms of both Lok Sabha seats and percentage of votes polled in its favour.[16]

The issues that became the punch line for the party to put forward its vision and action plan consisted mainly of such problems and rhetoric that would help in arousing people's nationalistic passion. Beginning with the drafting of its manifesto till the last day of election campaign, the party stuck to the core issues facing national defence and internal security. For instance, in highlighting its commitments for the unity and integrity of the nation, the party touched upon all the

---

[13] Rajdeep Sardesai, 'The BJP Juggernaut Is in High Gear', *The Hindustan Times*, 10 May 2019, 16.

[14] Romita Datta, 'Battle for Bengal', *India Today*, 20 May 2019, 52.

[15] Pratick Mallick, 'Poll Perceptions and Strategies in West Bengal', *Economic & Political Weekly* 54, no. 23 (8 June 2019), 10.

[16] Kumar Uttam, 'Behind BJP's Bengal Inroads, Month of Planning, Silent Toil', *The Hindustan Times*, 24 May 2019, 5.

vital aspects that tended to challenge the unity and security of India. Hence, right from Kashmir issue to that of cross-border terrorism, destruction of terrorist training camps across the border, menace of Naxalism and other insurgencies, and strengthening of the armed forces and other security apparatus, the party did not fail to lay stress on all these issues in any of the election meetings. In a way, the party, thus, was able to alter the discourse of election campaign by setting the agenda as per its convenience.

Although the Congress also tried to emulate the campaign strategy of the BJP, the implementation of its action plan could not be as perfect as that of the BJP. For instance, with a view to bolster its electoral fortunes in the crucial state of UP, the party went for appointing its seasoned and charismatic leaders as incharges of two distinct parts of the state. Accordingly, while Priyanka Gandhi Vadra was put in charge of eastern part of UP as the chief campaigner for the party, its young and charismatic leader Jyotiraditya Scindia was made chief campaigner for the party in the western part of the state. Side by side, party president, Rahul Gandhi, kept on visiting the state apart from holding electoral rallies in other parts of the country. However, the issues upon which the party based its campaign were patently negative as they sought to target Prime Minister Modi as a corrupt man despite no serious corruption charges being labelled against him.[17] Only after the assumed failure of the negative strategy, the party came out with its ambitious scheme of 'NYAY' seeking to guarantee an annual income of ₹72,000 in the bank account of each of the poor households.

Comparative analysis of campaign strategies of the BJP and the Congress shows stark contrast in both planning and execution. While the former was marching ahead with a well-planned strategy of raising only those issues and concerns that would have emotive appeal to voters, the latter began with a misplaced focus on demonising the mascot of the BJP as a corrupt man on

[17] Sunetra Choudhary, 'Chowkidar to Rafale, Cong's Graft Pitch Failed', *The Hindustan Times*, 24 May 2019, 2.

the basis of the Rafale deal. The fallacy of the most important plank of the Congress was proved disastrous when midway through the election campaign the Supreme Court on a petition debunked the Congress chief's claim that Modi has been proved corrupt in the Rafale deal. The engine of Congress's campaign machinery was, thus, punctured midway and the party had to look for some other plank to base its electoral strategy on. On the contrary, the BJP continued with its focus on security and related concerns throughout with only minor additions or deletions in speeches of its star campaigners as per needs of the local circumstances. The glaring mismatch between the campaign strategies of the two major contenders for power, in fact, set the stage for penultimate day when the voters had to make up their mind to cast their vote. Eventually, the poll outcomes proved the relative effectiveness of campaign strategies of the two parties. They also proved the inherent tendency of personalization of elections through the personas of both Narendra Modi and Rahul Gandhi, with the former eventually getting catapulted to the seat of power as the new epicentre of electoral politics in India.

Concluding Observations

The personalization of elections seemed to have taken deeper roots in the country with the unmistakable tendencies emerging out of successive general elections. A tendency that began from the days of the national movement ostensibly due to the reasons of public mobilization for making the anti-colonial struggle more formidable and result oriented eventually turned out to be the distinguishing characteristic of Indian democracy. What is more startling in this regard is the fact that the personalization of elections that was previously dominant in the case of the national elections also reached the political matrix of states with the weakening of the Congress Party over the years. In other words, as and as the Congress position in the political landscape of the country started getting marginalized, there emerged scope for the regional leaders to part ways from the Congress and form their own political parties that could help them become autonomous centres of powers in the states. This is, however, not to undermine the position of those parties and formations that emerged out of their ideological discord with the grand old party and had virtually raised banner of revolt against the Congress domination of the Indian political system right from the beginning. In this context, the position of the CPI as well as the Bharatiya Jana Sangh (BJS) has really been unique, and they have represented the other poles of the political spectrum in the country. But what is interesting about these parties is their propensity to get swayed by the national trend of personalization of politics and holding power primarily on account of this characteristic phenomenon. In other words, the tendency of the personalization of politics could surely be seen as the dominant feature of the Indian political system from which no party or formation could remain untouched. Rather, given the rich dividends accruing out of such a makeover of the political processes, personalization of elections has probably become the underlying feature of the Indian electoral system even for the times to come as could be gauged from the willing embrace of the phenomenon by almost all the major stakeholders of the Indian political system.

One cannot, however, rule out completely the possibility of derailment of democratic governance in India. In view of Ambedkar's warning in the Constituent Assembly regarding the rise of authoritarian personality,[18] if the leaders have access to unbridled power, election is a litmus test for the leaders and the political party they represent. The 1975–1977 Emergency shows how democracy was reduced to constitutional authoritarianism; it also underlines that given the strong roots of democracy, the reversal that was evident during those two years was short lived. There is, therefore, substance in the statement that democracy in India does not seem to be just 'top-dressing', as Ambedkar

[18] B. R. Ambedkar's speech in the Constituent Assembly on 25 November 1949, *Constituent Assembly Debates*, Book No. 5, 980.

characterized,[19] but one that has already struck deep roots in the Indian soil which is evident with the consolidation of a mindset in support of democracy. The strong opposition that confronted the regime that evolved in the wake of the Emergency is also a testimony to the view that it is difficult, if not impossible, to even undermine the democratic values that have become part and parcel of the Indian mindset. It needs to be emphasized that although the victory of a particular political party in elections suggests the critical importance of an individual or a set of individuals, it cannot nonetheless be a stepping stone towards creating conditions in which democracy is a casualty. In other words, as history has shown, attempts towards weakening the foundation of India's democratic governance were scuttled as soon as they became a serious threat to democracy. Fundamental here is the point that notwithstanding personalization of election and, in consequence, the political processes, there is hardly a threat to reverse the processes which are integral to the consolidation of democracy in India. This further means that democracy has its own resilience which is manifested in India on various occasions when it is threatened or sought to be undermined. Hence, the argument that personalization of election is an anathema to democracy does not hold much water since it is just a means to gain electoral victory in circumstances of cut-throat competition among the political parties and those seeking power.

[19] B. R. Ambedkar's speech in the Constituent Assembly on 4 November 1948, *Constituent Assembly Debates*, Book No. 2, 38. According to Babasaheb, 'democracy [in India] is a top-dressing on an Indian soil which is essentially undemocratic' presumably because of the prevalence of the divisive caste system.

3

Elections as Plebiscites

In view of the growing importance of the leader-centric elections in contemporary India, a new era of Indian politics is said to have emerged. The argument is simple: elections which are fought ideologically seem to have undergone a sea-change in India since the political parties, instead of defending their claim for power on the basis of the distinct ideological options, draw on the popularity of their leaders to garner votes. While the outcome of the first four national elections reveals the critical significance of the Congress' nationalist role, the elections that followed the 1967 poll presented a different picture. From the 1971 Lok Sabha poll, the leader especially of the pan-Indian political parties became far more important than their ideological priorities in securing votes in the elections. It was Indira Gandhi who remained an important vote catcher for the Congress Party, so long as she was on India's political scene; Rajiv Gandhi was a rallying point in 1984 Lok Sabha poll, which was held after the brutal assassination of his mother, the incumbent Prime Minister, Indira Gandhi. The trend was visible in the 1999 national poll, when the BJP gained votes, to a significant extent, by drawing upon the image of Atal Bihari Vajpayee as a capable prime minister, though it did not work in BJP's favour in the 2004 elections; in 2014 poll, the trend revived with the arrival of Narendra Modi as one who attracted voters to a large extent. The victory of the BJP and other NDA constituents was attributed to the charisma that Modi had in creating a stable support base for the conglomeration. The 2019 election was a continuity of the trend that seems to have struck roots in the Indian politics.

The above-detailed narrative of what became critical to Indian elections held so far is directed to argue that the recently held Lok Sabha polls were not just another elections but a kind of plebiscites or referendum on the nature of leadership. One must add a caveat here: a careful analysis of the elections in which leadership assumed tremendous significance reveals that, besides the importance of leaders, the voting behaviour was also governed by important slogans that captured the aims and objectives of the parties fighting for electoral victory. For instance, Indira Gandhi's slogan *garibi hatao* (removal of poverty) generated an electoral wave for the leader and also the political party that she represented. Similarly, the slogan to fight against the authoritarian Congress, which gained credibility in view of the pursuance of the so-called anti-people policies during the 1975–1977 Emergency, cemented a bond among the voters which was translated into votes against the incumbent Congress government. It also worked in Indira Gandhi's favour in 1980 Lok Sabha poll when viewpoints against political instability in the wake of the Janata Party governance between 1977 and 1980 became critical in Congress' success in winning a majority of seats in the Parliament. The rise of Modi as an apparently invincible leader in 2014 poll can be explained in terms of the BJP's success in ascertaining voters' support by creating a vote bank around the failure of the earlier governments in protecting the interests of the Hindu majority, besides, of course, by highlighting the scams and other corrupt practices in which the Congress ministers were also involved.

In order to capture and also analytically explain the rise and consolidation of plebiscitary politics in India, the chapter deals with the issues not only with reference to the prevalent context but also by drawing upon what exactly triggered the processes leading to the decline of the importance of ideological preferences in shaping voters' choice and the increasing significance of the leaders' charisma in creating a stable support base for the political party that gains strength. The aim here is also to test the validity of the argument that it was the leader who brought votes and not the ideological predilections of the political parties that presented before the voters a specific leader. In other words, the objective is to examine the assumption that ideology no longer remains critical in Indian elections.

Transformation of Indian Elections

India's experimentation with parliamentary democracy began on a promising note with most of its political institutions and processes working fairly in accordance with the desirable norms of such a system. For instance, when one looks at the electoral processes in the early phases of Indian democratic experience, it was clearly marked by a healthy environment in which different political parties put forward their views and opinions on different issues facing the country. As the basic issue at that time was the blueprint of nation-building, the plans and proposals of different political parties through their resolutions and manifestos provided ample information and inputs to electorate to assess the relative merits of their claims. Amidst the presence of a galaxy of leaders in the electoral fray with their distinct contributions in the national movement, the electors had abundant opportunity to consider the candidature of different leaders and cast their vote accordingly. What was noteworthy in these elections was that neither anybody tried to undermine the policies, programmes or promises of the other parties nor was there any attempt to raise emotive issues. Further, the elections were fought on a range of issues focusing on both the pressing needs of the people as well as imperatives of nation-building.[1] Though the unparalleled contributions of

[1] Sumantra Bose, *Transforming India: Challenges to the World's Largest Democracy* (Cambridge: Harvard University Press, 2013), 86.

the Congress made it the winning party for a long period of time, there was rarely any attempt by the party to make any election as a single-issue election.

However, unprecedented makeover of Indian electoral system from being rooted in a general broad-based debate and discussion on the pressing issues and challenges facing the country, and the probable responses of different contestants, to that of a single issue-based electoral process was witnessed with the arrival of Indira Gandhi on the political scene. Surrounded by political uncertainties both within and outside the party, she could not find any other method of salvaging her precarious position than to offer her persona as the best bet for the people to get rid of the vicious circle of poverty. Unsurprisingly, this gamble of Mrs Gandhi paid rich electoral dividends to her and emerged as a novel method of electoral manoeuvring by the people or parties short of any broader policy perspective on the issues facing the common people. In the successive years, the turn of events played out in such a way in the country that the general elections invariably got centred around one emotive issue that apparently made elections a high-stake battle, having potential of transforming the course of political history of India. Naturally, on all such occasions, people got motivated to vote en bloc for the betterment of the country that unmistakably resulted into bumper electoral gains for some and loss for other. This, in the long run, not only went on to strengthen the plebiscitary nature of Indian electoral system but also inspired the vulnerable leaders to raise such issues that could evoke emotive response from the common people.

Elections for the fifth Lok Sabha was argued to be different from the previous general elections on various grounds.[2] For instance, it was argued that instead of banking on the party organization as the foundation of electoral strategy, Mrs Gandhi was seeking to contest the election on her personal promises and charismatic appeal. At the same time, in the face of her

[2] E. P. W. Da Costa, 'Fifth Lok Sabha Polls: Three New Factors,' *The Times of India*, 09 January 1971, New Delhi, p. 9.

formidable challenge, the opposition parties hurried to form a combined platform against her, thereby brightening the possibility of putting up straight fight against Mrs Gandhi. Interestingly, for a Congressman, this election presented the great dilemma of choosing between Mrs Gandhi on the one hand and the syndicate on the other.[3] Given that Mrs Gandhi sought to fight the polls as a one-woman army, she did not wish to leave any stone unturned to not only project her positive promises before the people but also expose the weaknesses of the opposition. The gist of her campaigning strategy lay in branding the polls as monumental fight between her promise of *garibi hatao* and the ominous portents of the grand alliance of opposition parties.[4] However, such arguments and appeals of Mrs Gandhi to voters were not found to be quite impressive to the political analysts, primarily for reasons of localized nature of election campaigning in the absence of a system of mass media.[5] Nevertheless, the electoral campaigns of Mrs Gandhi were filled with emotional appeals to the electors along with her promises of bringing about a radical turnaround in the social and political fortunes of the poor and downtrodden sections of society. Amidst such a high-pitched and intensely personal campaigns, the stage was set for polling to constitute the fifth Lok Sabha.

Congress (R)'s performance in the fifth general elections had been reflective of its regaining the widespread support of different social and economic groups of people as had been during the period of Nehru. In other words, the relative decline of the party during the 1967 elections by losing support among certain social groups such as upper and lower castes had been

[3] Rakhahari Chatterji, 'Political Development in India: The State, Civil Society and Its Institutions—The First Half Century,' in *Politics in India: The State—Society Interface,* ed. Rakhahari Chatterji, (New Delhi: South Asian Publishers, 2001), 4.

[4] Rakhahari Chatterji, 'Democracy and Opposition in India,' *Economic & Political Weekly* 23, no. 17 (23 April 1988): 845.

[5] Myron Weiner, 'The 1971 Elections and the Indian Party System,' *Asian Survey* 11, no. 2 (December 1971): 1155.

effectively arrested, and the umbrella nature of the party was re-established under the leadership of Mrs Gandhi. At the same time, in the decisive battle over control of the legacy of the party, the syndicates were comprehensively voted out of existence. As a result, a new generation of Congress leaders, who did not have much support of their own among the electorate, came into existence under the commanding leadership of Mrs Gandhi. This depended on the charismatic leadership of Mrs Gandhi not only for electoral victories but also for any kind of intervention in public life in the name of the Congress Party. While on the one hand, all sorts of parochial considerations were wiped out of existence within the party, on the electorate pedestal, all the religious and caste groups voted for Mrs Gandhi in support of her unflinching faith in the socialist ideals and blueprint for social and economic transformations. Almost all the social groups appeared reassured of the protection of their interests under the leadership of Mrs Gandhi.

Indira Hatao

The introduction of unconventional elements in the electoral process was carried forward in a more concerted manner by the opposition parties in the next general election. The imposition of Emergency by Indira Gandhi government and the extreme excesses perpetrated during this period by police and other security agencies had created an atmosphere of abject dislike ranging to the extent of abhorrence against the incumbent government. So, when election for Lok Sabha was announced, different opposition parties not only coalesced together to form the Janata Party to take on the Congress in a united manner but also strategized their electoral strategy in such a way that the voters were given no second chance of thinking while voting against the government of Indira Gandhi. In other words, the opposition parties of all hues made it a point to focus on the excesses committed during the Emergency and, in turn, call for removal of Indira Gandhi government from the office as the only means of retrieving the democratic system in the country. This general election thus tended to consolidate the phenomenon of elections as referendums by reducing the entire electoral process to the single point of saving democracy by voting out the incumbent government.

The election to the fifth Lok Sabha that Indira Gandhi had won singularly by emphasizing on the single-point agenda of *garibi hatao* was, in fact, prefaced by a number of other radical measures such as bank nationalization and abolition of privy purses. Mrs Gandhi had indeed taken these measures as prelude to her masterstroke of *garibi hatao* slogan. Though the later turn of events blinded her wisdom to impose Emergency that culminated into untold excesses on the people in general and opposition parties and their leaders in particular, the basic fact remained that Indira Gandhi had won the previous election on the slogan of *garibi hatao*. Logically, therefore, in the sixth Lok Sabha polls, the opposition needed to have focused on the failure of her government to deliver on the promise of *garibi hatao* apart from the dark phase of Emergency and the under-mining of democratic rights and processes in its wake. But the opposition, for obvious reasons, chose to ignore all other issues and convert this election into a referendum on the Emergency imposed by the incumbent government to make people take revenge for the same by voting out the government, which actually happened, and the government was ousted from office.

The sixth general election, that way, was an opportunity for the opposition to repay Indira Gandhi in her own terms. If she could win the fifth general election on the strength of her magical slogan *garibi hatao*, now the opposition also replicated the same story by brushing aside all other plausible issues to make the electoral campaign centred on the emotive issue of *Indira hatao, loktantrata bachao*. As the election campaign progressed, the opposition war cry attained greater shrill, and the pitch for *Indira hatao* was raised to the extent on which Indira Gandhi had raised her slogan of *garibi hatao* to secure a landslide win in the previous election. The whirlwind tour of the opposition leaders in different parts of India echoed an unprecedented chord in raising the identical slogan of *Indira hatao*. This election was, thus, also converted into a single-issue election by the opposition, which the ruling Congress could not counter by coming up with any convincing rebuttal or counter narrative set by the opposition. The final outcome of the election was in the form of the people according their approval for the appeal of the opposition parties and voting the Congress out of power.

The tendency of converting elections into referendums was thus reinforced by the processes and results of the sixth general election.[6] Despite the presence of a number of equally, if not more, important issues with which the performance of the incumbent government could have been exposed, the opposition did not mind taking up those issues and tried to play that card which could have fetched the maximum benefit for it. Its concerted focus on impressing the people to decide whether they want the retrieval of democracy or allow lapsing the democratic system into authoritarian regime as experienced during the Emergency tended to make the election a single-point agenda of *Indira hatao, loktantra bachao*.[7] Accordingly, in such a charged atmosphere, common voters did not look at any other issue and took the election as an opportunity to cast his or her vote vis-à-vis saving the democracy by voting against Indira Gandhi government. This election's conversion as a referendum on the government of Indira Gandhi in general and Emergency in particular sharply narrowed down the choices of the people and paid rich political dividends to the opposition Janata Party, which was catapulted to power for the first time in the country.

Mandal and Mandir

The 10th general elections were held in the atmosphere of both hope and desperation. The failure of the government to complete its full term and internal ruptures that had kept the

[6] D. N. Dhangare, 'Sixth Lok Sabha Election in Uttar Pradesh—1977, The End of Congress Hegemony,' *Political Science Review* 18, no.2 (1979): 39.

[7] Aaron S. Klieman, 'Indira's India: Democracy and Crisis Management,' *Political Science Quarterly* 92, no. 2 (Summer 1981): 257.

government busy with its in-house management had provided the Congress the conventional argument to put before the voters that the opposition parties could never learn the art of running the government for a full term of five years. As a result, the party was buoyed to join the electoral bandwagon and aimed at bloating the charges made against it during the previous general election. The top leadership of the party including the prime ministerial candidate Rajiv Gandhi embarked upon the whirlwind tour of different parts of the country on the plank of providing a stable government at the centre, if the party is voted back to power. However, the party did face the stupendous task of convincing the voters, who had already been oriented towards the issues of Mandal and Mandir.

Riding on the wave of Mandal, the disparate parties forming the Janata Dal at that point of time began the electoral campaign with the renewed vigour by taking credit for making the vast majority of OBCs realize their long-cherished dream of joining the government jobs on the basis of reservations granted to them. This electoral argument of the Janata Dal was really able to cut much ice with OBCs particularly in the states of UP and Bihar, where the long traditions of socialist movement had already awakened a large mass of middle classes to claim their dues in the political and administrative cake. The Mandal issue, in fact, was taken by them as some sort of unprecedented empowerment through which a golden future would be looking at them. The leaders such as Lalu Prasad in Bihar and Mulayam Singh Yadav in UP tried to maximize the gains arising out of this historic decision of the V. P. Singh government. Thus, for the first time, the Janata Dal looked at replacing the Congress as the most significant gainer of the social churning taking place in the two critical states in the arithmetic calculations of the general elections.

Amidst these buoyancies of the two important stakeholders in the 10th general elections, the BJP naturally decided to consolidate its previous gains by reemphasizing Hindutva as the mainstay of its electoral strategy. The party was sure of expanding its electoral base in the Hindi heartland by countering the

Mandal wave by raising the Mandir issue with much more vigour than before. At the same time, the BJP tried to play down the caste-based appeal of the proponents of social justice in the name of calling for Hindu unity so as to regain the prestige and glory of the past. Thus, the bogie of cultural nationalism came as the readymade campaign strategy for the party to not only counter its opponents but also make a positive appeal to the voters to make their choice for the party. However, during these elections, like the previous ones, the parties, both the BJP as well as the Janata Dal, focused only upon the areas that had traditionally been their bastions from the past. Yet, apart from the Hindi heartland, the BJP extended its areas of influence to the western part of the country, particularly in the states of Gujarat and Maharashtra. Nonetheless, despite its best effort, the South still remained the region where the party could not extend its reach beyond a limit.[8]

The main battlefield for the 10th general elections though was thought to be the Hindi heartland but the decisive factor in the eventual outcome of the elections had been the voters of the southern and eastern parts of the country. As a matter of fact, the fragmentation of the voters in the northern states had been so intense that there could not have been any escape from the multi-polar contest in most, if not all, of the constituencies in these states. But the situation was markedly different in the southern and eastern states, where the lack of appeal of both the proponents of Mandal and Mandir did not entice them to try their luck in these states. As a result, the contest in these states remained traditionally poised between the rival regional parties with only the Congress making its presence felt in these states. Moreover, in many of the southern states, the regional parties were apparently having edge over the Congress, as the previous negative perception of the party did not disappear to the desirable extent. As a result, in the final reckoning, a number of the regional parties had put up great shows in these elections.

[8] James Manor, 'BJP in the South India: 1991 General Election,' *Economic & Political Weekly* 27, no. 24–25 (1992): 1269.

Ascendance of BJP

There also existed a lot of variation in the campaign strategies of different political parties during the 13th general elections. The BJP tried to enter the electoral fray with the twin strategy of containing any negative campaign against the party or the coalition by proving its innocence in the name of not getting ample opportunity to do much for the welfare of the people. But on the positive side, the party did not shy to capitalize on the Kargil War that the NDA government had fought against the Pakistani aggression in the hilltops in Kargil well within the Indian territory. Admittedly, the Kargil might be seen as a godsend opportunity for the BJP to show its resoluteness in taking on the challenges facing the unity and integrity of the nation. In fact, over the years, BJP had been strident in putting forward its argument for a resolute and firm handling of the issues posing any threat to the unity and integrity of the nation. But the party never got a chance to show to the people how capable was the party, to put its words in action whenever an occasion arose to this effect. Thus, much of the election strategy of the BJP during the 13th general elections depended on showcasing of the Kargil War as the proof of the determinate behaviour of the party in times of crisis facing the nation, either from within or outside.

The electoral scenario, therefore, appeared distinctly poised in favour of the BJP and the NDA in comparison to the opposition parties including the Congress and the Third Front. The only formidable challenge likely to arise before the ruling party was from the strong regional parties that had also stood their ground all through these years, as the BJP had done. So, throughout the campaign trail, the BJP had tried to tread a cautious path in such a way that it could put forward its views and appeals to the electorate without casting any aspersion, especially on the regional parties that could become the probable ally of the party in case it became short of majority in the Lok Sabha.[9] Moreover, the party focused on its core vote banks

[9] Yogendra Yadav, Sanjay Kumar, and Oliver Heath, 'The BJP's New Social Block,' *Frontline* 16, no. 23 (1999): 14.

in the Hindi-heartland states along with its areas of influence in the western parts of the country. In the rest of the country, the party banked on its allies to make most of these elections and augment the tally of seats in the Lok Sabha. For the opposition, while the Congress appeared in doldrums given the novice moves of the party president, the other parties remained engaged in their pocket boroughs at provincial levels. Thus, these elections appeared as the best-possible chance for the BJP to maximize its gains and help its allies all over the country to come up with handsome electoral results, so that the NDA could emerge as the coalition with at least working majority in the Lok Sabha.

In the 16th general elections, all the major contestants had very high stakes. But the most vital stake was that of the BJP for both ideological as well as tactical reasons. Ideologically, the BJP has been championing the cause of Right enmeshed in the framework of Hindutva ever since its formation in 1980. In the face of the Congress's Left of the Centre ideology, the BJP has been seeking to present an alternative to the ideology of the Congress by offering the Right of the Centre approach to almost all the issues and challenges facing the country right since Independence.[10] With the arrival of the forces of social justice on the political scene in big way in the aftermath of the implementation of the Mandal recommendations, the ideological landscape in the country got muddied with these forces eschewing the ideology of either Left or Right for the sake of social justice. Yet, the Congress's overt or covert collaborative political engagements with the Left from time to time has surely strengthened the Leftist genre of the party and imparted a distinct ideological space to it. What the BJP has been trying to offset is the dominance of this Leftist-leaning policies of the Congress Party by pushing that to political marginalization through electoral politics. The BJP had already made significant inroads in the Hindi heartland and replaced the Congress as the

[10] Pradeep Chhibber and Rahul Verma, 'Why the Congress Needs the BJP,' *The Indian Express*, 19 March 2014, 11.

dominant political player in these states. But the dominance at the Central level was yet to come.

Alongside the ideological pursuits, the BJP also wanted to present an alternative vision in terms of its radical views on the important issues and challenges facing the country. Given that the previous experiences of the NDA government under the leadership of Atal Bihari Vajpayee did not allow the party to materialize its vision of India owing to the coalitional nature of the government in which securing support for its agenda would not have been possible, the party was surely eying these elections as the stepping stone for it to arrive at the seat of power in New Delhi with comfortable majority of its own.[11] Moreover, with Narendra Modi declared as the prime ministerial candidate of the party, the leadership position of the party had already experienced a generational change in which the old guards no longer remained the shepherd of the party. As a result, these general elections were both a challenge and an opportunity for the second-generation leadership of the party to prove their mettle in running the party and making it acceptable to the people on the basis of the long-drawn avowed goals and objectives for which it had stood steadfastly over the years. So, for the BJP, the stakes in the 2014 general elections were as high as a matter of life or death. For, the third consecutive defeat at the national polls would have foretold the doomsday for the party from the political scene.

As the dominant party of the ruling coalition, stakes for the Congress in these general elections could not have been less, if not more, than that of the principal opposition party. As a matter of fact, the sliding down of the Congress Party on the electoral scale in the absence of a Gandhi–Nehru scion at the helm of the affairs had presumably convinced Sonia Gandhi to step in and take charge of the party at an opportune time. The veracity of her decision to become president of the party was proved somewhat right when she was able to cobble up

[11] Pradeep Chhibber, Harsh Shah, and Rahul Verma, 'The Art of Building Majorities,' *The Hindu*, 14 March 2017, 9.

the coalition in the name of the United Progressive Alliance (UPA) to offer a plausible alternative to the NDA. Further, her decision to decline the offer of the coalition partners to make her the prime ministerial candidate of the coalition and name her trusted aide Manmohan Singh had amply proved the political acumen of the 'foreigner' in protest against whom a number of senior leaders of the party had left the Congress. The political morale of the party in general and Sonia Gandhi in particular was enormously boosted when she was able to steer the coalition for a back-to-back victory in 2009 general elections as well. In such a situation, the third straight win for the party could surely have turned Sonia Gandhi into the persona of her mother-in-law who played a defining role in the Indian politics.

For the other parties, these general elections presented a win-win situation for two reasons. One, the regional and Left parties were sure that the straight fight between the two dominant national parties, the Congress and the BJP, would surely be an advantageous position for them. They appeared quite sure that the performance of the ruling party in these elections would not be as thumping as it was in the two previous general elections. The series of corruption charges against senior ministers of the government and the anti-incumbency wave after 10 long years of rule by the Congress appeared as the plausible reasons for them to be hopeful of Congress's dismal performance in these elections. Alongside, they were also expecting that the BJP, as the epitome of the Right-ideological perspective, would not be able to cut much ice with the teeming millions, given the social and economic orientations of such people to unhesitatingly go for the Left-leaning parties. Two, the regional and Left parties, after improving their tallies in the wake of the dismal performance of the two national parties, also looked to vie for their greater role in the national politics, as part of the ruling coalition that was likely to be constructed after the indecisive results of the polls. Thus, the stakes of the regional and Left parties also seemed to be very high, as handsome results in these elections could have secured them the passport for becoming the kingmaker at the national level. But the basic characteristic of these elections remains rooted in its conceptualization as a vote on the performance of the incumbent government.

Plebiscitary Democracy: Is This a Tenable Conceptual Mode?

As the above discussion shows, the argument in support of characterizing some of the specific Lok Sabha polls as plebiscites needs to be pursued while keeping in view the importance of some of the ideological priorities that the political parties put forward before the electorates to garner votes. There is hardly a one-size-fits-all formula to persuasively explain the electoral outcome in India; the issue is far more complex in which the appeal of the political parties to the voters is also couched around specific socio-economic goals that they are determined to realize once they are brought to power. A careful reading of the poll outcomes also suggests that it will be simplistic, for instance, to attribute the victory of the Modi government in 2014 and 2019 national elections to the magnetizing presence of Narendra Modi only, as the study of voting behaviour shows. There is more substance to the people's mandate than just being blindly swayed by personality cult. A charismatic political persona is a mere accessory to the leaders' track record of engaging fruitfully with the particularities of the socio-economic context that they are campaigning within. Nonetheless, elections remain an important conceptual tool to comprehend how democracy, which was introduced in India in the wake of colonial rule, became integral to the mindset that evolved in support of Westminster democracy. The process is complex but has steadily contributed to the consolidation of the foundation of democracy in India. Fundamentally, here are three important points that need attention. First, despite severe challenges from within and the consolidation and triumph of forces opposed to democracy in the neighbouring states, India's experience with democratic politics and government is rather successful. Not only elections are held regularly but there is a template that has become stronger as days pass on. Although the British democratic tradition contributed immensely to India's democracy, equally significant is the role of the Congress Party which was coterminus with the nationalist campaign for freedom in sustaining the democratic spirit of the populace, at least institutionally, since its inception in 1885. Not only did the Congress stalwarts champion and absorb the democratic values by being sensitive to the philosophy of Enlightenment, they played a critical role in legitimizing democratic rule as a whole. The general concern is not so much for the substance of political authority as for the mechanisms entailing elections, representation and mandate obtained through adult suffrage. They derive their sustenance from the Constitution, which provides for a specific structure of political life 'by allowing and encouraging (within limits) popular participation in the political system within a framework of rules, rights, structures and processes which must be broadly respected by both rulers and ruled'.[12] Here probably lies the reason why democracy survives in India, since it has sustained itself as a legitimate mechanism for realizing the ideal of self-rule, despite the challenges from both within and outside its geographical boundaries.

There is another peculiarity that deserves attention here: none of the political parties succeeded in election by being rigid in its ideological preferences. For instance, both Jawaharlal Nehru and his daughter, Indira Gandhi, despite having had socialist inclinations, never ever identified with the Left political parties, which means that they needed to be Centrist in their ideological inclinations to accommodate various kinds of ideological forces. Being Centrist, it was easier for the Congress in its earlier days to survive as a legitimate claimant of political authority. Notwithstanding their avowed commitment to right-wing ideals, the BJP's growing propensity for programmes geared towards generating mass acceptance (eg., *sabka sath sabka vikas*, i.e., collectively moving towards universal

---

[12] Achin Vanaik, *The Painful Transition*, 99.

development) is evident, as demonstrated in the 2014 and 2019 Lok Sabha polls. All this points to a gradual slide towards the middle of the political spectrum, which is a trend that has come up again and again in India's democratic past.

Second, in view of the complex scenario in which elections are fought in India, it is fair to argue that plebiscite democracy also contains an ideological battle that wages over the respective preferences by the political parties and their leaders. The long Congress rule ended partly in the 1967 State Assembly election, though till 1977, the party succeeded in retaining its authority in Delhi, presumably because of a stable support base that stood by. With the rise of popular regional leaders with multiple ideological predilections, there was a phase when it was believed that like the pattern that evolved in West Europe, coalition of political parties was the only option for forming a workable government.[13] The trend continues even today in some form or the other. In the 17th Lok Sabha poll in 2019, the BJP succeeded in winning a majority on its own, though by being respectful to the other constituents of the NDA, it did not throw away any of its partners. Core here is the argument that, in the present scenario, the principle of accommodating political parties with identical ideological inclinations continues to remain highly pertinent. Hence, the leading constituent of the BJP-led NDA has also emphasized the idea of *sabka biswas* (everybody's faith) in the conglomeration in power. What is evident here is the concern for all, which necessitates the acceptance also of viewpoints which may not conform to what the leading partner, the BJP, upholds. The idea that for electoral victory political parties are required to be accommodative seems to have struck organic roots in India, presumably because of the sociocultural diversity of the voters, which can also be ignored only to the detriment of the parties' prospects of winning.

[13] Bidyut Chakrabarty has dealt with this phenomenon in his *Forging Power: Coalition Politics in India* (New Delhi: Oxford University Press, 2006).

Continuity and Change

Successful holding of general elections over a period of seven decades, India's experimentation with democracy has undoubtedly borne fruit.[14] But these 17 elections also reflect the continuities of certain unmistakable characteristic features of the Indian democracy, despite witnessing a number of changes as per the imperatives of time and circumstances of particular elections. As a matter of fact, recognized as the largest democracy in the world, free and fair elections have been the foundational characteristic of Indian democracy. India has been able to successfully organize 17 general elections so far, the latest being held in 2019 itself. Though the Constitution stipulates that the lower house of Parliament would have a term of not more than five years, quite a number of times, premature general elections have also been organized in case of the fall of a government and the house unable to provide a stable government. There has also been an occasion in the country when the term of the Lok Sabha has been sought to be extended beyond the constitutional stipulations. Times have also been there when the scheduled elections to the Lok Sabha could not be held on account of the executive arbitrariness, as has been experienced during the period of Emergency in 1977. Thus, the regularity with which the general elections in India have been organized cannot be taken as a mean achievement given the multiple challenges arising out of different individuals and contingencies. But, after all, democratic process of the country has remained on the track braving all kinds of challenges.[15]

When the democratic system of government was envisaged for the country by the Constitution makers, apprehensions were raised in a number of quarters regarding the capability of the institutions and individuals to keep the process of democratic government intact, if not to talk of its deep rooting.

[14] Surjit S. Bhalla, *Citizen Raj: Indian Elections 1952–2019* (Chennai: Westland, 2019), 291.

[15] Prannoy Roy and Dorab R. Sopariwala, *The Verdict: Decoding India's Elections* (New Delhi: Penguin, 2019), 32.

The situation further seemed complicated for the alarmists on account of the introduction of a universal adult franchise as the guiding principle of Indian democracy. Such apprehensions of some people were presumably based on their perception of taking democracy and democratic processes as the monopoly of the Western countries. Moreover, they appeared convinced that the mass of people having all sorts of social and economic backwardness—poor, illiterate, caste ridden, having predominant primordial affinities and prone to all kinds of threats and allurements—could never succeed in making democracy a successful experimentation in their societies. Above all, the failure of democratic experiments in many other parts of the world have been the empirical cases for them to foretell the failure of the democratic experiment in the country. But having experienced the democratic government for over 70 years, Indians are now well in place to show the world how democracy is designed and implemented in the traditional societies.

The democratic experience of the people of India has not remained confined only to the elections for the apex bodies like the Parliament only. On the contrary, the democratization of the Indian polity has been sought to be taken to the lower possible levels. Thus, elections are held regularly to elect the representatives of the people at the state, district, block, village, municipality, urban centres, cooperative societies and everywhere else if that body or institution has been engaged in the management of the public affairs. For successful conduct of all these elections, appropriate bodies and administrative units have also been created at appropriate levels. In fact, the administrative and logistical paraphernalia of the election machinery have been so efficiently organized and managed in the country that a number of other countries in the world look up to India to assist them in organization of free and fair polls in those countries as well. Thus, the vision of the Constitution makers to make the Indian democracy successful and vibrant has been facilitated by the creation of competent machinery, provision of men and materials and design of standard operating procedures for conducting free and fair polls.

Elections may be considered as both the cause and effect of democratic process in the country[16], given that at the heart of democracy lies the election of the people's representatives to take charge of the government on behalf of the people electing them. Thus, election has indeed been the cause of democracy. In other words, the idea of democracy could simply not be visualized without thinking of the appropriate system through which the people would be able to articulate their opinions or views on the people likely to be their representatives. But the ingenuity of the people still has not allowed them to imagine any other institution or process through which the true representatives of the people could be identified and placed in the position of government. As a result, elections remain the basic system through which democracies attain functional vibrancy. However, the democratic processes also result in the refinement of the processes and methods of elections in such a way that constant innovations and creativities are experienced in the conduct of elections in different parts of the world. Elections, therefore, affect and get affected by the democratic processes in a number of subtle ways all across the globe. Insofar as India is concerned, elections have been an important factor in reinvention of the democratic institutions and processes in the country.

Concluding Observations

Indian elections have always been full of surprises right from the introduction of electoral democracy in the country after the promulgation of Constitution. For instance, when the idea of universal adult suffrage was accepted as the guiding principle of electoral democracy, the sceptics appeared quite sure that the country's experimentation with representative democracy would not be able to survive long, and it might sooner or later relapse into an authoritarian rule. But as the proceedings of the

[16] Ruchir Sharma, *Democracy on the Road: A 25 Year Journey through India* (New Delhi: Penguin, 2019), 107.

first general election were concluded and results of the general election started pouring in, it was quite clear to them that the people as well as political leadership of India were mentally prepared to accept elections as their *fait accompli,* and therefore, democracy would sooner become a way of life for them. Such an evolution of the democratic processes in India has been proved prophetic after that with the successful conclusion of 17 general elections despite a number of hiccups and occasional challenges before it. What has, however, remained an enigma before the scholars and analysts have been the unique characteristics that have become typical of Indian democracy. While a majority of these characteristics are unique to India, their role in ensuring the vibrancy of the electoral process in the country has been recognized as a valuable contribution of India towards better understanding of the democratic processes in the developing countries.

Roots of the emergence of elections as some kind of referendums on certain issues or leaders over the years could probably be traced to the birth of Indian democracy through the lineages of the national movement. For instance, even during the national movement, in order to make the struggle against the colonial rulers mass based, the Indian leadership, particularly Gandhi, found it prudent to pick up one or the other emotive issues to arouse public passion on it and make them stand up against the colonial rule. Thereafter, such a trend presumably continued even after Independence with the general electorate identifying a particular election with certain specific issue and framing its mind in that direction. This has obviously imparted a distinct character to the Indian elections, making them plebiscitary in nature, whereby the entire general public would appear to be swayed by their respective stands on such issues. Interestingly, despite the ambiguity on the fact whether such a character of the Indian elections would be propitious for the long-term health of democracy in India, the fact remains incontrovertible that the conversion of elections as a kind of referendum on the incumbent government or on the opposition claim of presenting an alternative vision of life for the common people has become a distinct characteristic of the Indian democracy. While previously such a phenomenon was identified as the product of the Congress Party and its leaders, with the emergence of the BJP and its leader, Narendra Modi, emulating almost similar kind of electoral rhetoric, it has now become a proven fact of the Indian democracy that the conversion of general elections into plebiscitary exercises probably suits all the stakeholders and, therefore, nobody feels distancing him or her from the strengthening of this phenomenon of the Indian politics.

In a nutshell, India's democratic experiment is a class by itself for a variety of reasons, as the discussion in this chapter has shown. Prominent among them is the idea that electorates are swayed by the magnetic personality of the leaders, who are well-equipped to carry the voters by drawing upon a specific ideological package. So, it has characteristics of a plebiscitary democracy. This is one part of the story. The other part is linked with the equal importance of the ideological preferences themselves, which also act decisively in charting out the way in which the voting behaviour is shaped. What is argued here is the point that a plebiscitary democracy entails a system of election in which the role of the ideological priorities is as important as the leader representing them. Conceptually innovative, this point of view clearly defends the point that given India's sociocultural disparate demography, the claim that leaders' charisma alone helps the political parties secure voters' support does not hold much water, since it is also built on the basis of the socio-economic packages that the electorates hope to receive in case the political party of their choice gains authority. In other words, the importance of personality cult may be a necessary condition for the electoral victory but can never be a sufficient condition unless voters are also persuaded to cast their votes in accordance with what is presented before them as appropriate for their future well-being. Hence, India, being defined as a plebiscitary democracy per se, does not seem to be persuasive, since voters do not necessarily vote for the candidates purely by being swayed by the leader's personality.

Based on empirical inputs, the argument suggesting that for a meaningful understanding of elections, especially in a strikingly diverse society, one is required to pay adequate attention to the processes which finally culminate in one's choice for a specific political party and its leader. Implicit here is the point that the leader in view of being highly charismatic can be an effective vote catcher, provided there exists meaningful packages for socio-economic gain which the voters readily accept. The Congress victory in 1971 and assumption of power by the BJP-led NDA following its success in the 2014 and 2019 national polls exemplify the contention in more than one way. And elections are thus proved to be a useful tool also to ascertain the conceptual validity of the claim that India is a plebiscitary democracy that itself is immensely important in reconceptualizing democracy as a phenomenon.

4

Ideological Churning

Ideological persuasions of different stakeholders have always been an important factor in shaping the outcomes of different elections in India. For instance, immediately after Independence, the ideological standpoints of different political parties ranged from the Left parties like the Communist Party of India to that of the Rightist Swatantra Party. In between the two, there stood the Congress as the Left of the Centre party with even the capitalists and erstwhile royals siding with the party, owing to its nationalist lineage. As the Congress could gain the mandate of the people to give shape to the broad contours of the social, economic and political system of India, other important ideology-based parties remain busy in gradually convincing the people of the veracity and appropriateness of their ideologies for the overall development of the country. What is remarkable in this context is the fact that for a long time it appeared that the ideological pendulum of the Indian political system remains essentially tilted towards the Centrist parties.[1] Therefore, the

---

[1] Achin Vanaik, 'Flexibility of Indian Centrism,' *Sunday Observer*, New Delhi, 28 April 1991, 13.

parties subscribing to other pure or extreme ideologies stood very less or no chance of getting catapulted to the centre stage of the electoral politics. But such an impression was shattered by the Left parties sooner than expected by succeeding in replacing the Congress as the mainstream political force in the states like Kerala and West Bengal and set an example of communist rule through winning the people's mandate by elections.

The aim of this chapter is to comprehend the relative importance of ideology and leadership in designing electoral strategies to catch the voters' attention. As results of the elections show, there is hardly a pattern in voting behaviour in India, presumably because there are multiple ideological packages that are presented before the electorates. In order to ascertain how ideology remains a cementing device in elections, the chapter also dwells on the processes culminating in how a leader creatively blends charisma and ideology to significantly persuade the voters in favour of one party or a collectivity of parties. By dwelling on the intricate sociopolitical churning, both during the interim period between two elections and on the eve of the poll, when the contestants place before voters what they propose to do if they win, the chapter also endeavours to assess whether ideology plays a critical role in creating a solid support base for the party and its nominees.

Congress and Centrist Ideology

Barring a few cadre-based parties rooted in their orthodox ideologies, the ideological base of the political parties in India has usually not been one of their trademarks. Such a situation may partly be explained with reference to the political process drawing its inspiration from the proceedings of the national movement. Given the fact that the primary concern of almost all the major stakeholders during the national movement was independence of India from the British colonial rule, they did not mind too rigid adherence to their ideological moorings. So much so that a number of political formations during that period did not have much to do with any kind of ideology as their purpose of existence was considered going beyond such a parochial consideration. This kind of situation was more pertinent in case of parties of organizations busying themselves in the protection and promotion of interests of their people, apart from fostering the cause of national movement. Nevertheless, there did exist at this time a few parties who were very much identified with their ideological purity. In this context, the Communist Party of India stood out prominently as the party with much adoration for its ideological roots. Similar position also existed for a few more political formations that sought to serve the interests of varying sections of society.

In case of the Congress, however, the ideological roots of the party were very varied and flexible in accordance with its avowed objective of keeping the goal of securing the independence from British imperialism at the top.[2] Moreover, the umbrella character of the party probably allowed it to accommodate people from all kinds of ideological persuasions who were willing to be part of the national movement. Interestingly, while the party began its forays in the national movement as the party of the elite and educated class of Indians vying for certain concessions from the British colonial government, the gradual domination of the party by the people with socialist ideological persuasions increasingly turned it into a radical political outfit, fighting not only for the cause of freedom but also social and economic reconstruction of India. The increasing domination of the party by the socialist leaders or its sympathizers sometimes brought the situation to such a pass that there appeared a condition of rift among the leadership of the party. But the commonality of the cause of national interest in terms of freedom acted as the cementing force that kept all its important factions together in their fight against the colonial rulers.

[2] Pitambar Datta Kaushik, *The Congress Ideology and Programme, 1920–1947: Ideological Foundations of the Congress During the Gandhian Era* (Bombay: Allied Publishers, 1964), 228.

After Independence, the entry of the party in the electoral fray came more as the champion of the national movement than a party professing any particular ideological perspective. The goodwill that the party had earned during the national movement apparently helped it secure its landslide victories in all the general elections that it fought under the tutelage of Nehru. Nevertheless, it was an open secret for all that the party's top leadership including Nehru was very much infatuated with the socialist ideology that the party tried to reflect in its policies and programmes. As the implied vision of the party was to direct the social and economic development of the country on the basis of socialist ideology, it went to the extent of declaring the establishment of socialistic pattern of society as its avowed objective. The adoption of the strategy of planned economic development as the mainstay of India's development paradigm was nothing but concretization of what the party had been professing for long. The later developments in terms of creation of a large structure of public-sector undertakings and community development for rural areas demonstrated the party's predilections for socialism as the ruling ideology of the time.

Though the Congress remained committed to the ideals of socialistic pattern of society as the fundamental feature of government policy, the party, under the leadership Indira Gandhi, sought to breach the delicate balance that was maintained during the times of Nehru, to make India look like a mixed economic system. In order to make her political objective of regaining control over the political loyalties of the common masses, she was hell bent on portraying herself as the champion of the cause of the masses. She, therefore, held no bar in her spree of dismantling whatever was vital on the part of the capitalist and propertied classes and robbed the royalties of their compensations that they appeared to be unduly getting from the government. She further wanted to reinforce her image as the messiah of the poor and downtrodden by floating the catchy slogan of *garibi hatao* that worked magically among the masses and catapulted her into political mainstream. Her tenure could thus be seen as the pinnacle of the socialist orientation of the party that received wholehearted support from the masses and helped her retain hold over the pulse of Indian electors over the years.[3]

Congress Party's tryst with the socialist ideology apparently came under strains with the arrival of Rajiv Gandhi on the political scene. When he disinterestedly joined the political bandwagon after the assassination of his mother, he did not have to strategize his political moves to win the election, as the sympathy wave in his favour gave him unprecedented majority in the lower house of Parliament. Moreover, his upbringing and socialization among the Western soul mates probably made him more inclined towards a mixed economic model rather than going for retention of the socialistic fervour of the party. Further, his focus on automation of governmental machinery and invitation to the private sector to play important role in the economic development helped in the dilution of the ideological depth of the party in favour of pragmatism. Thus, though his regime did not try to dismantle the vast range of public-sector undertakings, nor sought to bring about major structural changes in the economic system, it unmistakably laid the foundation for ideological flexibility in the party. Now, the party no longer seemed to be doggedly observing its commitment to the socialist ideology and readying to supplement it with pragmatism on the economic front. Over the years, the party has walked over to embrace capitalism as its favourite fad that continues even today. This seems to be a remarkable reinvention of the party, given its avowed acceptance of socialism as the ruling mantra for a long period of time.[4]

Varying Acceptability of the Left

Ideological predilections rooted in the Left have always been dominant discourse in the Indian politics since the days of the

[3] Sudipta Kaviraj, 'Indira Gandhi and Indian Politics,' *Economic & Political Weekly* 38, no. 39 (20 September 1986): 1698.
[4] Ravi Shankar, 'Congress Party: The Ideology Trap,' *The Indian Express Magazine*, 04 August 2019, 3.

national movement.[5] Two interrelated reasons may be discerned to explain this underlying phenomenon of the Indian politics. One, given the fact that many of the prominent leaders of the national movement were educated and trained in the Western countries, they could get a feel of the exploitative character of capitalist economic system, whose highest stage was reflected in the form of imperialism. These leaders, therefore, presumably became allergic to the exploitative capitalist economic system, and as its antithesis, they tended to embrace the socialist ideology as the only plausible ideology that could be practised in countries like India. Two, the social and economic conditions in the country were such that the mass of Indians used to live in conditions of abject poverty, apart from facing different kinds of social discriminations. In these circumstances again, the leaders felt that the only political ideology that could be appealing to the masses in enlisting their support not only during the national movement but also in the post-independent times would be no other than the Left ideology getting reflected in its varying form.

Though, in its early phase, the ideological predilections of the national movement were primarily rooted in the liberal ideology of the British traditions, as the national movement started getting radicalized, the predominance of the Left-leaning elements both within the Congress and outside started getting formidable. In this context, ideological persuasions of the Left got reflected in two distinct shades during the pre-Independence days. On the one hand, there was a large number of leaders who were totally devoted to the cause of Left ideology but decided to stay back in the Congress in order to strengthen the party as well as radicalize it from within so that the basic nature of the national movement became pro poor. In the course of time, these elements went to the extent of setting up the Congress Socialist Party as a powerful pressure group within the party. But on the

[5] Rajnarayan Chandavarkar, 'From Communism to "Social Democracy": The Rise and Resilience of Communist Parties in India, 1920–95,' *Science & Society* 61, no. 1 (Spring, 1997), 105.

other hand were a number of leaders who did not believe in the moderate face of the Left and sought to alter the political ambience through radical measures ranging to the extent of violent activities. What was common to both these Leftist groups was their unflinching faith in the Left ideology as the only valid ideological proposition in the face of the social and economic conditions of the country.

After Independence, when the first general election was announced, the simmering cleavages within the left oriented political formations started coming to the fore, resulting in the birth of a number of left-leaning political parties. Given the fundamental differences among these parties with regards to the basic issues facing the people as well as the nature of Indian State that came to replace the colonial rule, these parties could simply not think of any kind of poll adjustment or understanding against the monolith Congress Party. As a result, these parties contested the first general election on distinct symbols, putting up their candidates in different constituencies, albeit facing each other quite often. Though as the most organized and cadre-based party among the left-leaning political parties, the Communist Party of India could secure the highest number of seats in the first general election; the other parties were also not very far behind it in securing respectable percentage of votes and number of seats in Lok Sabha. That way, amidst the landslide victories of the Congress Party, the other political groups that could manage to put up some kind of fight against the Congress candidates were none other than the Left parties.

The Janata Parivar

The Centrist ideological position of the Congress was also embraced by the Janata Party after its formation in the course of struggle against the Emergency and the JP movement. The ideological milieu that the JP movement had created was translated in the repeal of a large number of draconian laws through the Forty-third and Forty-fourth Amendment Acts in 1978. In other words, the fact that the mounting public pressure resulted in the abrogation of laws supporting authoritarianism also confirms the critical role that social context plays in shaping a specific ideological stance. There is one fundamental conceptual point here: corruption and decline of ethics are dialectically interconnected; while the former has had 'variegated incidence in different times at different places, with varying degrees of damaging consequences',[6] the latter also unfolds gradually and is, thus, contingent on specific mindsets which either remain indifferent or supportive of some sort of malfeasance for private enrichment. There can, thus, hardly be a universal explanatory model, because this interrelationship is also context driven. For instance, in the erstwhile Licence–Quota–Permit Raj guaranteeing massive discretionary power to those holding public authority, corruption was considered to be the much-needed grease for the squeaking wheels of rigid administration. Gradually, the idea seems to have lost steam and the classical system of let things go became the normal pattern of political life of people.

In the mid-1970s, the efforts towards utilizing government machineries for personal gains provoked mass consternation, which was reflected in the JP movement. Challenging the ideological design of those in power, the campaign for JP's total revolution created, rather instantaneously, a constituency of support, presumably because of the abuse of authority by the powerful at the cost of the ordinary citizens. This was the main factor behind the massive campaign that JP had spearheaded in collaboration with political forces with incompatible ideological predilections. The lack of distinct ideological symmetry in the Janata Party, however, proved to be its nemesis, as the coalition parties and partners who had joined hands together very soon got exasperated from the party and it fell under its own weight.[7]

[6] Pranab Bardhan, 'Corruption and Development: A Review of Issues,' *Journal of Economic Literature* 35 no. 3 (September 1997), 1320.

[7] Madhu Limaye, *Janata Party Experiment: An Insider's Account of Opposition Politics, 1977–80*, vol. 2 (New Delhi: D. K. Publishers, 1994), 542.

Anti-Congressism as New Ideology

The ninth general elections facilitated the emergence of the anti-Congressism with renewed vigour in the Indian politics. In other words, the host of opposition parties that could not secure clear mandate from the electorate to form a non-Congress government did not wish to miss the opportunity offered to them to oust the Congress from the power at the centre, despite their not forming the government for themselves. This has indeed been the trait of the democratic politics that the political stakeholders espousing the cause of anti-Congress have always clamoured to oust the grand old party of India and replace with the non-Congress government. But none of these parties has ever been in a position to form the government on their own. As a result, whenever the opposition parties got a chance to form the government at the centre as in 1977, such a government would inevitably be a coalition of disparate political forces that would otherwise detest one another just as they do the Congress.[8]

The situation unfolding after the results of the ninth general elections were announced, which proved the long-standing belief of the analysts that for the opposition parties to come together for any meaningful purpose would only be to oust the Congress from power. But their ability to form and run a government at the centre, consisting of the host of parties, has always been in doubt. Interestingly, that has also been the saving grace for the Congress in that after every non-Congress government's fall, in the subsequent general elections, the party has been able to make a comeback as it did in the time of the first Janata government. Nevertheless, it is quite startling to see the anxiety of the opposition parties to ensure the exit of the Congress from power by all means. The situation had been more interesting in the aftermath of the ninth general elections

[8] Subir Sinha, 'Democratic Trajectories I: Congressism, Anti-Congressism and Composing the "people-as-a-whole",' in *Indian Democracy: Origins, Trajectories, Contestations*, eds Alf Gunvald Nilsen, Kenneth Bo Nielsen, and Anand Vaidya (London: Pluto Press, 2019), 101.

because of the system and mechanism through which the government was formed and allowed to run for whatsoever term it remained in office. Moreover, the internal bickering of the opposition coalition has also provided the Congress a chance to ensure that more than one prime minister enters the fray to run the opposition governments.

As in the case of the first Janata experiment, when the government of Morarji Desai fell, the Congress did not prefer to go for the outright elections. Rather, it prodded the desperate Charan Singh to stake his claim to form the government that the Congress would support from outside. It would then try to discredit the opposition conglomerate in such a way that in the ensuing general elections the electorate could be convinced that only the Congress Party could give a stable government that would be able to last the full term of office. The turn of events in the aftermath of the ninth general elections was a kind of action replay of the first Janata experiment with the same script and subtext of the political drama. That way, the Congress has always retained its relevance as the focal point of political process, whether it remains in government or in the opposition. In a way, the Congress exploits the sheer selfish interests of the opposition leaders as per its own calculations, so as to make most of the political drama enacted by the opposition leaders whenever they get a chance to form the government at the centre.[9]

The political scenario emerging out of these elections also demonstrated the need and acceptability of political expediency even on the part of the ideology-based parties whose avowed declarations are torn apart once it comes to join hands for the sake of anti-Congress government at the centre. Clearly, after the failure of the Janata Dal to secure a working majority in the Lok Sabha to form a government, there was also the possibility before the president to invite the leader of the biggest party in the house to form the government.

[9] R. K. Sinha, 'Anti-Congressism roots go deep,' *The Pioneer*, 11 August 2015, 7.

Given that the Congress had emerged as the biggest party in the house, the opposition feared that if they did not cobble up the numbers, the ball might be rolled out in the court of the Congress. Therefore, the ideologically diametrically opposite parties, such as the BJP and the Left combine, wasted no time in making up their mind to prop up the government of V. P. Singh from outside. This was a unique proposition in the Indian democracy when the ideologies of the parties were given a go-by just to make sure that the Congress remained out of power at the centre.

While the trend of extending outside support to a government has been in vogue at the state levels for quite a long period of time, this phenomenon has generally been uncommon at the centre. Only on one or two occasions in the past had the governments been formed at the centre with the outside support of other parties. Even in those cases also, the support to the governments were strategic and could not last long. In other words, such outside supports to the minority governments were not part of any long-drawn strategy of the parties and appeared to be contingent in nature. But in case of the ninth Lok Sabha, the two ideologically opposed political parties took the deliberate and well-considered decision of supporting the V. P. Singh government from outside that could actually survive for a fairly long period of time. When this government fell, the Congress wasted no time in coming up with its deceitful plan of supporting the Chandra Shekhar government from outside, so as to gain time for strategizing its electoral plan as and when the elections take place.[10] Thus, the phenomenon of minority governments being supported from outside by a host of parties became the established norm of the Indian democracy.

In the deep rooting of the phenomenon of minority governments forming and surviving with the outside support of

[10] For an interesting account of the politics of the time, see Dipankar Sinha, 'V. P. Singh, Chandra Shekhar and "Nowhere Politics" in India,' *Asian Survey* 31, no. 7 (1991), 598–612.

a number of parties indeed betrayed the opportunistic characteristics of almost all the political parties. Ordinarily, it is quite often that a party or all the parties fail to secure a working majority in the lower house of Parliament. In that case, formation of the government becomes a challenge to overcome which the concerned parties need to evolve certain consistent position in consonance with their ideological and programmatic orientations. But evolution of such a normative trait in the country has obviously been sacrificed on the altar of the opportunistic desires and aspirations of almost all the political parties as they take such occasions to reorder their electoral strategies, so as to face the upcoming electoral challenge in a more systematic manner. These opportunistic moves on the part of the different parties are also conditioned by the fact that the production of a hung house in the aftermath of an election would, in most probability, be followed by the announcement of fresh general election, as the government of the day would not be able to complete its full term.

The formation of the governments, led by opposition parties at the centre beginning with the ninth general elections, has been taken as the maturing of the Indian democracy. The established norms of the older democracies have been that the governments or the ruling echelons need to rotate among the competing claims to the political power of the country, so much so that in many countries there has been made a constitutional provision prohibiting a single individual from even contesting elections for more than two terms for a particular political office. Though no such provision exists in India, it has been felt desirable that the rotation of governments need to take place in such a way that no party is able to hold the power at the centre for more than two consecutive terms. So, the reversal of the fortunes of the grand old party in the general elections at periodic intervals has been a positive signal for the vibrancy of the Indian democracy. That way, results of the ninth general elections had indeed been a pointer in the right direction as it provided the opposition parties a chance to form the government, albeit for a short span of time.

Ideology of the Right

Among all the political parties, the most significant gainer of these elections had been the BJP. Ever since its formation, the party had been trying to gain somewhat respectful, if not formidable, foothold in the electoral landscape. But the hegemonic influence of the Congress Party across the country did not permit any leg space for the BJP for the simple reason that the probable voters of the BJP could have been the ones that had also been the ardent supporters of the Congress. So, BJP's earnest efforts in creating a distinct wedge in the core voter base of the Congress, through its unique ideology-driven emphasis on Hindutva, had reached its probable target in the aftermath of the Rath Yatra of the party stalwart L. K. Advani.[11] Moreover, the clever move of the BJP had also polarized a large section of the Indian electorate, particularly the upper-caste Hindus, on the issues of Hindutva and Ram temple.[12] Thus, the political landscape during these elections had become so complex that the established discourses got decisively shattered, allowing the BJP a widespread acceptance across the different castes and regions. Consequently, the party was able to improve its seat tally remarkably from just 2 in the previous house to that of 85 in the ninth Lok Sabha that afforded it the critical position of kingmaker. The vote share of the party had also increased substantially to the tune of 11.36 per cent that had surpassed the combined vote share of the Left parties that had been in the mainstay of the political scenario of a number of states.[13]

[11] For a critical examination of Rath Yatra as a path-breaking event in the democratic process of the country, see Bidyut Chakrabarty, ed., 'Introduction' in *Whither India's Democracy?* (Calcutta: K. P. Bagchi & Co. 1993), 1–28.

[12] See, Y. K. Malik and V. B. Singh, *Hindu Nationalist in India: The Rise of the Bharatiya Janata Party* (New Delhi: Vistaar Publications, 1995), 189.

[13] For a lucid account of how the decline of the Congress has proportionally facilitated the rise of the BJP in different states, see V. B. Singh, 'Rise of the BJP and Decline of the Congress: An Appraisal,' in *Indian Democracy: Meaning and Practices*, eds Rajendra Vora and Suhas Palshikar (New Delhi: SAGE Publications, 2004), 304.

The democratic dynamics since Independence has ordained such circumstances in which the Congress Party has remained in power for a long period of time. The legacies of the national movement have, in fact, helped the party penetrate into the bottom of heart of the general masses in the country in such a way that majority, if not all, of them have become an avowed Congressmen. Cashing upon this goodwill of the people, the Congress could remain in power even after the departure of the leaders who really had taken part in the national movement and could be considered as the true inheritors of the nationalist legacy of the Congress. This, however, does not mean that there did not exist any kind of opposition to the Congress ideology and programmes. Rather, several streams of social, religious as well as political movements have been in vogue that espoused exactly the opposite cause articulated by the Congress. But none of the anti-Congress forces have been formidable enough to take on the Congress in an effective manner. As a result, they did not seem to be left with any other alternative than to join hands together to put up a combined fight against the Congress. Thus, anti-Congressism has been a constant factor in the Indian politics right from the 1960s. While its first meaningful articulation could be seen in the first Janata experiment of 1977, the ninth general elections have also witnessed the reiteration of the same sentiments in a different form.

With the political vacuum getting widened in different states, particularly in the Hindi heartland by the dwindling support base of the Congress, the party that eyed to step into the footsteps of the Congress had been the BJP. Amidst the ideological landscape getting mired into the competing claims of the Left parties, Congress as well as the parties standing for social justice to occupy the Leftist space, the BJP was obviously left with no other option than to go for consolidation of its Rightist ideology enmeshed into its long-standing demand for the construction of Ram temple in Ayodhya. As a matter of fact, the key ideological premise of Hindutva that had been a sort of article of faith for the party had virtually got crystallized at that time into its campaign for the construction of Ram temple at the birthplace of Lord Ram. Thus, amidst the powerful thrust of the proponents of social justice for awakening the latent political and social power of OBCs, the BJP sought to counterbalance these forces with its renewed and vigorous thrust towards bringing the issue of Ram temple at the centre stage of democratic politics in the country sooner than later.

On the political front, the greater consolidation of OBCs' votes on the part of the Janata Dal made the other claimants of their votes shaky, resulting into the initiation of the counter-moves on the part of the latter to galvanize the voters in their support. In this context, the most significant countermoves came from the side of the BJP, which felt threatened to lose its core vote bank if the different constituents of Hindu society started looking at each other with suspicion and disbelief. It, therefore, went on sharpening its Hindutva ideology so as to put it as the uniting force of the Hindu society in the face of the divisive politics of the rival opposition parties. That way, the entire electoral process during the course of the 10th general elections revolved around the issues of Mandal and Mandir with the other issues of national importance getting pushed into insignificance. Such polarization of the votes went to the extent of creating violent wedges among the different sections of the society, resulting in killings of one section of people by another and outbreak of the communal riots in different parts of the country, thereby vitiating the peaceful atmosphere in which the entire electoral exercise had to be completed.

The progressive strengthening of the hold of caste-based parties in the core states of the Hindi heartland has been sought to be countered by the BJP through its increasing and consistent thrust on the ideology of Hindutva as the hallmark of its appeal to the voters.[14] In fact, in order to present an alternative vision to the dominant Congress's ideological and

[14] Stuart Corbridge and John Harris, *Reinventing India: Liberalisation, Hindu Nationalism and Popular Democracy* (New Delhi: Oxford University Press, 2001), 133.

programmatic reach, the party insisted on taking up a number of such issues and concerns that went to strengthen its image of a Hindu nationalist party. The party argued for the adoption of cultural nationalism as the founding principle of the Indian polity in such a way that the traditional Hindu way of life is blended with the modernity of the time. During this period, the party sought to symbolize its thrust on the ideology of Hindutva and cultural nationalism by calling for the construction of a grant Ram temple at the site of his birthplace by removing the disputed structure standing at that place as the Babri mosque. Thus, the stridency of the party on the issue of Ram temple, apparently, provided it a long following among the upper-castes people, who identified themselves with the traditional glory of India.

Concluding Observation

India has always been a laboratory of various kinds of experiments. It is a matter of common knowledge that the rise and consolidation of democracy is a miracle in India in view of her diverse sociocultural texture. Many factors are cited. Prominent among them is surely the endeavour of the Congress stalwarts to ideologically couch the nationalist campaign. In order to organize the socioculturally divided people, it was perhaps the best means which they understood as soon as the struggle for freedom created a common template for all. It is, thus, fair to suggest that regardless of their differences, people from all walks of life participated in the movement that the Congress steered towards the goal. Being an umbrella organization, the Congress was also accommodative of ideologically diverse forces, which confirms how the goal acted decisively in mobilizing support for the freedom struggle. Despite being subject to strong criticism by his own colleagues within the Congress, Gandhi reigned supreme in so far as India's nationalist movement was concerned. Implicit here are two core points which will help us comprehend the complex character of the Gandhi-led anti-British campaign for political freedom. On the one hand, it reveals that nationalism as an ideology was largely effective in cementing a bond among the participants notwithstanding their different ideological inclinations. For those who held incompatible points of view appear to have been convinced that under those circumstances ideological differences should not be allowed to weaken the conglomeration for the principal goal of Gandhi's campaign. There was, on the other, an equally important aspect, namely the leading nationalist platform; the Congress was also not so rigid ideologically by being respectful to the distinct points of view the constituent wings nurtured. It was a quid-pro-quo arrangement, it seems, presumably because the nationalist activists privileged political freedom over any other considerations.

Once freedom was won, the trend continued presumably in view of the presence of those nationalists on the political scene who actively involved in the endeavour that finally led to India's freedom. Although nationalism remained an important ideological force in electoral battles, at least in the initial years after liberation, the political scene became gradually complex with the consolidation of other contrasting ideological priorities. For instance, the Socialists, Communists and also those championing caste identities and regional interests, which were allegedly under-represented or unrepresented, became important players in elections. Issues may have been articulated differently since the objectives of the political parties in fray differ from one election to another. Nonetheless, it also proves that their ideological inclinations in the form of specific socio-economic and political packages remain critical in garnering votes in elections. Basic here is the point that voters do not appear to decide a priori but contextually on the basis of their judgment, which is generally based on their assessment of the politico-ideological promises of the parties. Ideology is therefore paramount in elections.

As a detailed study of elections show, the political processes in the countries like India have always been prone to the massive ideological churning due to the absence of an organic evolution of political parties on the basis of their avowed ideological commitments. Moreover, the colonial past of these countries makes them wage a sustained and long-drawn national movement during which the party spearheading this movement emerges as the focal point of polity embracing, essentially a Centrist ideology, as it had to accommodate all kinds of interests and people within its fold. That way, Indian political process has been typically ideologically neutral, as the ruling party for a long period of time remained bereft of any orthodox ideological commitment despite its declared objective of establishing socialistic pattern of society. While the socialist commitments of the party remained in focus as long as the people who had participated in the national movement remained at the root of the party, the departure of such people from the scene and their replacement by new generation resulted into unavoidable ideological metamorphosis of the party, into a party of liberal economic beliefs.

Insofar as parties who had previously constituted the core of the opposition parties in earlier times are concerned, their ideological predilections have been more clear and forthcoming. For instance, the ideological moorings of both the Left and Right parties have been quite apparent, as they refused to toe the Congress line even during the national movement and preferred to charter a distinct course for them despite remaining committed to the cause of independence. Hence, the participation of these parties in the electoral processes have been quite on terms of their ideological clarity, and any vote for them had been counted as a vote for their ideology, apart from the personal or regional factors. Similarly, the electoral fortunes of different political parties have also not been uniform, as almost all kinds of ideologically committed parties have found chance to win the support of the people and form the government, either at the centre or in the states. Interestingly, the ideology of Right, which was not in the reckoning of electoral games a few decades ago, has now become the reigning ideology with its proponents getting astounding majority in the succeeding elections and marching ahead with their long-drawn plan of restructuring the basic contours of the society, polity and economy, despite stiff opposition from both within and outside the country.

Fundamental, here, is the argument that in Indian elections, ideology also plays a critical role in privileging one claim over another, which means that it is generally a decisive factor. It is also true that the charismatic leadership too is an important factor, as cursory look at the past elections demonstrates. With his personal appeal to the Indian voters, the BJP's star campaigner, Narendra Modi, sustained the tempo of anti-Congressism notwithstanding the coming together of his opponents both in 2014 and 2019 national polls. Here, the argument gets little complicated, since mere ideological appeal may not have been a sufficient condition for winning an election. This was also true to the 1971 election, when the personal popularity of Indira Gandhi as a saviour of the poor created a positive wave for the Congress Party which, however, lost its momentum, to a significant extent, in the 16th and 17th Lok Sabha polls, held in 2014 and 2019, respectively. The chapter is, therefore, a reconfirmation of the argument that elections in India, unlike what happens in the well-established Western democracies, are an occasion when voters and the parties interact with one another when ideology and also the leadership of the political parties act to cement a bond between them or cause a separation, which is reflected in the poll outcome. Does it happen fortuitously? The answer is both yes and no: yes, because under normal circumstance, the political parties keep themselves busy to sustain the support base by being involved in many regularly conducted political activities which give them dividends in elections, held at regular intervals; no, because of unforeseen situation, which puts a political party ahead of others. For instance, the astounding poll victory of the Congress in 1984 is largely attributed to the brutal killing of the incumbent Prime Minister, Indira Gandhi, which helped the party win maximum number of seats in the national polls, which would have been impossible, had the election taken place in normal circumstances. So, there is substance when one claims that elections in India are generally decided ideologically, but in extraordinary conditions that had, for instance, emerged following Indira Gandhi's assassination in 1984, ideology does not seem to be as critical as it is the case otherwise.

5

Eternity of Caste

Caste could be seen as one of the most important and perpetual determinants of electoral behaviour of common people in India. As various studies have shown, caste is a decisive factor in both parliamentary and State Assembly elections. Apart from those elections that took place in extraordinary circumstances, that caste remains significant in catching votes is established beyond doubt. One of the striking examples of how caste became a significant factor in Indian electoral contests is certainly the growing importance of the regional parties that drew exclusively on their caste appeal. For instance, with the implementation of the Mandal Commission Report in 1990, the regional political parties, especially in India's Hindi-speaking provinces, gained enormously by their promise to champion the socio-economic interests of OBCs. These parties defended their claim as fair, since despite being more than half of India's demography, OBCs had a share of meagre 5 per cent of public jobs. The organized campaign for protecting OBCs' genuine concern resulted in the defeat of the Congress and victory of these regional parties. Core here is the point that caste determines the poll outcome in most of the elections except, perhaps, 2014 and 2019 national polls, when Hindutva succeeded in cementing a pan-Indian identity in which caste did appear to be as critical as in elections that took place earlier.

By focusing on how caste acts as a determinant in elections, the chapter dwells on this aspect to justify whether the claim is true or false. We must add a caveat here. It is true that the critical role of caste can conceptually be gauged, which, however, does not mean that a specific poll outcome can be attributed to caste appeal only because there are other complementary factors supporting the endeavour at securing votes for specific caste groups. The argument that is pursued here is about the relative, if not overwhelming, importance of caste in shaping the poll outcome in specific elections in India.

Caste in Indian Politics

Undoubtedly, one of the significant issues in Indian politics is certainly caste that, besides being a social marker, also provides a readymade form of organization which is critical for political mobilization in electoral politics. Caste is, as Nicholas Dirks informs, 'in fact not some unchanged survival of ancient India, not some single system that reflects a core civilizational value, not a basic expression of Indian tradition'. It is, he further adds, 'a modern phenomenon, that it is, specifically the product of an historical encounter between India and Western colonial rule'.[1] Colonialism was, for instance, instrumental in 'politicizing caste' for its own 'divide and rule strategy' that was articulated through a well-calculated reservation scheme. The nationalists' insistence on caste-based reservation had given 'the legitimacy' which the colonial state needed to justify the scheme as beneficial to the peripheral majority, who remained marginalized in the Hindu social hierarchy due to their birth in the so-called 'lower castes'.[2]

[1] Nicholas B. Dirks, *Castes of Mind: Colonialism and the Making of Modern India* (Princeton: Princeton University Press, 2001), 5.

[2] For a detailed discussion on the debates between B. R. Ambedkar and Gandhi, see Bidyut Chakrabarty, *Social and Political Thought of Mahatma Gandhi* (London: Routledge, 2006), 103–112.

In post-colonial India, caste continues to remain significant, though the members of the Constituent Assembly firmly believed that with democracy and modernization it would lose its importance. Far from losing importance, caste, however, continues to exert determining influence in Indian society. Not only is the caste most conspicuous marker of social privilege in India but political parties in modern India prefer to consolidate their support by aligning with one caste group or another. Caste has, therefore, become a significant criterion of electoral politics in contemporary India.

Rise of the caste politics has been witnessed over the two axes of Dalits and OBCs. Interestingly, upsurge of Dalits as a formidable vote bank has always engendered a renewed debate on caste as the marker of the social and economic indicator and its relevance in Indian politics as one of the most influential factors for democratic decision-making.[3] But the rise of the backward castes–those groups intermediate between SCs at the bottom and the Brahmins and Rajputs at the top—has radically altered India's political texture in recent times. In legal terms, these groups are known as 'Other Backward Castes or Classes' to distinguish them from SCs and Scheduled Tribes (STs). It was these OBCs who formed the social basis and provided the leadership of those parties which pushed the Congress Party out of power in 1967 in a large number of Indian states. In the 1977 national election, these OBCs were critical in sustaining the opposition to the Congress Party. In fact, the coalition survived so long as the OBC-led Lok Dal and the Socialist Party held the balance among the disparate conglomeration of parties, known as the Janata Party.

OBCs became a formidable group because of economic power which they got through land reforms and the Green Revolution; given their numerical strength, they also gained political power. What they lacked was administrative power. Hence, the Janata government appointed the Mandal Commission in 1978, which

---

[3] Rajni Kothari, 'Rise of the Dalits and the Renewed Debate on Caste in India,' *Economic & Political Weekly* 29, no. 26 (25 June 1994).

identified caste as the main denominator of backwardness. On the basis of state surveys, the Commission recognized that there were 3,743 specific castes which still remained backward. Though they constituted more than half of India's population, these castes were poorly represented in the administration, especially at the higher levels. Hence, to redress this imbalance, the Commission recommended that 27 per cent of the Central Government jobs be reserved for these castes. While defending its decision, the Commission thus argues:

> We must recognize that an essential part of the battle against social backwardness is to be fought in the minds of the backward people. In India Government service has always been looked upon as a symbol of prestige and power. By increasing the representation of OBCs in Government services, we give them an immediate feeling of participation in governance of this country. When a backward caste candidate becomes a Collector or Superintendent of Police, the material benefits accruing from his position are limited to the members of his family only. But the psychological spin-off of this phenomenon is tremendous; the entire community of that backward class candidate feels elevated. Even, when no tangible benefits flow to the community at large, the feeling that now it has its own man in the corridors of power, acts as a morale booster.[4]

In what is euphorically described as 'deepening of democracy', the Mandal recommendations remained the most critical input in grasping Indian politics in recent years. Recommending 'quota' for OBCs, the report is broadly a scheme for 'affirmative action' for socially underprivileged sections of society. By deciding to implement the Mandal Commission Report, submitted to the Government of India in 1980, the V. P. Singh government championed, as it were, the cause of 52 per cent of the population belonging to OBCs. Although the recommendations were accepted by the government in 1990, attempts were made in

---

[4] Backward Classes Commission, *Report of the Backward Classes Commission* vol. 1 (Delhi: Controller of Publications, Government of India, 1980), 57.

the past in according reservation to what was defined as OBCs. To fulfil a constitutional obligation, as Article 340 suggests, the government of India appointed the First Backward Classes Commission, popularly known as Kaka Kalelkar Commission, after its chairman in 1953. The Commission submitted its report in 1955, listing about 32 per cent of population as backward on the basis of caste identity. The Commission also identified 2,399 castes as backward. However, Kalelkar himself rejected the report when he placed the report for presidential assent saying that it would have been preferable to determine backwardness on 'principles' rather than 'caste'.

Although the reservation scheme was shelved at the national level, nearly all the states constituted their Backward Commission and legalized reservation in public services and educational institutions under state control. The Second Backward Classes Commission, known as the Mandal Commission, appointed in 1978, revived interests in formulating a national policy for OBCs. The Commission suggested that OBCs forming 52 per cent of population required special concession to correct the social imbalance. But the Supreme Court ruled that 'reservations cannot exceed 50 percent of the jobs.' So, the Commission reluctantly agreed to accept 27 per cent jobs for OBCs, though they constituted more than half of India's population. There was also a rider because the Commission also categorically stated that 'candidates belonging to OBCs recruited on the basis of merit in an open competition should not be adjusted against their reservation quota of 27 percent.' By implication, what it means is the fact that if the commission's recommendations are respected, half of the posts in the public sector and universities will be filled by people who could not get in on merit, provided they belong to 'the right castes'. As evident, the Mandal formula rests on two premises: (a) OBCs comprise a very large segment of India's population and (b) their representation (only 5%) in the public sector is abysmally poor. Hence, the recommendations ensuring 27 per cent reservations in central jobs and education for OBCs appear most appropriate. In contrast with the Kalelkar Commission, which took into account economic variables, among other criteria, the Mandal Commission Report changed the original philosophy of reservations by clearly identifying caste as the sole criterion for backwardness.

Whatever advantages the Mandal formula may have, reservation for the backward castes and religious minorities are directed towards maintaining a balance of power in the caste-divided India's social structure. As a scheme striving to strike a balance between the privileged upper castes and the hitherto neglected OBCs, the Mandal recommendation deserves appreciation. In reality, however, the better-off sections of OBCs would reap the benefit at the cost of the more deserving sections within these castes. To substantiate the argument, let us draw our attention to the caste dynamics in North India. Till the 1950s, domination was enjoyed in the rural areas by the AJGAR (Ahir, Jats, Gujjars and Rajputs) group. They gained remarkably in material terms after the Green Revolution, and all of them moved well and truly into modern sector. The intermediate castes, such as Kurmis, Koeris, Lodhas and others also benefited but not uniformly, and therefore, there is a considerable social and economic heterogeneity in each of these castes. Hence, the Mandal definition of 'backwardness' does not appear plausible in view of its obvious limitation of having ignored social and economic heterogeneity among OBCs. As a result, the benefits meant for OBCs are likely to be monopolized by the better-off and influential sections among these castes. In other words, 'the rhetoric of reservation is addressed to the mass of under-privileged, but their rewards are reserved for the affluent upper castes of the OBCs'. M. N. Srinivas, thus, argues that 'when a certain caste has political clout it should be excluded from the backward class list; otherwise, the richer members of the higher groups among the backward classes ... will hog the benefits which should have gone to the genuinely deserving backward classes.' [5] The political imperatives behind reservations are

[5] M. N. Srinivas, 'End of an Egalitarian Dream,' *Sunday Observer*, New Delhi, 12 August 1990.

thus apparent. What prompted the ruling parties to accept the Mandal recommendations is probably a well-calculated design aiming at mobilizing the support of the OBC elite.

By virtue of its unique status in the OBC society, its wealth, its relatively high educational level and its hegemony in a majority of caste councils, the OBC upper crust is viewed as the most significant power brokers in the Hindi heartland. So, the Mandal formula, designed to ensure social justice, is virtually a scheme for creating and sustaining a secure vote bank for the V. P. Singh-led National Front government. And since number counts in franchise today, parties, irrespective of ideology, strive hard to win the support of caste groups for electoral gains by promises whipping up caste sentiments. So, if caste has acquired a new lease of life in independent India, this is almost entirely because of the increasing use made of it in politics. The decision to implement the Mandal Commission report is just another effort to effectively draw on caste sentiments for victory in elections. The Commission is thus described as 'a caste commission' which is seen 'as a passport to power'. Whatever the future of the reservation plan, the Mandal formula has polarized the contemporary political forces more sharply than before. So, a mere acceptance of modern secular political idioms does not ensure their sustenance in a society which draws on feudal sentiments and primordial loyalties. It is not, therefore, strange that elections are conducted on caste calculations, the candidates are nominated on caste ratio and, as a consequence, patronage is likely to be distributed on caste basis and public policies are also to be tilted in favour of the caste-support base.

Despite sharp criticism and violent student fury directed against the Mandal Commission Report, the formula deserves serious attention as it strives to correct the injustice of centuries inflicted on the downtrodden in the name of the discriminatory *varna* system. Due to peculiar socio-economic transformation in India which had a long colonial past, the benefits, meant for the genuine backwards, are likely to go to the relatively better-off sections within OBCs. So, the Commission's aim of ensuring a greater equality for OBCs as such is sure to be defeated under the present circumstances. Unless it becomes a part of a comprehensive plan for development, the Mandal formula, despite B. P. Mandal's sincerity and devotion to the OBC cause, hardly makes sense in a situation in which the reservation plain is being utilized primarily for electoral gains. Yet, none of the political parties can be critical of the reservation scheme, perhaps due to adverse political consequences and also the political costs of opposing the scheme. Congress (R)'s performance in the fifth general elections had been reflective of its regaining the widespread support of different social and economic groups of people as had been during the period of Nehru. In other words, the relative decline of the party during the 1967 elections by losing support among certain social groups such as upper and lower castes had been effectively arrested, and the umbrella nature of the party was re-established under the leadership of Mrs Gandhi. At the same time, in the decisive battle over control of the legacy of the party, the syndicates were comprehensively voted out of existence. As a result, a new generation of Congress leaders came into existence under the commanding leadership of Mrs Gandhi, who did not have much support of their own among the electorate. They depended on the charismatic leadership of Mrs Gandhi not only for electoral victories but also for any kind of intervention in public life in the name of the Congress Party. While on the one hand, all sorts of parochial considerations were wiped out of existence within the party, on the electorate pedestal, all the religious and caste groups voted for Mrs Gandhi in support of her unflinching faith in the socialist ideals and blueprint for social and economic transformations in the country. Almost all the social groups appeared reassured of the protection of their interests under the leadership of Mrs Gandhi.

Caste dynamics of Indian politics was also in full play during the fifth Lok Sabha elections with varying political preferences of different castes and social groups. Three major conventional patterns of voting behaviour could be seen on the basis of caste before the emergence of caste-based parties during the decade of 1990s. First, high status, middle, Harijans and STs remained the steadfast voters of the Congress ever since Independence. Even among them, the most solid support came from the STs, who voted overwhelmingly for Congress (R).[6] That pattern continued in the fifth general elections as well with those caste or social groups shifting their loyalties to the personality of Mrs Gandhi instead of the Congress as an organization represented by syndicates.

Though the regional figures on the performance of Congress (R) show the pan-India appeal of Mrs Gandhi in garnering support for her radical policies, the variation in its performance in different regions is indicative of two major tendencies of political economy of India. First, relatively backward or poor regions such as the North and the East had been excessively receptive of the radical policy measures promised by Indira Gandhi to bring about a rapid social and economic transformation. Thus, sensing the bright prospect for certain degree of turnaround in their fortunes, the people in the two regions voted overwhelmingly for the party that helped it secure a high percentage of vote shares that transformed into good number of seats for the party in the Lok Sabha. Second, perceived animosity to the radical measures on the part of the erstwhile royals and other ruling classes in the western part of India, on the one hand, and the deep entrenchment of the regional parties in their respective states in the deep South, on the other, did not allow the Congress (R) to have a walkover over its rivals in these regions. As a result, both the vote share as well as the number of seats secured by Congress (R) in these two regions did not supplement each other in the same measure as had been the case in the rest of the two regions.

[6] Llyod I. Rudolph, 'Continuities and Change in Electoral Behaviour: The 1971 Parliamentary Elections in India,' *Asian Survey* 11, no. 12 (December 1971): 1128.

Consolidation of Caste Politics

The fragmentation of the Indian society for the sake of votes could, thus, be said to be the most significant transformation that the 10th general elections brought about in the democratic India. However, amidst the claims and the counterclaims of the different political parties as standing for the cause of the people of their own castes or religions, certain sections of people remained committed to their traditional patrons and leaders, irrespective of the political manoeuvring by other political parties. In this context, the performance of the Bahujan Samaj Party (BSP) in these elections could be said to be remarkable, as the core cadres of the party consisted mainly of the persons belonging to SCs and that too of certain sub-groups even among them. In other words, the social churning that had apparently started with the implementation of the Mandal Commission recommendations failed to have any impact on the core vote bank of the BSP that had stood with the party making it win a number of seats in UP. That way, the parties like BSP had tended to act as the stumbling block in the way of the proponents of social justice because they thought of retaining their independent identity in the social and political arenas.

The decline of the Congress as the dominant political party had unleashed various kinds of social forces that sought to claim the political space vacated by the grand old party of India.[7] But the ideological and programmatic fault lines among the different social and political groups had been so many and so profound that they could not think of evolving a common strategy or platform to take on the Congress. Hence, during the ninth general elections, while the different non-Congress parties appeared united in their resolve to dislodge the Congress from the seat of power at the centre, they could not agree on whom to anoint as the prime minister once the Congress was defeated in the battle of votes. Consequently, when the final results of the

[7] M. L. Ahuja and Sharda Paul, *1989–1991 General Elections in India: Including November 1991 By-elections* (New Delhi: Associated Publishing House, 1992), 63.

ninth general elections were declared, the scenario of a hung Lok Sabha had put the opposition parties in a quandary. Leader of a minority party was made the prime minister with the Left and Right parties extending their support to him from outside. But the political bickering among the major players of the electoral politics in the country continued unabated during this period that eventually not only led to the downfall of the government but also unleashing of new trends in the Indian politics, whose primary focus remained embedded in arousing the primordial affinities of the people and reap the electoral dividends like never before in the electoral history.

Based upon the numerical preponderance of OBCs, the most spectacular impact of the primordialization of the democratic process had been felt in the populous and key Hindi heartland states of UP and Bihar. Interestingly, for a long period of time after independence, these two states had been the bastions of the Congress, as long as the party was able to keep intact its strategic balance among the different caste groups of these states. But with the gradual erosion in the universal support base of the party, the political space vacated by it started getting occupied by the proponents of social justice and Hindutva. The proponents of the social justice had virtually got a shot in their arm with the plank of OBCs reservation. The latent political and social ambitions of OBCs got aroused by the state-level leadership of these caste groups that eventually transformed into a number of regional political outfits in different states. After the disintegration of the Janata Dal at the national level, these regional parties emerged as the formidable political forces in UP and Bihar, upstaging the well-entrenched political parties like the Congress.

The party for which the 10th general elections were likely to prove a matter of life and death was none other than the Janata Dal.[8] The basic reasons for such high stakes of the

[8] Lewis P. Fickett Jr, 'The Rise and Fall of the Janata Dal,' *Asian Survey* 33, no. 12 (December 1993): 1153.

party in these elections were three. One, it consisted of such sporadic group of regional straps who would have remained part of the party only in case the party would become part of any ruling dispensation, so that they could enjoy the power for longer periods of time. Next, the party had played its most valuable card of social justice in the name of Mandal Commission recommendations, and the failure of this card to produce desirable results for the party would have reduced them to where they used to exist decades ago. In the end, the party also wanted to put forward the argument that the fall of the government was for the valuable cause of protecting the secular fabric and interests of the minorities for which the minorities needed to support the party en masse. But the grand plans of the party fell flat on the face of the sympathy wave in favour of the Congress and it remained confined to just 69 seats as compared to the handsome victories of both the Congress and the BJP.

Marginalization of Caste as an Electoral

The period of the 11th and the 12th elections had been the period of the rise of the hitherto latent sections of the society, for whom voting in the general elections was more a ritual than a thoughtful decision. But with the caste-based mobilization by the parties propounding the case of social justice getting increased stridency in the electoral system, these castes became aware of the value of votes and what their votes could do for them. That had been the turning point that made the electoral system substantive rather than ritualistic. While the deepening of democracy had already been a good track record in the south, the new churning that had been introduced by the unleashing of the forces of social justice had their electrifying impact on the intermediary castes in the Hindi heartland. In this process, almost the entire system of politics and the electoral system underwent radical transformations. Not only the established patterns of voting, voter mobilization and identifying the vote with the caste identity of an individual was highlighted, this also resulted into the formation of a number of new political parties. As these parties sought to expand their social and political base rapidly, among the masses of their caste along with the strategic alliance with other pliable castes, this gave birth to an unconventional band of leaders who hitherto had remained oblivious of the political forays. That way, the deepening of democracy introduced an altogether new pattern of electoral politics that had drastically been different from the traditional format of politics being practised by the parties like Congress. This period, therefore, resulted into the greater strengthening of the position of the caste-based parties and proportional reduction in the strength of the Congress.

On the whole, the 11th and the 12th general elections were reflection of the changing paradigms of the democratic politics of India. The old idioms and values of the party system, electors, political alliances and voting behaviour of the common electorates had undergone subtle transformations during these elections. The grand old party had silently given space to the parties that had been almost unknown or out of existence just a few years back. But gradually, they had come up as the main actors in the political discourse of the country. In this regard, the cases of both the caste-based parties as religion-based parties had been striking. What was more interesting was the fact that these two sets of parties initially emerged out of anti-Congressism that had been the underlying theme of the democratic politics for a long period of time. But once they were able to oust the Congress from the mainstream of the democratic politics, they themselves became staunch rival, and the subsequent elections had become the fight between these two sets of parties. However, in their sustained rivalry, the BJP had definitely marched much ahead of the caste-based parties. The 11th and the 12th general elections had, in fact, been the launching pads for the BJP which got ample opportunities during these elections to test the waters in order to ready itself for bigger strides in the times to come.

The period of the UPA rule could be seen as the phase of consolidation of coalition politics.[9] The social and religious churning taking place during the decade of 1990s in the country had tended to rupture the established norms of democratic politics in terms of caste, class and religious groups acting as conventional vote banks of different political parties. The obvious outcome of this churning had been in terms of massive disintegration of the traditional social support base of the Congress Party with a large section of almost all the social groups such as the upper castes, OBCs, Dalits, Adivasis and even the urban middle class deserting the Congress. As a result, riding on the support of their distinct castes along with contingent voters such as Muslims, a number of regional political parties, particularly in the Hindi heartland, emerged as formidable political force in various states. The BJP also took advantage of subtle disintegration in the traditional Congress vote bank. Consequently, it not only improved its seat tally in the Lok Sabha from 2 to 200 but was also able to enter into strategic political alliances with a number of regional parties to augment its seats in the Lok Sabha. The formation of the Vajpayee government in the aftermath of the 13th general elections was the distinct electoral gain the BJP could secure by strategic positioning of its fixtures in different parts of India.[10]

But the Congress could neither discern the gradual disintegration in its traditional vote bank so minutely, nor was it able to come out of the hangover of its hegemonic presence over a long period of time. In such circumstance, it was simply out of place for the party to enter into any sort of electoral alliance with the regional parties in different states to make up the deficiency in its vote share after the departure of a number of preponderant social groups from the fold of the party. Hence, the stage was set for the 14th general elections

[9] For a lucid account of the coalition politics in India, see Chakrabarty, *Forging Power.*
[10] Mukulika Banerjee, 'Sacred Elections,' *Economic & Political Weekly* 42, no. 17 (28 April 2007): 1558.

with different opposition parties readying themselves to take on the incumbent BJP and its alliance partners in various states on their own. Resultantly, the 14th general elections were a multi-cornered contest in which, apart from the BJP and the Congress, the regional parties or Left parties also entered the fray with formidable candidates. The outcome of these elections came as a shock for the BJP-led NDA, as the incumbent government failed to secure a majority in the Lok Sabha. This presented the golden opportunity before the opposition parties to leave no stone unturned in keeping the NDA out of the power. But the moot question before them was to arrive at a consensus leader whom they could present as their prime ministerial nominee.

BJP and Caste

The loss of the BJP and the Congress in the 13th general elections had been made merry by the regional parties both in the Hindi heartland as well as other parts of the country as well. But the most fragmented electoral outcome could be seen in the state of UP, where the whopping number of seats for the Lok Sabha was shared majorly by the different stakeholders. In other words, the electorate of UP, even by now, could not overcome the primordialization of their political affinities and continued to vote as per their caste calculations or loyalties. Thus, the two important regional parties of the state came out with good show in the 13th general elections. While the Samajwadi Party (SP) rode on the support of the its traditional vote bank of Yadavs, the other important party, BSP, could win as many as 14 seats riding on the support of SCs. In view of the soft Hindutva exhibited by the Congress during the reign of P. V. Narasimha Rao, the Muslims in the state had deserted the party to vote for the SP and BSP, depending upon the winning ability of the candidate. The performance of the Left parties had traditionally been confined to their strongholds in West Bengal and a few other states, while the splinter group of the Congress, the Nationalist Congress Party (NCP) headed by Sharad Pawar, could also put up an impressive show by winning eight seats in these elections.

The outcome of the 13th general elections had a number of serious implications for Indian democracy. At the outset, the most formidable element established by these elections had been that the time for the rise of the Right had arrived. The vision with which the BJP was set up in 1980 had more or less now been accepted by a large majority of the population. Though the BJP did have a number of such foundational beliefs and value premises which would not have made it acceptable to its electoral allies, the party had indeed been able to retrofit its short-term as well as long-term agenda in such a way that its acceptability across the political spectrum of the country increased manifold, thereby allowing it a foothold even in those areas that had previously been a no-entry zone for the party. Interestingly, the party did not abjure its basic resolves and values such as Hindutva, Ram temple, abrogation of Article 370 and adoption of the uniform civil code, among others. What it actually did was to put them on the backburner so as to present its liberal face before both, the electorate as well as its NDA allies and outside supporters. This strategic retreat of the party had played the pivotal role in helping it manage a comfortable majority in the Lok Sabha and form the government with a firm resolve and resolute mindset of governing the country.[11]

The confidence with which the BJP had been able to form the government at the centre by cobbling up a comfortable majority, thanks to the unconditional support of the Telugu Desam Party (TDP), was striking.[12] No other non-Congress party or alliance had earlier been able to form the government with such exuberance and clear vision as the BJP did in 1999. This was reflective of the growing confidence of the party,

[11] Paul Wallace and Ramashray Roy, *India's 1999 Elections and 20th Century Politics* (New Delhi: SAGE Publications, 2003), 187.

[12] Bob Hardgrave, 'The 1999 Indian Parliamentary Elections and the New BJP-led Coalition Government', available at https://web.archive.org/web/20081011235012/http://asnic.utexas.edu/asnic/hardgrave/Elections1999.html (accessed on 19 July 2019).

not only in its abilities to meet the challenges of running a coalition government through its deft handling of its allies but also exhibited its belief in the veracity of the commitment with which its allies and partners had joined hands with it in forming the government. The obvious result of such a resolve produced the unprecedented distinction of the NDA government being the first non-Congress government to last its full term in office. This distinction has imparted a new vibrancy and flexibility into the Indian democracy, which has generally been observed as the bastion of the Congress Party. The successful running of the NDA government for its full term proved that the Indian democracy has matured enough to experience the rule of non-Congress parties and alliances with the same degree of commitment to the constitutional values and norms that need to be followed in order to maintain the sanctity of the democratic institutions and processes. Thus, with the NDA government, the Indian democracy seemed to have entered into a new phase of maturity and vibrancy.

In conceptual terms, two ideas seem important here: on the one hand, elections in India are a mirror to see how political processes are shaped and articulated. Hindutva rose in importance following the demolition of the Babri Masjid in 1992, which also led to the increasing importance of the BJP and its partners in the NDA. In other words, Hindutva generated an appeal to the Hindus who emerged as a well-knit community and voted en masse for the NDA, since it was considered to be an appropriate platform for protecting their distinct socio-ideological goals. As a consequence, the 1992 event also led, on the other hand, to a horizontal division among the voters: Hindus and Muslims in particular became compartmentalized as distinct sociocultural communities. The poll outcome, however, did not reflect the division so clearly. For instance, in 1999, the NDA assumed authority though, in terms of the proportion of votes, it did not succeed in bringing to it the majority of the voters, which means that even a large section of Hindus did not vote for the conglomeration that emerged as the sole custodian of Hindu interests and rights. The argument that the appeal to the Hindus as distinct from others did not appear to be as effective as the NDA conceived. This further confirms that the failure of the NDA to ensure the support of the majority of the Hindu voters shows the limitations of the argument seeking to explain its victory exclusively in terms of its success in building the so-called pan-Indian identity. There were other factors too which also created a wave for the conglomeration. We must not lose sight of another aspect here, which will help us grasp the sustained role of caste, regions and ethnicity. By securing votes in their favour, the parties opposed to the NDA also proved that there were politico-ideological forces that were capable of countering the Hindutva, which again reveals that caste continues to act as a cementing device, to a significant extent. India's political scene appears to have changed in 2014 in which the BJP-led combination captured power. Here too, besides Hindutva, the involvement of the incumbent Congress government in various scams created an opportunity for the BJP and its NDA partners. Broadly speaking, neither caste nor Hindutva seems to have acted decisively in shaping the 2014 poll outcome. The trend continued in 2019 Lok Sabha election, when the incumbent government was brought to power again. Here, too, the image of the Prime Minister Modi being a strong leader had also strengthened NDA's appeal for a second terms. What was, however, striking was also the success of the winning candidates gain support cutting across both caste and religious boundaries, justifying the argument that voting behaviour in India cannot be conceptualized in one-size-fits-all formula, presumably because of the socio-economic and culturally diverse demography. Hence, it will be conceptually erroneous to seek to explain India's elections in one format simply because of their complex texture due to equally complex socio-economic circumstances in which voters exercise their right to vote.

Concluding Observations

Indian democracy, since its inception, has been marked by certain degree of homogeneity in terms of the political culture as well as electoral behaviour of the people. In other words, the elections had never been the basis of social and political fragmentation of the Indian people. But the turn of events since the formation of the Janata Dal government under the leadership of V. P. Singh had tried to drive such a wedge in the minds of the Indian electorate that there emerged total fragmentation of the voters. The subsequent game of one-upmanship had stirred the social and political landscape of the country, producing a number of political parties based on their primordial affinities. By the time of the 13th general elections, such fragmentation of the Indian voting behaviour seemed to have become complete with a number of regional parties based on caste, religion, language, region, etc., making rich dividends out of the 13th general elections. The consolidation of the gains of the regional parties had proportionally resulted into the decline of the support base of the traditional parties such as the Congress. The impact of this fragmentation had been taken both ways by the political analysts. While this has famously been argued as the deepening of the democracy, such a tendency could also be perceived as destruction of the social and political cohesion with ominous portents for the long-term interests of both the people as well as the country.

At one level, elections in India are caste driven; at another, far more perceptive level, they are also governed by consid-erations other than caste. By dwelling on how caste acts in both ascertaining victory for some of the contesting political parties and also defeat for their opponents, the chapter has reinforced the point that one needs to take into account the complex socio-economic milieu before one makes a judgment. Here, there are three points that need careful attention: first, there is no denying that India is passing through processes of significant social, economic and political churning, which cannot be undermined while seeking to understand the voting behaviour. The increasing importance of OBCs in shaping the poll outcome is captured by an analyst as a silent revolution leading to the transfer of power from the upper caste to various subaltern caste groups which remained peripheral in the past in electoral arithmetic. It was a silent revolution because such a radical change was brought about 'peacefully', and the relative calm was 'primarily due to the fact that the whole process {was} incremental'.[13] Undoubtedly, it was a sea change in Indian politics which contributed meaningful socio-economic meta-morphosis. This was true, that the shifting of power created a context in which it 'petered into an endlessly involuted conflict of one subcaste with another {and} most anti-caste movements turn out to be ... merely anti-upper caste movements {happily excluding} those below them'.[14] The process was, thus, not without pitfalls, which is argued here by drawing attention to how various caste groups struggle among themselves to gain political ascendancy in India's competitive democracy. Second, the change is visible in voters' behaviour, which is reflective of how they normatively conceptualize the alternative ideological priorities which the political parties present before them. Implicit here is a persuasive explanation of why some political parties gain in elections and others fail, for instance, the success of the SP in UP in opposition to the BJP and the Congress before the 2017 State Assembly Election when the BJP had won a thumping majority. The trend was repeated in the 2019 Lok Sabha with the victory candidates in 62 of 80 parliamentary seats. The contrasting scenario, thus, substantiates the claim that given the peculiar voting behaviour, it is difficult, if not impossib'e, to conceptualize the importance (or otherwise) of caste in a straight-jacketed manner. Finally, in view of the critical role that caste plays in organizing socio-economically disparate groups, there is no way one can ignore this aspect of the Indian politics. Regional variations notwithstanding, caste continues to remain a cementing factor, as the election results demonstrate. The appeal of caste is sometimes so overpowering that it is suicidal for any party to completely ignore this aspect of electoral politics. In post-Mandal era, it does not seem odd for the political parties seeking votes to couch their appeal in such a way as gaining support sometimes from specific caste groups

[13] Christophe Jaffrelot, *India's Silent Revolution: The Rise of Lower Castes in North India* (London: C. Hurst & Co, 2003), 494.

[14] Pratap Bhanu Mehta, *The Burden of Democracy* (New Delhi: Penguin, 2003), 163.

and sometimes from a combination cutting across many caste groups. Whatever be the ways, the fact remains that even after more than seven decades of constitutional governance in India, the voting behaviour is, to a significant extent, conditioned by caste considerations.

Is caste, being pertinent in India's elections, a deterrent to the rise and consolidation of democracy in its true spirit and texture? The answer is a qualified yes, because caste, being a primordial device of group integration, stands in contradiction with democracy, which is the rule of the *demos* regardless of any artificial demarcation among them. A perusal of the past elections in India, however, shows that caste is primarily an instrument for bringing people together; in other words, it is a unifying device around certain politico-ideological claims. In this sense, since caste is an organizing tool, it has elements of bringing people together around some identical socio-economic concerns. In other words, caste does not seem to be exclusively an endogamous identity but one that has also transformed radically by creating a space for groups' identity on the basis of common socio-economic interests. So, caste is an interesting social entity, the nature of which is integrally connected with how democracy has evolved in India since its gradual introduction in the colonial era.

The Indian experiment of democracy is most innovative for at least two important reasons. First, by defying the classical conceptualization of democracy, the Indian counterpart redefined some of the fundamental assumptions on which the classical theorists based their theoretical ideas. This means that the rise and consolidation of democracy follows different trajectories in different socio-economic milieu. In other words, there is hardly one model of democracy which justifies the argument that one needs to be sensitive to the prevalent socio-economic context to provide a plausible explanation of why democracy thrives in India but failed in most of the former British colonies in the South Asian subcontinent. From this argument follows the second reason. As democracy is a struggle in which the *demos* participate as legitimate actors, it is conceptually wrong to comprehend their role in derivative wisdom. For instance, caste continues to remain important, but to understand its role in a traditional theoretical format will lead us nowhere, since it has undergone a sea change with the growing awareness of the people of being integral to governance. As contemporary studies reveal, the mass zeal for voting even in remote villages in India underlines how the idea of being recognized as an important actor inspires the voters with different caste identities to go to the polling booth for exercising their right. The political scene is not radically different from what we witnessed in the past. As caste groups have become critical to the electoral outcome, the political parties are also required to be respectful to their demands to garner their support. This is also an indication and confirmation as well of how a radical shift is slowly taking place in the normative domain: caste is no longer conceived as a deterrent to democracy, rather, it is complementary to its rise and consolidation in India.

6

Politics as Culture

Political discourse on the idea of India has now been dominated by what is called as 'cultural nationalism' pioneered by
the Hindutva forces led by the BJP.[1] This is in sharp contrast
to the Nehruvian idea of India rooted in secular credentials of
India, a hallmark of which has been the acknowledgement of
the first right of minorities on the resources and privileges of
the country. While such a perspective of the Congress and other
secular formations have consistently been chided by the BJP as
nothing but Muslim appeasement, in the electoral process this
standpoint of the former has benefited the party immensely as
the Muslims used to vote for it en bloc in conjunction with other
social groups that has ultimately made the Congress apparently
invincible political force in the country for a long period of time
since the beginning of electoral process.

With the consolidation of the Hindutva forces, secular
discourse of Indian elections has now been replaced with 'culture' emerging as the central theme of the Right-wing parties.

---

[1] John Zavos, Andrew Wyatt, and Vernon Hewitt, eds, *The Politics
of Cultural Mobilization in India* (New Delhi: Oxford University Press,
2004), 17.

Equating Hindutva with Indianness, they have indeed been able to generate such a narrative of cultural nationalism that secular discourse has stood discredited as nothing but Muslim appeasement to a large extent. On the positive side, politics as culture is sought to be reinforced with the invention of a number of Hindu imageries and symbols whose lineage could be traced to the pre-Muslim historical past of the country. On the negative side, the medieval period of Indian history is portrayed as the dark age in the annals of the country that had done nothing but undo the glorious past of the Hindus. On the extreme, this narrative calls for transforming the secular fabric of the country to make it a Hindu nation in such a way that Hindus should have preponderant position in deciding the course of history of the nation in place of Muslims being given priority over Hindus. As the main carrier of the cultural narrative, the BJP has indeed been able to drive its point of view in the majority of the people whose net result has been its astounding performance in the 17th general elections to win a majority of its own. Thus, cultural orientation in place of secular overtone has been an unconventional outcome of electoral politics of India over the last decade. The aim of the chapter is to show how Hindutva succeeded in garnering votes for the BJP and its constituents both at the national and regional levels. The poll results account for the growing importance of the appeal of Hindutva in recent years which was inconceivable in the heyday of the Nehruvian socialism. As well as the ideological appeal of Hindutva, the importance of pan-Indian leadership has grown beyond imagination. In other words, as the 2014 and 2019 national polls and other State Assembly elections firmly demonstrate, Hindutva gradually became a mainstream ideology along with the acceptance of the BJP leader, Narendra Modi, as perhaps the most effective in helping the poor by resorting plans to eradicate poverty.

Culture as Basis of Indian Politics

As against the individualistic and restrictive conceptualization of the idea of Hinduism, the notion of Hindutva was evolved by the radical elements of the Hindu revivalist movements. They take a more strident position on the history, philosophy, legacies and future perspective of the Hindu way of life in India. In fact, the proponents of the ideology of Hindutva tried to envisage a comprehensive blueprint for the reconstruction of the politico-cultural system in such a way that the Hindus would get an absolute preponderance in the affairs of the country. The ideology of Hindutva, therefore, moves beyond the confines of the religious and personal life of the individuals and seeks to reconstruct a whole new world for the Hindus by way of establishing the 'Hindu Rashtra'.[2] Over the years, it has turned out to be a distinct political ideology that vies with the secular credentials to have some degree of preponderance in the politico-cultural life of the people. The ideology of Hindutva was given the shape of a refined and viable, to some, theoretical construct by V. D. Savarkar in his various writings and speeches. Later on, this ideology was adopted by the Rashtriya Swayamsevak Sangh (RSS) as the intellectual input in its pursuit for the 'Hindu Rashtra' in India. Indeed, the entire band of Hindu Rightist political and cultural formations in the country draws its ideological sustenance from the ideology of Hindutva propounded by Savarkar.

Evolution and Firm Conceptualization of Hindutva

Savarkar began his conceptualization of the idea of Hindutva by seeking answer to the question, what could be considered as a Hindu.[3] He tersely proclaims that a Hindu could be anyone who considered this land of *Bharatvarsha*, from the Indus to the Seas, as his/her fatherland as well as his/her holy land that would be the cradle land of his/her religion. Further, he envisaged three fundamental bonds that would conjoin the Hindus as a common entity, namely *rashtra* (territory), *jati* (race) and *sanskriti* (culture). Thus, territorially, a Hindu is one who feels

[2] For an extremely critical analysis of the rise and growth of the ideology of Hindutva, see Jyotirmaya Sharma, *Hindutva: Exploring the Idea of Hindu Nationalism* (New Delhi: Penguin Books, 2003).

[3] This section draws on Bidyut Chakrabarty and Rajendra Kumar Pandey, *Modern Indian Political Thought*, Sage, New Delhi, 2009.

being attached to the geographical tract extending between the rivers Sindhu (Indus) and Brahmaputra, on the one hand, and from the Himalayas to the Cape Comorin, on the other. This geographical specification, indeed, becomes identical to what has traditionally been considered to be the land of India for centuries.

Racially, Savarkar considered a Hindu as the one 'whose first and discernible source could be traced to the Himalayan altitudes of the Vedic *Saptasindhu*'. Such a racial demarcation of the Hindus was seemingly not meant to claim any sort of superiority of the Hindus in comparison to the other races in the world but to distinguish them from others. Moreover, Savarkar pronounced that the trait of Hindutva encompassing the life of the inhabitants of this part of land would remain indelible as the impulse of his/her Hindu blood would make him/her feel the pride of being a Hindu. As he writes,

A Hindu believing in any theoretical or philosophical or social system, orthodox or heterodox, provided it is unquestionably indigenous and founded by a Hindu, may lose his sect but not his Hindutva—his Hinduness—because the most important and essential which determines it is the inheritance of the Hindu blood. Therefore, all those who love the land that stretches from Sindhu to Sindhu, from Indus to Seas, as their fatherland and consequently claim to inherit the blood of the race that has evolved, by incorporation and adaptation, from the ancient Saptasindhu, can be said to possess tow of the most essential requisites of Hindutva.[4]

Culturally, Savarkar maintains that a Hindu must feel the pride and commonality of his/her cultural roots with the other people of Hindustan. As he explains,

Hindus are bound together not only by the tie of the love we bear to a common fatherland and by the common blood that

[4] V. D. Savarkar, *Hindutva*, 6th ed. (Bombay: Veer Savarkar Prakashan, 1989), 90–91.

courses through our veins and keeps our hearts throbbing and out affection warm, but also by the tie of the common homage we pay to our great civilization—our Hindu culture, which could not be better rendered than by the word Sanskriti, suggestive as it is of that language, Sanskrit, which has been the chosen means of expression and preservation of that culture, of all that was best and worth-preserving in the history of our race. We are one because we are a nation, a race and own a common Sanskriti (civilization).[5]

Savarkar, thus, provides for a complex criterion to ordain a distinct identity and character to the Hindus in the Indian society.

Savarkar's construction of Hindu identity is *territorial* (the land between Indus and the Indian Ocean), *genealogical* (fatherland) and *religious* (holy land). The Hindu Rashtra is, therefore, more of a territorial than religious nationalism because Hindus represented a cultural and civilizational synthesis which is more 'a secular-rationalist than a religio-fundamentalist construction'. This particular conceptualization was also an outcome of a specific politico-ideological debate that unfolded with the propagation of Muslims being a separate nation which got a concrete shape in the 1940 Lahore Resolution when Pakistan was formally conceptualized and demanded. So by highlighting the cultural aspect of Hindu Rashtra, Savarkar, one of the first pioneers of Hindu nationalism, strove to provide a persuasive alternative to the Muslim League's insistence on Muslims being socio-culturally different from their Hindu counterparts. This was the beginning of the institutionalization of Hindu nationalism or Hindutva on the basis of what Savarkar construed as the essence of Hindu culture.

Savarkar's Hindu nationalist design can be said to have been largely contextually contrived for two reasons: on the one hand, he raised his voice in opposition to the nationalist mainstream in favour of a point of view that did not have the importance that it deserved. As history has shown, given the

[5] Ibid.

hegemony of constitutional liberalism which Gandhi and his colleagues in the freedom struggle had upheld, other alternative socio-ideological priorities had hardly had a presence. There was another reason, on the other, attributing the growing acceptance of Gandhi being the supreme commander left no chance for ideologues holding contrary views. This further gave a fillip to the mainstream nationalists largely undermining the endeavours, made by those who while challenging Gandhi and the Congress nationalists, sought to evolve an alternative mode of conceptualizing nationalism. In such a context, it was not a mean achievement when not only did Savarkar articulate a persuasive set of ideas supportive of Hindu nationalism, he also succeeded in creating an ambience in which it became a real nationalist alternative.

Hindutva as a Creed of BJP

Political forays of the BJP have always been rooted in its commitment to Hindutva ideology. As a matter of fact, when the RSS decided to make an indirect debut in politics, its offspring and BJP's previous incarnation the BJS began to challenge the Nehruvian idea of India rooted in socialism and sought to reconstruct the post-Independence social, economic and political order as per the ancient Indian traditions. However, given the formidability of the Congress in the political landscape, the BJS could not cut much ice with the people and remained a peripheral player in the electoral politics. Despite the best efforts by the party leaders as well as the top brass of the RSS, the BJS could never emerge as a political force to make any difference to the political texture. This naturally induced a rethink in the leadership of the party and that eventually resulted in the founding of the BJP as the successor of the BJS.

Initial fate of the BJP also appeared jinxed as the party could not put up a strong fight in the general elections. But with the gradual weakening of the Congress Party and creation of certain degree of vacuum in the political landscape, the party could sense an opportunity to consolidate its position. But the most important challenge the party faced in this regard was from the caste-based parties seeking to monopolize the Congress space in the crucial states of the North India, and the BJP was required to reinvent its strategy of overcoming this bottleneck. Thus, the progressive strengthening of the hold of caste-based parties in the core states of the Hindi heartland has been sought to be countered by the BJP through its increasing and consistent thrust on the ideology of Hindutva as the hallmark of its appeal to the voters.[6] In fact, in order to present an alternative vision to the dominant Congress's ideological and programmatic reach, the party insisted on taking up a number of such issues and concerns that went to strengthen its image of a Hindu nationalist party. The party argued for the adoption of cultural nationalism as the founding principle of the Indian polity in such a way that the traditional Hindu way of life is blended with the modernity of the time. During this period, the party sought to symbolize its thrust on the ideology of Hindutva and cultural nationalism by calling for the construction of a grand Ram temple at the site of his birthplace by removing the disputed structure standing at that place as the Babri mosque. Thus, the stridency of the party on the issue of Ram temple apparently provided it a long following among the upper-caste people who identified themselves with the traditional glory.

With the fall of the successive governments, a number of parties had started taking the fluid situation as the opportune time for them to reposition their electoral strategies, while the others remained busy in the game of government formation. In this regard, the perspective of the BJP had been quite different from others. Undoubtedly, the successive efforts of the party to form government at the centre had been sabotaged by the opposition parties. In other words, every time the BJP was able to form the government, the opposition parties had always

[6] Blom Hansen Thomas and Christophe Jaffrelot, eds, *The BJP and the Compulsion of Politics in India* (New Delhi: Oxford University Press, 1998), 7.

joined hands with one another to ensure the downfall of the government. Thus, the government formation experiences of the BJP in the previous times had been very unpleasant. So the party was now left with no option than to buy time out of the skirmishes taking place among different Janata offshoots and evolve a concerted strategy that could catapult it to power at the centre. In this move, the party was greatly assisted by the formation of governments at the centre with the support of either the regional parties or the Congress. Thus, the rise and fall of different governments did take place but the blame game among the different stakeholders did not affect the BJP and it busied itself in going for fresh elections.[7]

Amid the social and political churning that had become the hallmark of this phase of electoral politics of India, the most significant gainer in terms of seats had definitely been the BJP. In fact, this phase might be seen as the reinvention of the BJP from being a fringe element of the Indian politics to become the nucleus of the political system. However, two significant pointers of the time could be seen as the important terms of discourse of BJP's rise to the top of the system. With the appeal of the cultural nationalism cutting ice with the different social groups, particularly the upper-caste people who once constituted the core support base of the Congress, the party had consistently been improving its tally of seats in the Lok Sabha. As the figures in Table 6.1 indicate, the party could improve its seat tally from 161 in 1996 to 182 in the 1998 general elections. But the growing acceptability of the BJP on the part of the people did not go well with the other political parties who stood in clear competition with the BJP in cornering the benefits arising out of the social and political churning. For instance, in the beginning, the parties that came into open alliance with the BJP had been just a few except its traditional ally, the Shiv Sena. The social justice based parties

[7] Oliver Heath, 'Anatomy of BJP's Rise to Power: Social, Regional and Political Expansion in 1990s', *Economic & Political Weekly* 34, no. 34–35 (12 August 1999), 2516–2517.

tried to portray the BJP as some sort of untouchable but the electors had something else in mind.

Learning the hard lessons from its first tryst with power at the centre, the BJP re-strategized its political arithmetic in such a way that its acceptability among the mainstream political parties increased. The party could very well realize that the major difficulty with other political parties had not been with the Rightist approach of the party but with its enmeshing the Rightist ideology with the ideology of Hindutva along with its discordant views on a number of controversial issues facing the country. The fear of the other parties, thus, did not emanate from their distrust in the Rightist ideology but with the Hindutva and other controversial positions taken by the BJP on different issues such as the Ram temple, status of Jammu and Kashmir within the Indian union and the uniform civil code, among others. Even on these issues, the other parties did not seem to be uncomfortable with the BJP for the sake of any other concern but the fear of desertion of the Muslim voters who had been key to their electoral performances in both state and national elections. Thus, the basic mantra left for the BJP was to tone down its insistence on the controversial issues and find a common ground to gel with other political parties.

The political scenario during the last few years had been such that the political disintegration of different social groups had become almost complete between the competing political claims such as the proponents of social justice, the Hindutva-based parties and the political formations thriving on the basis of local or regional issues and concerns, especially in the southern and eastern parts. During this churning, the BJP had indeed been able to arouse the Hindutva orientation of a large section of the society but its monopoly on this emotive issue had been so complete that it did not leave any scope for any other political party to eye the votes likely to be cast on the basis of the Hindutva persuasions. On this count, the only exception could be seen in the form of the Shiv Sena which has been able to maintain its vibrancy in the Maharashtra politics despite playing the same electoral tune as that of the BJP. But for other opposition political parties, Hindutva became as alien ideology as that of staking claim for the Nehruvian socialism as their own preserve.

The BJP, in order to expand its social and political acceptance, on the one hand, and earn more and more allies, on the other, embarked upon the twin strategy of keeping its hard-line political stances such as Hindutva, Ram temple and its perspectives on other controversial issues as its long-term guiding principles, but remaining ready to present a liberal or accommodative face to its allies and to the general masses on the practical pedestal. In other words, the party performed a very delicate task in a wonderful way by retaining its strident approach to its foundational issues but on the ground remained a pliable, accommodative and liberal political party with which the liberal, Centrist and Rightist political forces can align with in the short term. Personality wise, while L. K. Advani represented the hard face of the party in a seemingly uncompromising manner, the soft face of the party was put forward in the shape of Vajpayee as a malleable and sweet personality ready to mix and work with any political party falling within the broad ideological spectrum of Rightist orientation. With this strategy, the party could win a number of allies and partners that eventually made the party head the ruling alliance after 1999 general elections to complete the full term in office.

Sixteenth General Election and Resetting of the Agenda

The coalition government that the BJP formed after the 13th general election could not provide it the required opportunity to reset the agenda of social, economic and political reconstruction as per its vision of ancient Indian cultural traditions due to the pulls and pressures exerted by different coalition partners on a constant basis. But such a situation could well be washed out in 2014 due to the formidable majority that the party enjoyed among its coalition partners under the leadership of Narendra Modi. The party now got an opportunity to translate the promises it made to the people into reality by pushing for structural reconfiguration of vital bodies and institutions that formed the core of the Nehruvian vision of India. In this context, the most significant alteration made by the BJP government was in terms of replacement of the erstwhile monolith Planning Commission by a brand new idea called the NITI Aayog. The formation of the NITI Aayog, in fact, also reflects the political and ideological dispositions of the government of the time. The Planning Commission was fruition of the long-held socialist ideas of a dominant section of the Congress led by Jawaharlal Nehru. Now, with the waning away of the socialist orientations in the development discourse, and its replacement with the neoliberal economic agenda, the political context of the formation of the NITI Aayog has been sought to be provided by the ideas of the non-socialist national leaders such as Mahatma Gandhi, Dr Bhimrao Ambedkar, Tiruvalluvar, Pt Deendayal Upadhyaya, Sankar Dev and Swami Vivekananda. In the Cabinet Resolution adopted on 1 January 2015, to establish NITI Aayog in supersession of the Planning Commission, these leaders were quoted to provide intellectual and ideological justification for the reorientation in the developmental discourse of the country. For instance, the Cabinet Resolution opens with the quote of Mahatma Gandhi: 'Constant development is the law of life, and a man who always tries to maintain his dogmas in order to appear consistent drives himself into a false position'.[8] Thus, the long-standing purpose and rationale of the Planning Commission has been discarded at the stroke of a pen.

The political and economic philosophy that lay at the root of the formation of the NITI Aayog has been drawn from the ideas of social and spiritual leaders closely associated with the ideology of Hindutva. Taking the ideas of Deendayal Upadhyaya as the foundational precepts of the NITI Aayog, the Cabinet Resolution embraces *Antyodaya* as the ultimate purpose of economic development. It says that in a country like India where

[8] Cabinet Resolution adopted on 1 January 2015 (New Delhi: Cabinet Secretariat, Government of India, 2015).

a large section of society is still poor and survives on subsistence needs of life, the economic development would not be complete unless each and every individual's life is touched and improved by fruits of such economic development. Moreover, in accordance with the philosophy of Antyodaya, the pattern of economic development needs to be such where the fruits of economic development should reach first of all to the poorest of the poor. At the same time, the inequalities based on gender, caste, class as well as economic and regional disparities are simply unacceptable in a democratic country. Hence, the model of development for a country like India should be such in which the equality of opportunity should be balanced by the ideas of inclusive and comprehensive development in which no sections of society are left outside the framework of development discourse. The developmental strategy followed so far in the country has not been able to achieve the desired agenda of balanced and inclusive development.

Hence, what the Cabinet Resolution argues for is the adoption of 'a Bharatiya approach' to development. Given the context and contents of the Cabinet Resolution, the Bharatiya approach to development may have two aspects—negative and positive—insofar as planning as the mainstay of socio-economic development in India is concerned. One, the Bharatiya approach negates the ideological influences of the alien socio-economic and political philosophies on the development discourse in India. In other words, there appears to be a subtle critique of the ideology of socialism that underpinned the entire idea of the Planning Commission which has been considered to be alien to the Indian ethos. As the Cabinet Resolution notes,

Perhaps, more importantly, the institution must adhere to the tenet that while incorporating positive influences from the world, no single model can be transplanted from outside into the Indian scenario. We need to find our own strategy for growth. The new institution has to zero in on what will work in and for India.[9]

[9] Ibid.

In a way, thus, the government's position on the institutions like Planning Commission appears to be quite paradoxical. On the one hand, the government wants to free the institutions of development from any alien ideological baggage like socialism. But, on the other, the way the idea of NITI Aayog has been mooted and the kind of structures and functions envisaged for it, there remains no doubt that it would be imbued with the ideological thrust of the neoliberal economic thinking.

The other significant dimension of the Bharatiya approach to development is rooted in relooking at the focus of development strategy in India through the lens of Antyodaya, as conceptualized and propagated by Pt Deendayal Upadhyaya. Thus, instead of orienting the focus of economic development towards creation of infrastructure industries and affording the public sector the position of commanding heights of the economy, the Antyodaya philosophy seeks to focus on the equal and inclusive distribution of the outcomes of the economic development. Elaborating the concept of Antyodaya, the Cabinet Resolution outlines,

> Antyodaya or uplift of the downtrodden where the goal is to ensure that the poorest of the poor get the benefits of development. Inequalities based on gender biases as well as economic disparities have to be redressed. We need to create an environment and support system that encourages women to play their rightful role in nation-building. Equality of opportunity goes hand in hand with an inclusiveness agenda. Rather than pushing everyone on to a pre-determined path, we have to give every element of society—especially weaker segments like the Scheduled Castes and Scheduled Tribes— the ability to influence the choices the country and government make in setting the national agenda.[10]

In order to contextualize the formation of the NITI Aayog in place of the Planning Commission, the Cabinet Resolution lists out a number of forces that have been found to be lying

[10] Ibid.

at the root of transforming India. Among them, the first factor has been the reinvention in the role of the government in the era of liberalization and globalization. It has been argued that in the changed scenario, the role of the government needs to be defined in terms of being an 'enabler' rather than a 'provider' of goods and services to the people. Accordingly, instead of government acting as the lead actor in the theatre of economic development, it has to play the role of ensuring enabling legislation, policymaking and regulation. Similarly, in the field of agriculture, there has been drastic transformation in the situation from being a food-deficit to a food-surplus economy in the aftermath of the Green Revolution. Hence, there has been a call for moving ahead from food security to opting for a mix agricultural production to secure a remunerative venture for the farmers. In such endeavours, the private sector is likely to play an increasingly significant role in a growing competitive environment not only in India but in the world as well.

The changed economic landscape in India has not only been marked by rapid innovations and improvements in the scientific and technological inventions but also radical alternations in the social capital, that is, population base of the country. The Cabinet Resolution identifies four distinct sections of Indians who would act as the bedrock upon which the economic prosperity might be constructed: middle class; entrepreneurial, scientific and intellectual class; non-resident Indian community and small business. These groups of people are assumed to possess their unique potential for contributing to the growth story of India in case they are properly channelized and given adequate opportunities. For instance, regarding the potential of the middle class of Indian society, the Resolution notes,

India's middle class is unique in its size and purchasing power. This formidable group is increasing with the entry of the neo-middle class. It has been an important driver of growth and has enormous potential on account of its high education levels, mobility and willingness to push for change in the country. Our continuing challenge is to ensure that this economically vibrant group remains engaged and its potential is fully realised.[11]

Likewise, the other components of the social capital have also been acknowledged for their outstanding prowess and inherent capabilities to spur the economic activities. It has been premised in the Cabinet Resolution that the real challenge for the government lies in identifying the true nature and quantum of the contributory growth potential of these groups of people. Only then, their potential can be channelized for spurring the economic activities that may land India in the comity of developed nations of the world.

The slow and subtle process through which the BJP has been trying to materialize its avowed goal of rooting the economic and political life in which what is calls the cultural ethos has also been reflected in a number of other avenues of governmental functioning. In other words, the party's vision of taking politics as culture has found its complete acceptability on the part of the electorates now that the party has emerged as the epicentre of electoral politics in the county. This rapid stride in the electoral fortunes of the party has also helped it spread its reach to all nooks and corners with the perceptible vision of making the march of politics rooted in the cultural roots of the people rather than taking the imported ideas as the preferred reference point for the people. Politics as culture is thus an indelible mark that the party has sought to leave on the political landscape in place of the secular patterns of life that the Nehruvian legacy had left on the psyche of the people. Further blending the cultural ethos of India with the religious overtones of Hindutva seem to have worked wonders for the party as the mass of people including the ones belonging to the middle and backward castes have tended to accept that as the appreciable way of life and voted for the BJP to replace the Congress as the hegemonic ruler.

[11] Ibid.

Contemporary Scenario

In contemporary times, BJP's vision of politics as culture has taken the curious extension in the spheres of national security and resolution of the long-standing issues that threaten the unity and integrity of the nation right since the times of Independence. Moreover, the party has been trying to extend its forays in the areas and sections of people that had hitherto remained outside the reach of the party. In this context, the poll promises of the party during the 17th general election and its spirited fight in the states like West Bengal where the party was unsuccessfully trying to get a foothold presented a wonderful example of the futuristic vision of the party. That way, the 2019 general elections saw the clear continuation of the long-drawn beliefs and priorities of major political parties in terms of their avowed electoral promises presented in their manifestos. The BJP has unfailingly been a champion of a nationalist vision for country in which in the place of social and economic issues of the people, priority has been accorded to the issues concerning national defence and overall security scenario. In its election manifesto, named 'Sankalp Patra' (Dossier of Commitments), the party offered 75 promises that it would attempt to fulfil by the time India turns 75.[12]

Indicating its intent of according top priority to unity and integrity of the country over the issues of social welfare and economic development, the first set of promises related to the core issues facing the internal security and external defence of India. Curiously enough, party's long-standing promise of getting Ram temple constructed at Ayodhya got only passing reference in face of the muscular nationalistic promises getting focus over all other issues.[13] Although the party indeed offered a number of welfare measures for the farmers, such promises were

[12] Bharatiya Janata Party, *Sankalp Patra: Lok Sabha 2019*, available at https://www.documentcloud.org/documents/5798075-Bjp-Election-2019-Manifesto-English.html (accessed on 12 June 2019).
[13] Kumar Uttam, '"Nation First" Approach Won the Day', *The Hindustan Times*, 24 May 2019, 2.

surely not in the mould of socialistic freebies offered during the heyday of the Congress. Rather, the manifesto aimed at inching towards the 'New India' in which nothing would probably come without a price.

BJP's campaign strategy was overwhelmingly centred on the personality of its charismatic leader and Prime Minister Modi. But apart from Modi, the party also banked upon the massive electoral tours of its President Amit Shah as well as other party heavyweights.[14] A remarkable aspect of the campaign strategy of the party was to focus on those areas where it could sense bright prospects of bettering its previous records of seats in addition to paying sufficient attention to its traditional strongholds lying mainly in the Hindi heartland and western part of the country. For instance, the party could very well visualize fair prospects for it to have a strong foothold in the hitherto unexplored territories in eastern part of India with special stress on West Bengal.[15] It began with weaning away dissenter leaders of the TMC like Mukul Roy who acted to mobilize a number of TMC supporters in support of the BJP.[16] Moreover, the party stationed one of its very seasoned strategist to be in charge of the state on a long-term basis so as to have the feel of ground realities of the state, issues and challenges faced by the people, governmental responses to their problems and how the party could convert the public disenchantment with the ruling party into its favour. Such a master stroke of the party really worked well in the state and it was indeed able to emerge as a formidable force in the state in terms of both Lok Sabha seats and percentage of votes polled in its favour.[17]

The issues that became the punch line for the party to put forward its vision and action plan consisted mainly of such problems and rhetoric that would help in arousing people's nationalistic passion. Beginning with the drafting of its

[14] Sardesai, 'The BJP Juggernaut'.
[15] Datta, 'Battle for Bengal'.
[16] Mallick, 'Poll Perceptions'.
[17] Uttam, 'Behind BJP's Bengal Inroads'.

manifesto till the last day of election campaign, the party stuck to the core issues facing national defence and internal security. For instance, in highlighting its commitment for the unity and integrity of the nation, the party touched upon all the vital aspects that tended to challenge the unity and security of India. Hence, right from Kashmir issue to that of cross-border terrorism, destruction of terrorist training camps across the border, menace of Left-wing extremism, especially Naxalism and other insurgencies, and strengthening of the armed forces and other security apparatus, the party did not fail to lay stress on all these issues in any of the election meetings. In a way, the party, thus, was able to alter the discourse of election campaign by setting the agenda as per its convenience. The promises made by the party have pointedly gone well with the people who rewarded it with the majority of seats in the 17th Lok Sabha.

Assessing BJP's Weltanschauung (Worldview)

Speaking before the national executive of the party in April 1998, Advani remarked: 'Every step forward in our steady march from a marginal party in 1951 to the mainstream party in 1998 has been made possible by our uncompromising commitment to nationalism'.[18] The BJP positioned itself in the national politics as the party which put the interest of the nation before everything else. Beyond the integrity and security of the country's physical boundary, this commitment also meant unflinching faith in its unique cultural paradigm. It is the stress on the latter that has distinguished it more clearly from other political formations. This was defined aptly by Advani in his presidential speech before the party's national council in October 2004:

> We are a party with a difference, precisely because we are firmly wedded to a set of core beliefs. Our political priorities, strategies and tactics may be fashioned by the issues of the day but our ideology remains constant. The BJP is first and

18 *Presidential Speeches* (Part II), Party Documents, 309.

foremost a 'nation-first' party. We are a party of nationalism. Our politics is determined by the litmus test of what is good and desirable for the nation. The BJP is the party of cultural nationalism. We believe that Indian nationhood stems from an underlying cultural oneness. Some of us call this sense of nationhood *Hindutva*; Pandit Deendayal Upadhyaya also called it *Bharatiyata*. I am saddened that from being a description of the core of our nationhood, Hindutva has been misrepresented to denote a political approach. Hindutva is a sentiment; it is neither an electoral slogan nor should it be confused with religion.[19]

He also clarified that the BJP had never abandoned its ideology, whether in 1974, when the BJS agreed to join the JP movement or in 1998, when the NDA was formed with a national agenda for governance that did not include issues like Ram temple or Article 370 or uniform civil code: 'The fears are unfounded. Ideology is a commitment to certain principles. It is what defines our approach to political questions. The political priorities of the day are, however, determined by other constituency and need a context'.[20]

It is in this context of cultural nationalism, and sometime in the wider context of national integrity, that the party adopted icons who were not strictly part of its ideological fraternity, for example, Gandhi, Sardar Patel, Subhas Chandra Bose or more recently, Ram Manohar Lohia, A. P. J. Abdul Kalam or Ambedkar. At another level, the talks of multiple nations within India or the idea of India with multiple identities is something that the BJP fights wholeheartedly treating it as complete anathema. The idea of one nation, one culture adopted first by the BJS continues to dominate BJP's philosophy too: 'India is multilingual, it is multi-religious; but it is still one nation. Indians are one people'.[21] This larger idea of 'unity within diversity' is

[19] *Presidential Speeches* (Part I), Party Document, 8.
[20] Ibid.
[21] Advani's presidential speech, National Council, BJP, 2–4 January 1987, *Presidential Speeches* (Part II), Party Document, 149.

not something new, or propounded solely by the BJP, but the BJP has used it more effectively and frequently to connect with the emotional chord of average Indians.

It sees the modern concept of secularism, imported through a Eurocentric view, a complete misfit to the Indian conditions, something which it perceives as being responsible for making the intellectual debate lopsided or making the idea of cultural nationalism look retrogressive. It believes that this lopsided understanding of Indian culture and religions, developed through indiscriminate usage of the term secularism, has encouraged political 'minorityism' besides inculcating an inferiority complex (and even hostility) towards the Hindu essence of Indian life. The party feels that it is 'the perverse interpretation' of secularism and 'consideration of electoral expediency' that have made political leaders ignore the silken bond of one country, one culture.[22] At a more general level, this is seen as encouraging distaste for Indianness and India's traditional past:

Inclusion of stories from the Ramayana and Mahabharata in our text books make our pseudo-secularists fret and fume in rage. I have known politicians opposing the recitation of Mira Bhajans and Rama Charit Manas from the radio on the ground that they create a Hindu ethos. At the National Integration Council meeting in September 1986, objections were raised to lighting of lamps while inaugurating government functions and breaking of coconuts to mark the launching of a new ship. The objectors would rather have us imitating the western practice of cutting a tape, and smashing a champagne bottle. Truth is that for many politicians and intellectuals, secularism is only a euphemism to cloak their allergy to Hinduism.[23]

The pledge to be signed by members joining the BJP for the first time asks them to subscribe to the concept of 'secular state and nation not based on religion', following non-discrimination

[22] Ibid., 151.
[23] Ibid.

based on caste, sex or religion, and not observing or recognizing untouchability in any shape or form.[24] While this clearly recognizes that the party is not a supporter of a theocratic state, it draws a clear distinction between the English term 'religion' and the Indian term 'dharma', the latter signifying a broader connotation to mean moral and ethical order. Taking this argument a step further, the party believes that in sharp contrast to Pakistan which declared itself an Islamic state, 'India gave to itself a secular Constitution because it was Hindu. Theocracy is alien to traditional Hindu polity'.[25]

Concluding Observations

Electoral politics in India has become the domain where the creative perspectives of life are presented by the political class. The public reception of ideas eventually provides the much-required political force for them to get reflected in the governmental policies and programmes. In this case, the classic case has been the Nehruvian socialism which could indeed supersede the Gandhian vision of life for Indians in the post-Independence period due to the landslide electoral victories that Nehru could win in the three consecutive elections during his lifetime. In the later course of the Indian politics, the shape of things more or less remained hovering around the ideas, systems and institutions ordained by Nehru. That way, the alternative of life provided by the Right-wing parties, particularly the BJS and the BJP, could not attract the attention of the people in the face of the hegemonic influence of the Left-leaning policies and programmes. However, the idea of politics as culture has always remained the alternative perspective, that is, to come to the forefront given the availability of propitious situations. Such circumstances started getting in the way of the BJP after the progressive weakening of the Congress and disintegration of the other opposition parties. In this regard, the decisive moment for

[24] www.bjp.org/var/assets/reg-form/Membership%20Application%20 Form,pdf (accessed on 21 June 2019).
[25] Advani's presidential speech, 152.

the party came in 2014 when it was comprehensively voted to power in the 16th general election without lowering its guard on its crucial ideological beliefs and convictions including portraying politics as culture to reshape the basic contours of the social, economic and political life once the party is voted to power. The gains of the party cornered in 2014 were indelibly deepened in 2019 by brushing aside the counter-narratives of the politics as culture and professedly proclaiming the party's commitment to cultural nationalism and rebuilding the nation as per the cultural ethos of the past in conjunction with its judicious blending with the contemporary perspectives.

As India's nationalist history shows, the national movement drew on the dialectical interconnection between culture and politics. The 1905–1908 Swadeshi movement was, for instance, an account of how those who campaigned for the revocation of the first partition of Bengal justified their participation as a service to the Mother Goddess. It was, therefore, not surprising that Bankim Chandra Chattopadhyay's *Ananda Math* was hailed as an inspirational novel. Rabindranath Tagore captured this dimension in his 1916 novel *Ghare Baire* which presented before the readers the increasing importance of cultural affinity in cementing a relatively permanent bond among the nationalists. In his novel *Gora*, published in 1910, Tagore also identified how focus on Hindu cultural ethos created a communal chasm between the Hindus and their Muslim neighbours. Basic here is the point that culture and politics remain dialectically connected, as India's past has demonstrated. By reiterating that culture continues to be effective in bringing people together around some commonly accepted cultural values and principles, the BJP can be said to have recreated an ideological design that appears to have lost its significance with the consolidation of the so-called Nehruvian socialist-secular inclinations.

There are three points that merit attention to understand the steady rise of the BJP in India as a pan-Indian party by couching its mobilizing strategy around India's distinctive cultural identity. *First*, it is clear that the Nehruvian idea of India, despite being hailed as guiding force for independent India, did not seem to have had a universal appeal; it was accepted at a time when the Hindu nationalist ideas remained marginalized due to the overwhelming support that the Congress leaders had largely because of their contribution to India's freedom struggle. In other words, Hindu nationalism failed to generate adequate support primarily because of the prevalence of the nationalist euphoria that evolved with the attainment of independence in 1947. *Second*, there was also a crisis of leadership which was a serious handicap for those seeking to champion Hindu nationalist ideas. Syama Prasad Mookerjee of the BJS endeavoured this by raising the discriminatory Article 370 of India's Constitution which was not pursued as vociferously as was expected due to leadership vacuum. This is not, therefore, surprising that the BJS and the BJP in its initial years never became a formidable opposition to the Congress and the ideology that it represented. *Third*, the credit for making the BJP a pan-Indian alternative goes to the young leadership that set out a powerful voice drawing on the Hindu nationalist ideological priorities. As the post-1992 poll results show, that the BJP became a party of large following was firmly established by its growing popularity among the voters. There is also substance in the argument that the so-called Muslim appeasement by the Congress and its failure to address the genuine socio-economic grievances of the Hindus created a constituency for the BJP in India presumably because of its explicit concern for the majority community. On the whole, the BJP success is attributed to its ability to popularize Hindu nationalist ideas which remained peripheral in the past for partisan reasons. There are, therefore, reasons to pursue the claim that Hindu nationalism, in its contemporary form, continues to act decisively in shaping the electoral choice of the majority in India despite being dismissed as sectarian by those espousing the Nehruvian ideological inklings.

7

Regional Electoral Divergences

Electoral politics in India is characterized by a strong regional divergence. An analytical account of the first four national elections justifies the conceptually defensible 'one-dominant party' syndrome since the Congress had won both the State Assembly and Parliamentary elections. The scene underwent a sea change with the victory of regional and non-Congress political outfits in various State Assembly elections in 1967 that has been the case till now. Implicit here are two complementary arguments: on the one hand, the post-1967 electoral trends created a new template for voting behaviour suggesting that the voters preferred political parties other than the Congress in the regions or provinces. Here, on many occasions, the pan-Indian party failed to muster adequate support with the growing popularity of the regional parties and their leaders. On the other, the new template is conceptually significant since it led to the increasing importance of regional issues which the all-India parties could not afford to ignore as it was likely to undermine their support and those political parties with which they were aligned for electoral advantages in specific elections. This is, in short, 'regionalization of Indian politics'; regionalization because the regions have become critical players in Indian politics which is required to understood differently by drawing attention to the peculiar unfolding of the socio-political processes at the grassroots. Besides being a study of how the processes evolved, the chapter also seeks to conceptualize the phenomenon with reference to its contextual roots since the gradual decline of the Congress as an umbrella party. In other words, the failure of the Congress to adequately represent the local interests created a legitimate space for the regional outfits as capable of championing the regional aims and objectives. Dwelling on regional electoral divergences, particularly since 1971 Lok Sabha poll, the chapter is both a narrative and an attempt to plausibly explain the phenomenon with reference to the rapidly transforming socio-economic circumstances along with the changing ideological voices. The aim here is to identify how a careful analysis of the poll outcome will help us understand the gradual transformation of Indian democracy. It is evident that a process has started to consolidate 'regionalization of national politics' and 'nationalization of regional politics' which means that regions and the nation are dialectically interlinked. For a better grasp of the enigmatic nature of election, both at the national and regional levels, one is required to pay adequate attention to this dialectical interconnection; otherwise, our understanding shall remain terribly incomplete, if not prejudiced.

Congress and Regionalization

Trends towards regionalization of Indian politics had started emerging right since the decade of 1950s itself with the states like Kerala presenting definite signals of weakening of the Congress in the state and emergence of the CPI as the claimant to power.[1] However, regionalization as a widespread phenomenon of electoral politics could become a formidable fact of Indian elections during the decade of the 1960s only when

[1] Narendar Pani, 'Regional Nationalism: Challenge to National Parties', *The Times of India*, 16 May 1996, 7.

the internal divisions within the Congress led to its decisive fall from the position of the monopolizing political force to that of a party struggling for its united existence. The formation of coalition governments led by opposition parties in a number of states after 1967 elections ingrained the regional elements in the electoral politics in an irreversible manner. Further, in a weakened position, Indira Gandhi tried to form coalition governments in certain states like UP so as to take political mileage over her opponents. That way, the regionalization of politics in India came out in open only after the departure of Nehru from the scene and disintegration of the Congress Party by vertical split. While Indira Gandhi walked away with a majority of stakes at the central level, the regional satraps of the party found themselves in a marginalized position and preferred to dabble into regional politics, thereby giving new vigour and substance to regionalization of politics.

The 1967 experiment brought about far-reaching changes in Indian politics in two fundamental ways: *first*, the days of the single-party majority were over and replaced by a coalition of parties, not purely on the basis of ideological compatibility but for a desire to push the Congress Party out of power. In the formation of coalition, defection was an important ingredient and most of the parties were adversely affected except those parties to the far right and left which maintained their organizational integrity through discipline and ideological consistency. So the period, 1967–1969, proved to be a transitional stage or interregnum in politics illustrating the rise of a new phase where coalition of parties became an inescapable phenomenon. *Second*, anti-Congressism gained ground with the 1967 elections and the idea that the Congress Party was invincible seemed to have exhausted its potential. Anti-Congressism was defined in a very vague manner so as to catch on all the parties opposed to the Congress. This was probably how the major communist parties, including the CPI(M) and the CPI, shared the platform with the dissident members of the Congress while forming the United Front government in West Bengal. What drove them to support even the ideologically incompatible partners was perhaps the national democratic ideology of diverse class interests in order to trounce a major political foe, the Congress. Whatever the theoretical justification, the primary goal was to rout the Congress. The high priest of anti-Congressism was Ram Manohar Lohia who, as Kothari argued, 'devoted himself to the mission of destroying the Congress monopoly of power by uniting all anti-Congress forces in the country'.[2] Lohia succeeded in his mission and the Indian polity was clearly divided into two opposite camps of those supporting the Congress and those who were opposed to it.

This was an era of possibilities. The Congress lost power and for its revival, it had to renew itself keeping in mind the changed nature of Indian polity. Similarly, the opposition parties translated the sentiments against the Congress into an opportunity whereby the Congress was pushed out of power in majority of Indian provinces (9 out of 16 states). Yet their euphoria for electoral victory over the Congress was short lived. So this was also an era of political uncertainty where none of the major political parties was sure of its fate in future India. Despite being characterized by uncertainty and chronic political instability, the period, 1967–1969, was therefore a clear break with the past since it created a definite space for coalition politics as opposed to mono-centric single-party rule. The event of coming together of parties with diverse interests was thus a part of wider democratic processes whereby a new wave was crystallized with a far-reaching impact and significant consequences on future political articulation. In addition, coalition is inevitable because the basic shift that has occurred in Indian politics cannot be glossed over.

The 1971 National Poll and Its Aftermath

The general election that catapulted Indira Gandhi to the centre stage of Indian politics also pioneered the emergence of a number of formidable regional forces that could become

[2] Rajni Kothari, *Politics in India*, reprint (New Delhi: Orient Longman, 1986), 183.

some sort of permanent fixtures on the political landscape. In this regard, the context of the 1971 general elections appeared to be quite indicative. Amidst the multiple challenges facing the government of Indira Gandhi, what seemed to have tilted the scale in favour of the general elections was the successive defeat of one after another of the state governments led by her party. For instance, in September 1970, the alliance between Congress (R) and Chaudhary Charan Singh's Bharatiya Kisan Dal broke down leading to fall of the government in UP. This development was taken by Mrs Gandhi as a kind of alarming bell because it indicated that now the regional satraps are also taking her party as relatively weak and vulnerable to political manoeuvring on their part. Her apprehensions proved true sooner than expected when there appeared a kind of action replay of the incidents of UP in Bihar in December 1970. These events led to serious apprehensions in the minds of the Congress (R) leadership that political power at the provincial levels had fast been slipping out of the hand of the party. For party leaders, there appeared a clear likelihood that the chain of events set on in UP and Bihar might expand to other states as well, leading to the erosion of power of the party in large parts of India. State of things, thus, appeared to be getting out of control for Mrs Gandhi to arrest as she did not have so many options. One way out available for her was to go for political manoeuvring and realignment of political forces at both national and provincial levels. But such activities were not likely to bring about any long-term benefit for the party. So she was left with no other option than to sacrifice her minority government and go for general elections.[3]

Comparatively, the most dismal performance of the Congress (R) was experienced in southern states where the gain of regional parties ate into the overall seat share of the party.

---

[3] Atul Kohli, 'Power and Powerlessness: India's Democracy in a Comparative Perspective', in *State Power and Social Forces: Domination and Transformation in the Third World*, eds Joel Migdal, Atul Kohli, and Vivienne Shue (Cambridge: Cambridge University Press, 1995), 193.

For instance, Dravida Munnetra Kazhagam (DMK) was indeed able to maintain its hold on the Dravidian politics in Tamil Nadu that stymied the sweep of Congress (R)'s wave in the state. Similarly, good performance of a regional party, Telangana Praja Samithi, in the Telangana region of Andhra Pradesh did not allow the Congress (R) to have a walkover in the electoral battle in Andhra Pradesh. As a result, the South contributed the least number of seats out of its total seats spreading over the four states. The seat-wise break-up of the gains of Congress (R) in different regions is also, more or less, reflected in the vote share of the party as percentage of total votes in a region. The most interesting part in this regard is the highest percentage of votes secured by the party in the western region though the seat share was highest in the northern region. Such an apparent paradox between vote share and number of seats may be explained by the multi-cornered contest in the northern states as compared to the relative unity of the opposition parties in the West. For East and South, the vote share of the Congress hovered around respectable 36–37 per cent which translated in good number of seats for the party.

An important feature of the 1971 general election had been Mrs Gandhi's obvious gamble of delinking the Lok Sabha elections with the elections of State Legislative Assemblies in order to discourage the regional issues from influencing the national elections. But despite earning a landslide for Mrs Gandhi, such a gamble could not fulfil her aspiration of separating national and regional issues from working at cross purposes with each other. In the final analysis of the results of the 1971 elections, it was well established that in many of the states, the runner up in terms of popular vote was not a national but a regional party proving that a large number of people were still swayed by regional considerations despite the national character of the election.[4] Thus, the regional factors remained

[4] Myron Weiner, 'The 1971 Elections: India's Changing Party System', in *The Indian Paradox: Essays in Indian Politics by Myron Weiner*, ed. Ashutosh Varshney (New Delhi: SAGE Publications, 1989), 228.

formidable determinants of voting behaviour of the people despite the delinking of Lok Sabha and Vidhan Sabha elections. It was, in fact, these regional feelings that later emerged as the strong base of anti-Congress political formations in different parts of India.

The growing wave of regionalization was, however, halted in the course of the general elections held in 1985 after the assassination of Indira Gandhi. The historical victory of the Congress in these elections not only surprised its leadership including the prime minister but also upset the composition of the lower house in such a way that a regional party like the TDP emerged as the largest opposition group with 30 seats in the Lok Sabha whose leader was to be appointed as the leader of opposition. In other words, the victorious march of the Congress Party led to the decisive trouncing of most, if not all, of the opposition parties such as the BJP, the Janata Party and the Lok Dal. These grand old parties of Indian politics were reduced to insignificance in the Lok Sabha. Among the Left parties, the CPI(M) could succeed in keeping its support base intact to some extent in its traditional bastion of West Bengal by winning a respectable number of 22 seats. However, the other important Left party, the CPI could not withstand the Congress wave and could manage to win only six seats with a meagre 2.6 per cent of votes polled. In this regard, an interesting trend had been the mismatch between the percentage of votes polled and the number of seats won by different opposition parties.[5] For instance, despite securing 7.74 per cent of votes polled, the BJP could win only two seats as compared to Indian Congress (Socialist) which won four seats despite securing only 1.52 per cent of total votes polled.

The sweep of the Congress Party continued even after the conclusion of the general elections in December 1984. The deferred elections of Assam and Punjab were held later in early 1985, in which the winning streak of the Congress continued

[5] T. C. Bose, 'The Eighth General Elections and the Indian Polity', *Indian Journal of Political Science* 47, no. 1 (January–March 1986): 142.

though not with the same momentum in which it had won the main general elections held in December 1984.[6] Since both the states of Assam and Punjab were marred by social movements and terrorism, respectively, the parties spearheading and/or having sympathetic outlook towards these issues emerged as the major gainers of the elections. Thus, the major gainer of Lok Sabha polls in Assam had been the Asom Gana Parishad, the novice political party of college and university students of Assam whose nominees cornered majority of Lok Sabha seats in the state. Similarly, in Punjab, the Congress was taken as the spoiler of the cause of Sikh state and, therefore, the star of the Lok Sabha elections in the state emerged to be the Shiromani Akali Dal (SAD) that won majority of seats in the state. Despite the adverse situations in the two states, the Congress was able to add 10 more seats to its swelling kitty of 404 seats in the Lok Sabha. Thus, in the final composition of the eighth Lok Sabha, the Congress commanded the unprecedented majority of 414 seats that made its leader Rajiv Gandhi the most formidable personality of Indian politics of the time.[7]

Regionalization through Janata Clan

The imposition of Emergency by Indira Gandhi government and the JP movement against this tyrannical move turned out to be the momentous phase of Indian electoral politics. The JP movement brought to the fore a number of leaders and social forces that eventually became the fulcrum of regional politics. While the formation of the Janata Party was an important landmark in the political history of the country, its disintegration leading into formation of a number of other parties went a long way in the consolidation of regional politics. However, the real push towards regionalization came in the course of

[6] Vani Kant Barooah, 'Incumbency and Parliamentary Elections in India: An Analysis of the Congress Party's Electoral Performance, 1962–1999', *Economic & Political Weekly* 41, no. 8 (3 March 2006): 744.

[7] Iqbal Narain, 'India in 1985: Triumph of Democracy', *Asian Survey* 26, no. 2 (February 1986): 258.

the ninth general elections. In other words, the ninth general elections facilitated the emergence of the anti-Congressism with renewed vigour in the Indian politics. In other words, the host of opposition parties that could not secure clear mandate from the electorate to form a non-Congress government did not wish to miss the opportunity offered to them to oust the Congress from the power at the centre despite their not forming the government for themselves. This has indeed been the trait of the democratic politics that the political stakeholders espousing the cause of anti-Congress have always clamoured to oust the grand old party of India and replace with the non-Congress government. But none of these parties has ever been in a position to form the government on their own. As a result, whenever, the opposition parties got a chance to form the government at the centre, as in 1977, such a government would inevitably be a coalition of disparate political forces that would otherwise detest one another just as they do for the Congress.

Irrespective of the motivations for different leaders to leave the Congress, the fact of the matter has been that over the years, they turned out to be bitter adversaries of the party they originally belonged to. Besides these former Congressmen, there have also been a large number of leaders and parties who have traditionally harboured antipathy to the Congress Party on account of their ideological predilections. The prominent among them could be the BJP whose espousal of the cause of Hindutva has always kept it on a different pedestal than the Congress throughout.[8]

During this period, the political churning was also taking curious turns with different national and regional political parties desperate to expand their base in their respective areas of influence. In their electoral pursuits, the most formidable challenge was undoubtedly the pan-India presence of the Congress Party that had been able to corner most of the Lok

[8] Christophe Jaffrelot, *The Hindu Nationalist Movement and Indian Politics* (New Delhi: Penguin, 1996), 379.

Sabha seats in the eighth general elections. Moreover, the apparently ideologically rival parties such as the BJP and the Left parties were also trying to augment their seats in the lower house of the Indian Parliament by riding on the anti-government wave in different parts of the country. Amidst such a climate of political flux, the most shrewd and subtle moves came from V. P. Singh who successfully tried to align his Jan Morcha with a number of regional parties such as the TDP in Andhra Pradesh, the DMK in Tamil Nadu and the Asom Gana Parishad in Assam, among others. These electoral alliances of the disparate parties in different parts of the country clearly provided them an edge over their rivals, particularly the Congress, in the electoral fray. Subsequently, in the ninth general elections, the opposition parties had indeed been able to make good fortunes at the cost of the Congress as a result of which the party in power lost the elections with a hung verdict being delivered by the people to constitute the Parliament.

One of the less impressive performers in the 1989 general elections could be seen in the form of the host of regional parties that could barely hang on to mark their presence in the new house. In fact, the losses of the Congress did not seem to convert into gains for the regional parties. Moreover, in a number of states where the stakes of the regional parties could have been higher, the Congress Party did not perform as badly as it did in the Hindi heartland. As a result, barring the All India Anna Dravida Munnetra Kazhagam (AIADMK) from the deeper South, no other regional party could secure even a double-digit seat in the Lok Sabha. This was a striking phenomenon given the fact that in the previous house when all the mainstream political parties and forces were made to bite the dust in the electoral fray in the wake of the sympathy wave for Rajiv Gandhi, it was the TDP that had defied that wave and emerged as the main opposition party in the eighth Lok Sabha. But in these elections, the party had to contend with just two seats. Furthermore, the powerful regional parties such as the Shiv Sena, the Akali Dal and the DMK, among others, failed to capitalize on the failures of the incumbent government to improve their tally in the new house ostensibly because of the sociopolitical dynamics of different states.[9]

Regionalization in Post-Mandal Period

Apart from the national parties, the regional parties also had a lot of stakes in the 10th general elections particularly for those whose fortunes had dipped remarkably in the previous general elections. In this context, the case of the TDP and the Shiv Sena stood out prominently. In other words, in the elections for the ninth Lok Sabha, the two parties had failed to perform as per their prowess in their respective strongholds of Andhra Pradesh and Maharashtra. But these parties had indeed been able to make a spectacular comeback in the 10th general elections improving upon their previous tally. Besides them, the two other parties that had been able to maintain consistency in their performance were the BSP in UP and the AIADMK in Tamil Nadu. The tally of the six seats of the Jharkhand Mukti Morcha (JMM) had later become the saving grace for the government of the Congress at the time of the trust vote that the party faced on the floor of the Lok Sabha. The good performance of these parties showed their resilience to put up a grand show irrespective of the directions the national politics was likely to take.[10]

The elections for the 10th Lok Sabha offered a number of creative inputs in the conceptualization of democratic experience. The prelude events of the elections were of great significance in the reinvention of Indian democracy. Before these elections, the vital national interests of the country were considered as something sacrosanct. But during these elections, in the game

[9] Pradeep Kumar, 'The National Parties and Regional Allies: A Study in the Socio-Political Dynamics', in *Political Parties and Party Systems*, eds Ajay K. Mehra, D. D. Khanna, and Gert W. Kueck (New Delhi: SAGE Publications, 2003), 302.

[10] Yogendra Yadav, 'Reconfiguration in Indian Politics: State Assembly Elections, 1993–95', *Economic & Political Weekly* 31, no. 2–3 (13 January 1996): 96.

of one-upmanship, the political parties went to the extent of causing subtle harms to the vital interests of the society. During much of the campaigning for these elections, the resort to primordial affinities of the people turned out to be norm of the electioneering for almost all the political parties. As a result, the democratic process had entered into a phase of competitive populism in which one party was ever ready to counter the moves of another party by evolving matching contexts and pretexts to win the votes of the masses. In such a scenario, the parties that held on to the developmental and programmatic discourses appeared to be at the receiving end. Further, the regionalization of the political process also forces the challenge of stability and durability of the government at the centre as one party securing a working majority in the Lok Sabha becomes a remote possibility. Anyway, these elections did experience the greater primordialization of the democratic process that set the terms of democratic upsurge in the times to come. Interestingly, the caste-based electoral mobilization did yield good results for the parties like the Janata Dal. But in the later years, the growing appetite of the caste-based mobilizers for greater political clout had eventually led to the undoing of the parent party itself. Consequently, the party system got regionalized and federalized with the regional satraps taking the centre stage in the government formation at the central level. The impact of the caste-based mobilization was, in fact, more vigorous and yielding at the levels of the state. For instance, in the states like Bihar, the caste-based parties like the RJD was able to win three consecutive elections for the State Assembly and remain in power for an interrupted span of 15 years. But at the central level, such politics reached the points of saturation sooner than the states. In the later general elections, the regional divergence became quite apparent.

Recent Trends

While this tendency had been relatively less in the case of the Congress, this proved to be the nemesis of the Janata Dal which by the 1998 general elections had almost lost its existence as almost all the major constituents of the party preferred to leave the party and form their own party. The residue of the party though continued to be called Janata Dal, its electoral performance in the general elections proved to be dismal and the party eventually was driven out of existence. On the other hand, the prominent leaders of the Janata Party went ahead with leaving the party and came up with their own parties having distinct names as per the basic thrust with which the party had been formed. For instance, in UP, Mulayam Singh Yadav left the Janata Dal to form his own SP which eventually emerged as one of the most formidable parties in the state. However, the highest number of parties springing from the Janata Dal came up in Bihar. So while Lalu Prasad parted ways with the Janata Party to form his pocket borough in the name of RJD, Nitish Kumar ditched his original party to form the Janata Dal (United). Apart from that, the Samata Party was also formed under the leadership of George Fernandes and Jaya Jaitley. Similarly, various offshoots of the Janata Dal also came in Haryana and Karnataka, apart from others.[11]

The Congress had traditionally been enjoying the support of the different sections of society in almost all parts of the country given the nationalist legacy of the Gandhi–Nehru family.[12] During this period, in the absence of any Gandhi–Nehru patriarch at the helm of affairs, the party also suffered a number of splits with many of its prominent leaders leaving the party and forming their own parties. In this regard, two cases of departure from the party left deep mark on the electoral performances of the party in these elections. One of the major departures from the party might be seen in the form of G. K. Moopanar leaving

[11] Suhas Palshikar, 'The Regional Parties and Democracy: Romantic Rendezvous or Localised Legitimation?', in *Political Parties and Party Systems*, eds Ajay K. Mehra, D. D. Khanna, and Gert W. Kueck (New Delhi: SAGE Publications, 2003), 329.

[12] For an insightful analysis of the social profile of the Congress voters, see Anthony Heath and Yogendra Yadav, 'The United Colours of the Congress: Social Profile of Congress Voters, 1996 and 1998', *Economic & Political Weekly* 34, no. 34–35 (1999): 2518–2528.

the party and forming his Tamil Maanila Congress. Moopanar was one of the pillars of the party in Tamil Nadu and had worked for a number of years as party general secretary. He was considered as the representative of the southern state of Tamil Nadu and the party used to be recognized in that state through his persona only. His departure, therefore, left a deep dent in the electoral prospects of the party in the state from which it could never recover during the subsequent 2–3 general elections. Another notable departure from the party had been that of a number of leaders to form a new party in the name of Indian National Congress (Tiwari) after the party veteran N. D. Tiwari. This incident also compromised with the electoral prospects of the party in the states such as UP and Madhya Pradesh. Thus, the sagging fortunes of the party tended to dip further with a number of its prominent leaders leaving the party.

Amidst the splits and departures from the mainstream parties, the BJP was busy looking for dependable allies in different parts of the country. The party's performance in the different general elections since its formation had convinced the leadership of the party that the party's restrictive social support base and confinement of its areas of influence to only the Hindi heartland states, and that too with less influence in the populous states of UP and Bihar, would not allow the party to secure as much success as it desired. But the party also felt constrained by a number of factors to spread its area of influence to other areas.[13] In such a situation, the only option left for the party was to hunt for more and more alliance partners who could be roped in to act as the prelude to party's entry in those states. So keeping the support of its traditional allies such as the Shiv Sena and the SAD intact, the party did succeed in garnering the support of as varied parties as that of the Samta Party from Bihar to that of the Haryana Vikas Party from Haryana. Although the party also extended overtures to a number of other parties as well, many of these parties refused to respond to the overtures

[13] Pradeep K. Chhibber, 'Who Voted for the Bharatiya Janata Party', *British Journal of Political Science* 27, no. 4 (1997): 637.

of the party. Nevertheless, the party was indeed able to expand its social and political base in the country by riding on the back of different regional parties.[14]

Amidst the shifting loyalties of different parties and individuals, the plight of the splintered groups of the Janata Dal seemed quite interesting. Given the large number of parties formed out of the splintered groups of the party, these parties faced a multiple number of choices to determine their future courses of action. For instance, in view of the ally hunting of the BJP, a few of the parties did respond positively to the overtures of the BJP and formally became part of the NDA. On the contrary, certain parties found it comfortable to cosy up with the grand old party and, therefore, entered into strategic partnership with the Congress. The most important and durable partner of the Congress Party has indeed been the RJD of Lalu Prasad Yadav. At the same time, a number of parties such as the SP under the leadership of Mulayam Singh Yadav had decided to become partner of the Third Front spearheaded by the Left parties, especially CPI(M). The decision of the SP to join the bandwagon of the Left parties had been dictated by their ideological affinities. Finally, some of the splintered parties of the Janata Parivar decided to keep their identity intact by not joining any of the available options. Thus, the electoral scenario during the two general elections had been so complex that it was not easily known as to which party had been with which alliance at a given period of time. For instance, a number of parties that had been with the NDA in the 1996 general elections had quickly switched sides to leave the NDA by the time of the 1998 general elections to make better electoral gains (Table 7.1).

The relatively less number of seats won by the two claimants of the central power, the Congress and the BJP, had ultimately turned into the gains of the other national parties as well as the regional parties. This is clearly indicative of the deepening of

[14] M. P. Singh and Rekha Saxena, *India at the Polls: Parliamentary Elections in the Federal Phase* (New Delhi: Orient Longman, 2003), 187.

TABLE 7.1	Position of Different Parties in the 1996 and 1998 General Elections	
Parties	**Seats (1996)**	**Seats (1998)**
BJP	161	182
Congress	140	141
Janata Dal	46	6
Left parties	52	48
Tamil Maanila Congress	20	3
DMK	17	6
BSP	11	5
SP	17	20
TDP	16	12
Samata Party	8	12
Shiv Sena	15	6
Haryana Vikas Party	3	1
AIADMK	00	18

Source: Computed from the *Statistical Report on 1996 and 1998 General Elections* (New Delhi: Election Commission of India, 1996 and 1998), available at https://eci.gov.in/statistical-report/statistical-reports/ (accessed on 19 July 2019).

the democracy in India so much so that the gravity of power had probably shifted from the national parties to that of the regional parties. Moreover, the performance of the Left combine had been stupendous in these elections as they had been able to put up a marvellous show. The combine had been able to win a whopping number of 59 seats in which the share of the CPI(M) itself was 43. The regional parties such as the RJD in Bihar, the SP and the BSP in UP, the DMK in Tamil Nadu, the Biju Janata Dal (BJD) in Odisha and the NCP in Maharashtra had emerged as the formidable forces to leave their mark on the political scene even at the central level. Such kind of result proved that the era of single majority party rule at the centre had by and large been over as the regional and the other national parties could not be overlooked in shaping the nature of government at the centre by the two major national parties, the Congress and the BJP. Thus, these results laid the background for drastic restructuring of the nature of government formation at the centre with the Congress emerging as the nucleus of the new system and the regional parties taking sides with either the UPA or the NDA.

The 2014 national poll saw a resurgence of the BJP which had a comfortable majority with 282 Lok Sabha seats and its partners in the NDA had secured victory in 54 parliamentary seats. With approximately 38 per cent of popular votes in its favour, the BJP established its claim as a formidable player in elections. Nonetheless, the fact that the NDA partners, primarily the regional political parties, continued to remain integral also proves the extent to which they were taken seriously by the leader of the conglomeration. It is true that the regional political parties did not seem to be so critical then in the formation of the government given BJP's majority in the Parliament though by being integrally connected with the winning coalition, they remained relevant in governance. The trend did not appear to be different in the 17th national election, held in 2019. With victory in 303 Lok Sabha seats, the BJP sustained its popularity among the voters; by securing 38 per cent popular votes, it has moved to 'the centre of Indian politics'.[15] By winning in 58 parliamentary seats, the NDA partners enhanced their tally in 2019 election in comparison with its share of 54 seats. The NDA received nearly 45 per cent of votes which is the highest vote share by any of the pan-Indian conglomeration of parties in any of the earlier national polls since the formation of the BJP in 1980. The Congress-led UPA failed to regain its popularity and had won only in 91 parliamentary

[15] Sanjay Baru, 'Right Moves Closer to Centre', *The Economic Times*, New Delhi, 27 May 2019.

constituencies. A perusal of the 2019 poll outcome suggests that (a) despite the fact that the regional political parties no longer remain as pertinent as in the past in helping the pan-Indian political parties to constitute a majority on the floor of the Parliament, it is hardly a deterrent to remain integral to the winning combination and (b) by accepting the regional parties as partners in governance, NDA's leader, the BJP, has upheld the view that they, being representative of the regions, cannot be ignored which is also a definite step towards realizing federalism in its true spirit.[16]

Concluding Observations

The regionalization of electoral politics has been considered as a kind of reinvention of electoral politics in India given the dominance of the Congress as the hegemonic party for more than two decades. However, such a state of affairs would not have seemed improbable to an analyst who would have seen the rise and consolidation of the Congress Party in the context of the national movement. In other words, given the legacy of the national movement and great role played by the party in winning independence, it was not surprising that it could rise as the party of the country. But the vast social, economic, cultural, regional, linguistic and all other sorts of diversities, Indian political system was destined to be as much diversified as possible. Hence, when the monolithic structure of the Congress Party started falling apart, the regional satraps of the party could very well get the chance of asserting their regional identities and emerge as important players in their respective states. At the same time, certain states, particularly in southern India, having illustrious traditions of regional politics have also played a critical role in regionalization of electoral politics.

[16] We have dealt with this issue in Bidyut Chakrabarty and Rajendra Kumar Pandey, 'Predominance of the Right', in *Reconceptualizing Indian Democracy: The Changing Electorate* (New Delhi: SAGE Publications, 2020), 187–223.

The pinnacle of regional divergence was reached with the unleashing of the forces of social justice that virtually wiped out the Congress Party and fragmented the nature of Indian polity till the rise of the BJP as the epicentre of the political system at the national level. The net result of the regionalization of electoral politics is the emergence of coalitional nature of political process in which the regional parties have started playing a crucial role in making and sustaining the central government while retaining their autonomous space in the states. But the emergence of the BJP as the single majority party in Lok Sabha after the 17th general election has apparently halted the regionalization of electoral politics though the regional electoral divergence remains intact to a large extent even till date.

Ideologically, less catholic and politically more accommodative, the pan-Indian political parties are now favourably inclined to accept the regional outfits to form government at the union level. This is also suggestive of 'federalization of Indian politics' because the regional parties representing the regional interests have become integral to the articulation of national policy designs as well. By accepting the relevance of the regional political parties, the BJP thus defended the point by saying, '[t]oday, regional parties are important partners in the task of governance at the national level. This [enabled] the Union Government to address regional aspirations more effectively and thus prepare India for the challenges of the new century'.[17]

That regional political parties cannot be ignored is now firmly established. In the 2014 Lok Sabha poll, despite being the party with maximum number of parliamentary seats, the BJP had to draw on the support of the NDA partners which allowed the conglomeration to dislodge the Congress-led UPA coalition. As evident, the idea of coalition has struck roots in

[17] *Political Situation*, National Executive Meeting on 3–4 November 1999, New Delhi; Bharatiya Janata Party, *BJP Resolutions (Political), 1980–1999* (New Delhi: Office Secretary, Bharatiya Janata Party, 2000), 312.

two different ways: on the one hand, the consistent failure of the national parties including the Congress and the BJP to win even a simple majority in Parliament creates a clear possibility for a coalition with the willing partners to constitute a government; the remarkable success of the parties with regional roots is also, on the other, illustrative of a decline of the pan-Indian parties for their inability to articulate 'the regional voices'. So the increasing viability of coalitions is the outcome of a complex sociopolitical churning indicative of a new model of governance ruling out the single-party rule completely. The centre is now restrained by the regions or states to such an extent that, argues an expert, 'there is hardly a national party on the political horizon'. The national parties, whether the Congress or the BJP, have become increasingly 'regionalized'. The centre is now region dependent for its survival. The political career of region has thus 'swung from a state of dependence on the Centre to one of being in a position to bring decisive influence on it'.[18] What are the consequences of shifting power to the regions? Given the well-entrenched processes of centralization under the Congress governments, the growing de-centring of power is certainly a corrective step to restore the vitality of democratic institutions and federal character of the Indian Constitution.[19] Regional issues can amicably be sorted out through conscious democratic processes rather than through an imposition from the centre. The fragmentation of power is an opportunity of relocating India's democracy in a perspective in which the region-specific issues are equally important. By underlining the importance of the regions in its formation and continuity, the NDA coalition is thus a significant event in India's recent political history.

[18] T. V. Sathyamurthy, 'State and Society in a Changing Political Perspective', in *Class Formation and Political Transformation in Post-colonial India*, ed. T. V. Sathyamurthy, vol. 4 (Delhi: Oxford University Press, 1996), 473.

[19] For details of this argument, see M. P. Singh and Douglas V. Varney, 'Challenges to India's Centralized Parliamentary Federalism', *Publius: The Journal of Federalism* 33, no. 4 (Fall 2003): 1–20.

Following the rise of the regional parties as formidable partners in governance, the constituent states in federal India are growing strong gradually and steadily. Not only are they now capable of articulating their demands effectively, but they have, on occasions, become decisive in policymaking. Politically, it seems to be a sign of 'adulthood of Indian states' which may create the US confederate type polity with strong units and a centre as a mere monitoring instrument. The adulthood of states is not, at all, a romantic conceptualization of growing importance of Indian states but is premised on a particular variety of 'political consciousnesses', drawn on inherent diverse sociocultural realities of India as a 'nation'. There are instances which may be cited to substantiate that adulthood disrupts national integrity and hence despicable. But a thorough study of the so-called 'disruptive movements' championing regional autonomy may reveal that the outcome would have probably been otherwise had they been dealt with differently at the outset. To put it bluntly, the carefully crafted tendency to 'essentialize' multicultural Indian identity boomeranged and the sooner it is understood by those who preside over India's political destiny, it is better for the country.

There is a related point here. There is a fairly strong opinion to suggest that politics in India continues to be governed by traditional idioms and values. This is probably true if we interpret the growing importance of caste and other primordial loyalties literally without comprehending their articulation in conjunction with the socio-economic and political reality. Caste or religion is representational and, hence, its importance in political mobilization. And apart from consolidating a group identity, caste and religion provide a critical meaning to the individuals located in a wider collectivity. So the idioms which may be mistaken as 'traditional' are actually modern presumably because they are rooted in processes, linked with the growing democratization of the political system in its most complex form. So it would be wrong to suggest that increasing importance of primordial loyalties in conceptualizing political in India leaves no scope for modern politics to strike roots.

What is correct to argue, however, is that modernity[20] in Indian politics is a very complex admixture of various influences, drawn on the past as well as present experiences and there is, therefore, no straightforward way to easily delimit its domain. This is where the challenge lies.

---

[20] Dipesh Chakrabarty provides a critical account of modernity in his *Habitations of Modernity: Essays in the Wake of Subaltern Studies* (Chicago: University of Chicago Press, 2002), xix.

8

National versus Local

Elections are a conceptually vantage point to understand voters' responses in State Assembly and parliamentary elections. Broadly speaking, it was not visible in the first three general elections when the Congress Party had comfortably won both the assembly and national elections. For the first time, the 1967 election to the state legislature radically altered India's political template; there was an outpouring of anti-Congress sentiments which was translated into votes in elections. The Congress miserably lost to the opposition. In order to understand the transforming tapestry of the Indian politics, the chapter is devoted to the analysis of this phenomenon. A careful assessment of the voting behaviour reveals that the electorates are guided by different ideological considerations while voting for the elections to the State Assembly and Lok Sabha, respectively. By seeking to understand why it is so, the chapter is also an attempt to evolve a persuasive conceptual framework to comprehend how and why voters vote the way they do.

Conceptual Underpinning

The available study of the electoral outcomes since the 1967 State Assembly elections confirms that the voters generally tend to vote differently which means that they do not have the same criteria for their choice. Implicit here are two fundamental points: on the one hand, it is now fair to argue that since voters are sovereign, at least when they cast votes in specific elections, they decide whom to vote on the basis of the criteria that they deem appropriate. In other words, that the voters exercise their choice according to their priorities is a persuasive argument. This is probably the reason why, on many occasions, the political party that secures a majority in the assembly loses miserably even in the state that it governs. On the basis of this, one is persuaded to believe, on the other, that there is hardly a one-size-fits-all formula insofar as voting behaviour in India is concerned. This perhaps shows that election results are determined by the prevalent socio-economic context that keeps on constantly changing. Fundamental here is the idea that voters' decision varies from one occasion to another suggesting that it is also context driven. This is well captured by an analyst who, thus, argues that the concept of representation is essentially

> microcosmic. The members of the representative assembly are not to act as trustees for the nation, nor are they to act as delegates for local interests, nor are they to embody the sovereignty of the nation. Their essential function is to constitute, in themselves, a microcosm of the nation, so that if ... they pursue their personal interests, they will reach decisions which will maximize the happiness of the whole community.[1]

Explicit here is the idea that representatives are not independent of the electorates when they discharge their role as the latter's spokespersons, and they are guided by the primary concern of ensuring happiness of whom they represent. This is clearly a Benthamite conceptualization of how the representatives are expected to behave while performing their assigned role. What is emphasized here is also the claim that the representatives, while acting on behalf of the electorates, usually privilege the

[1] Birch, *Representation.*

community interests over their partisan interests. Here, J. S. Mill's conceptual point is very pertinent. According to him,

Democracy is not ideally the best form of government … unless it can be so organized that no class, not even the most numerous, shall be able to reduce all but itself to political insignificance, and direct the course of legislation and administration by its exclusive class interest'.[2]

What is argued here is that democratic governance involves representation of electorates' socio-economic and political interests; the representatives need to rise above their selfish desires in order to fulfil their role for contributing to the common welfare. There are two factors then which are critical in this design: on the one hand, the representatives are required to be respectful to the demands that their respective constituencies generate, which, on the other, means that they are also expected to sacrifice their partisan aims for the sake of their wider concern for the communities they represent. In the Indian context, the situation has become little complex with the rise of the regional political parties since it is believed that the pan-Indian political parties do not pay adequate attention to the local issues. This is, therefore, not a mere accident that in course of India's journey as a democratic polity, several regional political parties gained momentum at the cost of their all-India counterparts. In other words, with their rise on India's political scene, the RJD in Bihar or SP in UP, the DMK or the AIADMK in Tamil Nadu, or the TDP in the former Andhra Pradesh or the TMC in West Bengal or Shiv Sena in Maharashtra became integral to Indian polity presumably because for the electorates, they were well-equipped to effectively voice the local demands in the public domain. The trend that had begun in 1967 continues even today which further defends the argument that perhaps due to the failure of the pan-Indian political parties, the claim of the regional political parties as effective instruments for fulfilling the local

---

[2] J. S. Mill, *Consideration on Representative Government*, 3rd ed. (London: Longman, 1865), 164.

demands is, thus, readily accepted. We must add a caveat here since there are occasions when the pan-Indian political parties had won in the province by largely championing the specific demands of the areas in which they sought votes. For instance, the success of the Congress in the 2018 in Madhya Pradesh was largely attributed to its commitment to take care of the local interests which were clearly undermined by the incumbent BJP government there. Although the Congress government did not last long presumably because of its failure to sustain the support of the majority of the members of the legislature, the 2018 victory is a testimony to the argument that chances of winning for the pan-Indian parties are higher once they take the local issues far more seriously. Core here is the point that there is hardly a universal model to plausibly explain the electoral victory of the political parties in the fray; the chances of electoral victory are directly linked with how the contestants couch their campaign strategies and their role once they are elected in many public forums, including the legislature.

Delinking of Parliamentary and Assembly Elections

The inauguration of representative democracy in the country in 1950 began with the proposal of holding simultaneous polls for Parliament as well as State Legislative Assembly elections. Accordingly, the first elections for the higher legislative bodies took place in the country in 1952. The practice of simultaneous polls continued till the fifth general election when to wriggle out of the tough situation, Indira Gandhi decided to delink the parliamentary and assembly elections. The context of delinking the two polls was typical of the time. With the objective realities standing against her and strengthening of the opinion in support of going for fresh elections within her party, Mrs Gandhi unhesitatingly recommended for the dissolution of Lok Sabha to the president. Further, in order to ward off any misinformation campaign being mounted by her opponents regarding the motives for premature dissolution of Lok Sabha, she took to a special radio broadcast to address the common people and explain them the rationale for such an unprecedented move in the annals of the Indian parliamentary system. In the memorable address to the nation, she averred:

There comes a time in the life of a nation when the government of the day has to take an unusual step to cut through difficulties in order to solve the pressing problems with which the country is beset. The present is such a time. Therefore, on the advice of the Council of Ministers, the President has dissolved the Lok Sabha before its full term. In a parliamentary democracy this is not unusual but in India it has happened for the first time. Why did we do this when it is conceded from all sides that our government could have continued in power for another fourteen months? It is because we are concerned not merely with remaining in power but with using that power to ensure a better life to the vast majority of our people and to satisfy their aspirations for a just social order.[3]

Indira Gandhi took this opportunity to showcase her tremendous efforts towards bringing about an egalitarian social and economic order in the country through the radical measures such as bank nationalization and abolition of privy purses along with the initiatives for land reforms. For her bold and unconventional decisions, her personality was likened to that of a 'parameter-altering leader'.[4] At the same time, she also came down heavily on her opponents whom she described as reactionary forces to put the blame on them for sabotaging her efforts for social and economic reforms. She emphasized,

in the present situation, we feel we cannot go ahead with our proclaimed programme and keep out pledges to our people. The attempts to accelerate the pace of social and economic

[3] Publications Division, *The Years of Endeavour: Selected Speeches and Writings of Indira Gandhi, August 1969–August 1972* (New Delhi: Publications Division, Government of India, 1975), 75–76.
[4] Susanne H. Rudolph, 'The Writ from Delhi: The Indian Government's Capabilities after the 1971 Election', *Asian Survey* 11, no. 12 (October 1971): 963.

reforms have naturally roused the opposition of vested interests. Reactionary forces have not hesitated to obstruct in every possible way the proper implementation of these urgent and vitally necessary measures. Power in a democracy resides with the people. That is why we have decided to go to our people and to seek a fresh mandate from them.[5]

Thus, she sought to put the things in perspective before the people so that the imperatives of election are clear to them and they are able to exercise their franchise in a prudent and considered manner. Her speech in the backdrop of dissolution of Lok Sabha reminiscences the approach of her father to establish a direct dialogue with the common people of India in extraordinary and difficult times. This address helped portray a picture of Mrs Gandhi as that of the harbinger of social and economic revolution which the reactionary elements of society are not allowing. Logically, what, therefore, was needed was a resounding mandate to the prime minister so that nothing is allowed to come in her way of bringing about remarkable social and economic transformations in the country. She was, thus, able to reap rich electoral harvest by separating national from the local.

Coalitional Phase of Electoral Politics

The imposition of Emergency in 1975 had indeed provided a solid opportunity for the people to raise their voice against the government and seek restoration of democracy in the country. Hence, it was not unusual that JP had launched a successful crusade against the internal Emergency which resulted in its revocation in 1977. The campaign was fair because it was against the efforts of a select political leadership to debase governance for its partisan mission. In other words, by challenging the authority that took away the constitutionally guaranteed democratic rights, JP had articulated a voice for re-establishing

[5] Ibid.

the republican spirit of the Constitution. It would not be an exaggeration to suggest that Emergency was a paradox of history since it was 'as much a constitutional response by Indira Gandhi to the constitutional means as the opposition parties had adopted, to unseat her'.[6] The Emergency, thus, provided an experience that brought out very clearly that the Constitution contained provisions in it that could both enhance the democratic rights of the people and be used to deny even the constitutionally endorsed fundamental rights. Nonetheless, the proclamation of Emergency had created a context in which the issue of ethics in governance was not only raised but was also sought to be conclusively addressed. JP can, thus, be said to have set in motion processes whereby the importance of a moral code of conduct for the public personnel was forcefully reiterated. The paradoxical nature of Emergency and JP's successful mobilization against the excesses raise an open-ended question, if one seeks to comprehend those two tumultuous years in independent India's recent political history.

The context of the 1977 general election was, thus, patently provided by the anti-Emergency struggle of the people. The Emergency was a constitutional act, so was the challenge that the opposition parties had mounted on the prevalent political authority If Emergency was a Constitution-endorsed design of authoritarianism, then it was not a deviation from the rule of law; hence, those who proclaimed escaped condemnation. Similarly, the opposition parties were within the constitutional bounds when they protested by undertaking what the ruling authority had dubbed as unconstitutional means. A very piquant situation had emerged. Whether the governing elites indulged in unethical practices while declaring an Emergency following the constitutional provisions is definitely a question that cannot be answered conclusively. Likewise, the fact that the mass endeavour towards unseating the Congress was drawn on fulfilling the basic constitutional rights further complicates

[6] Ananth V. Krishna, *India since Independence: Making Sense of Indian Politics* (New Delhi: Pearson, 2011), 143.

the issue. In either of the cases, the rule of law was not grossly violated although its application seeking to realize the whimsical personal preferences of the leadership was certainly contrary to the fundamental ethical values from which the Constitution of India derives its sustenance. Hence, in the elections that followed the lifting of Emergency, the police brutalities against the people became the burning issue. The election was fought on the catchy slogan of remove Indira Gandhi and save democracy that worked magic throughout the country, thereby catapulting the Janata Party in power.

Interestingly, the 1984 general elections were fought on the issue of national security. The Congress sought to present the assassination of Mrs Gandhi as the gravest challenge to the national security of India given the prevalence of insurgency and terrorism in certain parts of the country. Since terrorism in Punjab seemed to be at its peak at that time and the assassination of Mrs Gandhi was directly related to the happenings in Punjab, it was argued that her assassination was a direct threat to the national security posed by the forces active to destabilize the country and undermine its democratic polity. As a natural corollary of such an argument, the voters were called upon to vote in favour of the Congress Party under the leadership of Rajiv Gandhi to show their resolute resolve to thwart any challenge to the unity and integrity of the nation. However, such arguments and exhortations of the Congress leaders appeared just as attempts to rationalize the sympathy wave that was sufficiently visible in all the nooks and corners of the country in support of the Congress Party. Mrs Gandhi's assassination was taken by people as an irreparable loss to the first family of the country, and therefore, the scion of that family, Rajiv Gandhi, must be given a landslide victory in order to prove the point that the country is united against that family in safeguarding the unity and integrity and ward off all attempts at destabilizing the country. Amidst such a charged atmosphere, the unprecedented victory of the Congress Party under Rajiv Gandhi appeared a foretold story that got translated in a mammoth majority for him in the Lok Sabha.

In the later years, concerted opposition to the Congress on the part of other parties has been one of the significant characteristics of Indian politics. The hegemonic nature of the party that ruled for a long period of time in the post-Independence period owing to its legacy of the national movement has created a kind of aversion among almost all the opposition parties irrespective of their areas of influence. Interestingly, there is no denying the fact that a majority, if not all, of the opposition parties as well as their leaders did have some kind of direct or indirect association with the Congress in the past. But they left the Congress Party at different points of time for different reasons. For instance, no less than a leader like V. P. Singh, the person who replaced Rajiv Gandhi as the prime minister after the 1989 general elections and was one of the towering personalities of the Congress holding as important ministries in the Rajiv Gandhi government as that of defence and finance, decided to leave the party just before the ninth general elections. The primary reason for Singh to leave the party was probably his shrewd calculation to become the catalyst of the anti-Congress political forces in the country in the wake of the party and its leader Rajiv Gandhi facing serious allegations of corruption epitomized by kickbacks and scandals. In other words, as the public opinion during that time appeared to be turning against the Rajiv Gandhi government, Singh found it as the most opportune time to leave the party and become the public hero.

Clearly, a majority of the leaders who left the Congress at different points of time apparently took that step on account of their selfish motives though they tried to portray their departure from the party as a step in the broader public interest. For instance, while a number of leaders left the Congress during the time of Indira Gandhi on the pretext of saving democratic ethos of the party from the dynastic portents of the party, several leaders departed from the party during the time of Rajiv Gandhi to take the high moral ground of not being part of the corruption that was alleged to have marred the party and government at that point of time. In the meantime, a number of regional satraps had also left the Congress to form their regional parties as they did not see any future for them by being part of the grand old party.[7]

In the second half of the 1990s, the democratic polity of the country experienced a number of unprecedented social and political churning that virtually set the tone of the electoral politics in the times to come. The progressive weakening of the Congress had unleashed all kinds of social forces to show their prowess in carving out a distinct space for them in the political landscape of the country. In this regard, the democratic processes in the country showed varying traits in different parts of India. For instance, while in the northern states that constituted the core of the Hindi heartland, the juggernaut of social justice had rolled in such a way that a number of parties sprung up drawing their lineage from the Janata experimentation to become the exclusive claimant of the sizeable votes of their particular castes.[8] When they found that their own caste votes were proving insufficient to help them secure a majority in the State Legislative Assemblies or propel their national dreams to arrive at the centre stage of the national politics, they sought and succeeded in forging a formidable alliance with the floating groups like the Muslims, thereby replacing the Congress as the ruling party in the states. The progressive strengthening of the hold of caste-based parties in the core states of the Hindi heartland has been sought to be countered by the BJP through its increasing and consistent thrust on the ideology of Hindutva as the hallmark of its appeal to the voters. In fact, in order to present an alternative vision to the dominant Congress's ideological and programmatic reach in the country, the party insisted on taking up a number of such issues and concerns that went to strengthen its image of a Hindu nationalist party. The party argued for the adoption of cultural nationalism as the founding principle of the Indian polity in such a way that

[7] Jaffrelot, *The Hindu Nationalist Movement*.

[8] Aditya Nigan, 'India after the 1996 Elections: Nation, Locality and Representation', *Asian Survey* 36, no. 12 (1996): 159.

the traditional Hindu way of life is blended with the modernity of the time. During this period, the party sought to symbolize its thrust on the ideology of Hindutva and cultural nationalism by calling for the construction of a grand Ram temple at the site of his birthplace by removing the disputed structure standing at that place as the Babri mosque. Thus, the stridency of the party on the issue of Ram temple apparently provided it a long following among the upper-caste people who identified themselves with the traditional glory.

Amidst the fast pacing of the social and political churnings in the North, the southern and eastern parts of the country remained engrossed with the regional orientation of the democratic politics. Majority, if not all, of these states had by now witnessed the rise of formidable regional parties that thrived on the anti-northern sentiments, on the one hand, and the politics of the clientele, on the other. Given that the configuration of the Lok Sabha seats in these states would not allow them any stake to become the power holder at the centre, they surely tried to extract as much political mileage out of their electoral strength in the Lok Sabha as possible. Thus, this period of democratic politics in the country also offered a distinct space to the southern states that acted to decide the fate of the governments at the centre. During this period, the domineering nature of the northern states in the political landscape appeared to be shaky given the fragmented nature of votes in the key northern states. As part of game of one-upmanship, the country witnessed so many persons becoming the prime minister within such a short span of time.

Ideological Roots of National versus Local

The Indian political landscape from the very beginning has been a mosaic of various ideologies and competing claims and counterclaims of varying interests of the society. However, the formidability of a particular ideology or interest in order to become the authoritative value of the society has always depended on the circumstances prevailing at a particular period of time as well as the imperatives of the general interests of the nation and its people. For instance, during the national movement, the most important objective of all the major political groups, irrespective of their ideology and the general interest of the nation and its people, revolved around the country getting complete independence from the colonial rule. So all the political formations used to work among the people to awaken them for the cause of waging a sustained struggle against the colonial rulers so that the independence of the country could be hastened. But given that the Congress was in the forefront of the national movement, it became the political formation to attract the mass support of people drawing on the active participation of almost all sections of the people. This does not mean that other ideological groups did not remain actively engaged in waging struggle against the colonial rule. What is being argued here is that the presence of all other groups in the national movement remained marginal only in the face of the formidability with which the Congress was able to carry the cross of the national movement. But in the course of time as and as the other ideological groups got opportunities to prove their worth among the people, they started getting wider public support and later became countervailing forces to the hegemonic presence of the Congress.

The same analogy could probably be drawn with regard to the rise of Right on the political horizon of the country. The people with ideological persuasions rooted in the Right have always remained active in the political life of India. But their presence in the country could not become significant for the obvious reason that the political mainstream in India has always been tilted towards the Left given the infatuation of a large number of Indian politicians with the Left ideology. At the same time, a distinct approach towards the issues and challenges facing India could be discerned between the Left and the Right since Independence. For instance, on the vital issues of national importance, the Left has always been strident in pushing forward their point of view in comparison to the Right that has preferred the incremental approach. The situation after

Independence took the curious turn of prominence of the Left with the coronation of Jawaharlal Nehru as the prime minister. An ardent believer in the Left ideology, Nehru, from day one, did not conceal his predilections towards the Left in both his words and deeds. It was, therefore, not surprising that soon the Left ideology driven plans and programmes began to roll out. But amidst all such fast pacing of the policies and programmes towards the socialistic pattern of society, the Right elements in the Indian politics remain committed to their ideology and kept working silently to convince the larger masses of the veracity of the alternative perspective or vision. Although the ideology of Right in the country has been articulated by a number of political parties, the most effective articulation of the Rightist ideology in the country has been put forward by the erstwhile Jana Sangh, the predecessor of the BJP. Despite remaining the marginal force in the political spectrum of the country for a long period of time, the formidable rise of the Right could be seen in the aftermath of the 1999 general elections.

Given the ideological stridency of different stakeholders, the 14th and 15th general elections have been important events in the democratic process of the country for they helped in the consolidation of a number of tendencies that have previously been practised as marginal activities. For instance, the Congress has been shying away from entering into any electoral alliance with any of the major political parties till the 13th general elections. But when its best efforts to secure even a working majority in the Lok Sabha after the 14th general elections could not yield desirable results, the party was forced to accept coalition as the fait accompli of not only the party but the country as well. Since that time, coalitional nature of the democratic politics in the country has come to become the underlying phenomenon in such a way that even the parties that are able to secure majority in the respective houses are finding it difficult to eschew the coalition and feel duty bound to carry on with the alliance partners. Had this not been the case in the country, the two successive governments formed by the NDA at the centre under Narendra Modi as prime minister would patently have been called the BJP governments as the party have indeed been able to secure a comfortable majority on its own in the lower house of the Parliament and would not need support of any of its coalition partners for formation of the government.

Multi-polarity of Indian Elections

The 14th general elections took place in 2004 in the backdrop of the overconfidence of the incumbent Vajpayee government deciding to go for snap poll even before it completed its term in office. The overdose of publicity and inflationary portrayal of the successes of the government by a few of the party functionaries as well as government officials had presumably made Prime Minister Vajpayee to go for the renewal of the public mandate to rule for another term of five years. But this gamble of the prime minister proved counterproductive as the BJP as the dominant partner of the coalition along with other coalition partners suffered massive defeats in the elections. Although no party or coalition could secure even a working majority in the lower house of the Parliament, the Centrist and the Left of the Centrist parties did join hands together with the Congress to oust the NDA government from power. Subsequently, a new political alliance was formed in the name of the UPA under the chairpersonship of the Congress President Sonia Gandhi to cobble up a working majority in the Lok Sabha and stake claim to form the government at the centre. In the wake of Sonia Gandhi refusing to become prime minister, her nominee Dr Manmohan Singh was elected as the leader of the UPA conglomerate and became the prime minister. Later, in the 15th general elections held in 2009, the UPA was again able to win the mandate to rule for another five years. Thus, the 10-year rule of the UPA in the wake of the 14th and 15th general elections imparted distinct features to the democratic processes. The present chapter seeks to critically examine the major transformations brought about by these two general elections in the Indian democratic experiences.

Although all the general elections in India have been important landmarks in the political history of the country, some of them have proved to be turning points in the sense that their outcomes have altered the political texture in fundamental ways. The criticality of such elections lay both in reversing some of the long-standing trends or conventions of the electoral dynamics or heralding newer tendencies having potential to reshape the Indian political landscape in a refreshing manner. Such elections are usually in contrast to the general elections that have tended to perpetuate or facilitate continuation of the long-standing phenomena of Indian politics. That way, the 16th general elections held in 2014 may be considered as a defining event for a number of reasons. Although the hegemony of the Congress in the Indian electoral politics has already been ruptured through the electoral victories of the non-Congress-led political formations in several general elections in the past, the decisive victory of the BJP-led NDA in 2014 has tended to marginalize the Congress to such an extent that it appeared unbelievable that the party that stood routed now has been the epicentre of Indian politics so much so that the entire spectrum of the Indian party system has famously been described as nothing but the Congress system. However, more than the unprecedented routing of the Congress Party, the 16th general elections are recognized more as the momentous event that catapulted the political Right on centre stage of the Indian politics.[9]

Till these elections, while no one denied the gradual ascendance of the Right on the political firmament of the country, very few, if any, could foresee such a formidable rise of the Rightist forces to become the fait accompli of India. In comparison to the Congress Party that has remained the ruling party of the country for a large number of years with handsome majorities in both houses of the Parliament, the previous role of the Right in formation of the government at centre appeared to be shaky and untenable given the large number of coalition

[9] Suhas Palshikar and K. C. Suri, 'India's 2014 Elections: Critical Shifts in the Long Term, Caution in the Short Term', *Economic & Political Weekly* 49, no. 39 (2014): 43.

partners that joined hands together to form the government. Although the government led by former Prime Minister Atal Bihari Vajpayee could indeed complete its full term, the internal fissures of the coalition remained visible throughout the four plus years during which the government lasted. But the 2014 general elections have tended to make such unimpressive performances of the BJP in the Lok Sabha elections a matter of the past. With Narendra Modi presented as the prime ministerial candidate of the party in these elections, the support for the party on the part of the common electors of the country has been so convincing that the results of these polls appeared most surprising in the electoral history of the country.

The circumstances preceding the 16th general elections presented a complex scenario in which all the political parties operating at different levels geared themselves up for reaping rich dividends out of the ensuing elections.[10] In such a scenario, the stakes of different political parties, both ruling and opposition ones, have become quite high. These stakes appeared embedded in the social, economic and political milieus in which different claimants to power sought to position their perspectives during these elections. The social churning in the country that has had begun with the implementation of reservation for OBCs was still being tried to be made relevant by the proponents of social justice, particularly in the Hindi heartland. The rise of the hitherto marginalized sections of Indian society has indeed imparted a new texture to the body politic of the country.[11] But amidst the resurgence of these classes that have immensely facilitated the realignment of the political forces in the numerically preponderant states of UP and Bihar, the parties like the Congress remained in the forefront of the electoral dynamics

[10] For contemporary nature of party system in the country, see Pradeep Chhibber, Francesca Jensenius, and Pavithra Suryanarayan, 'Party Organisation and Party Proliferation in India', *Party Politics* 20, no. 4 (2014): 489–505.

[11] Satish Deshpande, 'Caste in and as Indian Democracy', *Seminar* 677 (January 2016): 29.

of the country banking upon the mosaic of political forces in different parts of the country. At the same time, the regional parties, particularly in the southern and eastern parts of the country, also appeared ferocious in keeping their social support bases intact to put up a robust show in the ensuing elections. But the party that has been gearing itself to spoil the electoral march of the incumbent forces has undoubtedly been the BJP.

Concluding Observations

The simultaneity of elections for Parliament as well as State Legislative Assemblies has emerged as one of the major determinants of electoral outcomes in the country. Over the years, the caste and ideology have also emerged as a significant normative goalpost of the parties such as the BJP and the Left parties in the country. While the Left parties tried to combine their ideological predilections with class perspective of Indian politics, the BJP has tried to conjoin the ideology of Hindutva with the caste dynamics of Indian politics. Interestingly, while the social support base of the most, if not all, of the major political parties in the country has been expanding or contracting depending upon the electoral promises or leadership patterns of different parties, in the case of the BJP, such an observation could not be held with much conviction. For, the social support base of the party has traditionally been confined to the relatively less numerical social groups of Brahmans and Banias. Even among the two, only Banias have been argued to be steadfast in extending their unflinching support to the BJP ever since its inception. Brahmans have not been the original supporters of the BJP given their earlier support to the Congress even from the days of the national movement. In such circumstances, the constrictive social support base of the BJP has been proving to be its nemesis in getting a majority on its own in the Lok Sabha. The party has, therefore, sought to trigger the realignment of the social forces in the country by putting forth the ideology of Hindutva in the face of the forces of social justice and economic empowerment represented by caste-based parties and the Congress Party, respectively. The ideology of Hindutva has, in fact, been presented as the cementing element that could bind all the social groups within the fold of the party just by virtue of them being Hindu first and harbouring other social markers of identity later. This has been a calculated gamble that the party played amidst its two previous consecutive defeats. But since the caste could not be a national factor for any party to win an election, hence there has been stiff opposition from regional parties to reintroduce the simultaneity of polls despite the strong pitch for the same on the part of the BJP.

Democracy in India is peculiarly textured in many ways. Prominent among them is the growing ascendancy of an electorate that has judiciously exercised the voting rights in elections after elections to prove that the voters remain sovereign. This is a peculiar feature which appears to be an odd if Indian democracy is sought to be conceptualized in the liberal mould of classical theories of electoral democracy. What is, thus, distinctive about Indian democracy is the continuity of the system of democratic governance in circumstances which do not seem to be supportive of its growth according to the classical theorists. A perusal of the trajectory of democracy in India not only confirms but also elucidates the assumption that there is hardly a one-size-fits-all formula in this regard. The argument is justified in light of the articulation of voters' response, especially since 1967 State Assembly elections which saw, for the first time, the rise and consolidation of non-Congress political parties with a view to dislodging the Congress Party from the seats of power. On the surface, it appeared to be just a change of political guards though its implications were significant. The 1967 general elections ushered in a new era in Indian politics.

The changing texture of democratic governance in India reveals that democracy is hardly a static concept, and hence, it cannot be persuasively conceptualized in derivative theoretical format. India's contextual peculiarities need to be taken into account to explain the equally peculiar nature of her democracy. As shown above, regional parties, with clear concerns for local interests, became integral to the articulation of a national voice which also helps build a regional voice with national concern. In conceptual terms, the growing ascendancy of the regional parties brought about a radical change in the texture of Indian politics that has led to 'nationalization of regional/local interests and regionalization of national interests'. Implicit here is the idea that regions, by being introduced to the national issues, are now drawn to the nationalist arena which did not appear to be as significant as it gradually became. Similarly, by insisting on being sensitive to the regional issues, the nation cannot afford to ignore the regions or its constituents. For instance, the issue of intrusion of outsiders in India is reported to have radically altered the demographic composition of the provinces such as Assam and West Bengal (bordering Bangladesh) where the 2019 Citizenship (Amendment) Act was both a source of consternation and happiness. Politico-ideological issues are, thus, articulated accordingly. This may not be the case in other provinces in India presumably because the alleged illegal entry of the migrants had hardly any direct impact there. Hence, the Hind heartland may remain immune from the skirmishes that West Bengal and Assam, in particular, experience so often. Nonetheless, the citizenship issue is no longer confined to the regions; instead, it is now a national issue. Hence, the argument is offered to suggest that regional issues cease to become regional, but, on occasion, they become national. Similarly, the 2019 surgical strike in the terrorist camps in Balakot in Pakistan just immediately before the election in some of the provinces created a bonhomie among the Indian citizens since it demonstrated India's military capability vis-à-vis her neighbour. As many studies on the increasing popularity of the BJP in the 17th Lok Sabha poll show that had there been no Balakot surgical strike by the Indian Air Force, the election results would not have been the same. The example is illustrative of how a national issue shaped the voting behaviour in the last Lok Sabha poll, held in 2019. What is argued here is the contention that national and local are dialectically intertwined as the electoral responses in elections since 1971 amply demonstrate. It is, therefore, fair to argue that instead of explaining in a specific derivative mould, one should draw on the contextual peculiarities to arrive at a plausible explanation.

The above-detailed discussion of the peculiar voting behaviour is both an endorsement of how the nation interacts with the local and vice versa, especially during elections. Notwithstanding several politico-ideological waves in many elections in favour of a specific party or a conglomeration, the fate of the contestants is decided on the basis of a creative blending of local and national issues; their importance may have been varied; nonetheless, there was hardly a situation, especially since 2014 elections, when those seeking office defended their claim exclusive on either local or national issues. The idea is conceptually plausible since the voters support a political party on the basis of their own socio-economic and political priorities which also means that the issues that are determinant here may not be same for all. Here also lies the justification of the argument defending the point that voting behaviour is largely context driven which further upholds the view that for a plausible comprehension of how voters vote, one is required to study the context in which a particular set of issues gain importance, while the others do not. So in the ultimate analysis, instead of compartmentalizing the national and local issues, one needs to be sensitive to the context in which they become critical to voters' choice. And, only then, a fair understanding of how elections are fought and won shall be possible.

9

Historicity of Identity Politics

As one's socio-economic identity still remains relevant in one's electoral choice, it cannot be ignored altogether for a meaningful study of India's political texture and processes. By dwelling on socio-economic churning in contemporary India leading to the consolidation of identity politics, the chapter is an attempt to unfurl the complexities of the processes that are critical to its articulation. In view of the critical importance of individual socio-economic identity in political mobilization, the chapter also seeks to put forward an argument suggesting that a mono-causal explanation focusing solely on identity seems to be vacuous in view of the complexities of the political processes in which the electoral voice is articulated.

Socio-economic Identity and Electoral Politics

Just like the 1992 demolition of the Babri mosque that radically altered the texture of Indian politics, the introduction of reservation in public employment for OBCs brought about dramatic changes in conceptualizing political in the Indian context. The reservations seemed to have lost its momentum except that nearly all the states constituted their Backward Commission and legalized reservation in public services and educational institutions under state control. Appointed in 1978, the Second Backward Classes Commission, known as the Mandal Commission, revived interests in formulating a national policy for OBCs. Reservations were born out of a concern to remedy injustices which deprived certain sections of an equal opportunity to raise themselves in the socio-economic hierarchy. In order to create 'an inclusive Indian identity', the post-Independence Indian leadership favoured 'policies of discrimination' as instruments 'to offset the advantage, enjoyed by some, and to equalize opportunities at the starting line'.[1] Seeking to rectify the social imbalance due to the age-old economic deprivations, the Mandal formula seeks to give 27 per cent reservation to a total of 3,743 OBCs in government jobs. What it, therefore, means is the promotion of the backward castes that will also be entitled to a much bigger slice of 'an already meagre employment cake'.[2] The violent student riots, led primarily by the privileged upper castes that swept the entire North India after the announcement, seemed explicable in view of the perceptible threat to the upper-caste hegemony in the white-collar world. South India was hardly affected probably because of the long tradition of non-Brahmin movement there.[3] The recent violence over the extension of the controversial scheme shows the extent to which the idea of reservation has itself become repulsive to the assertive section of the upper castes. In the immediate aftermath of Independence, reservation was mandatory for the SCs and STs as it is directed 'towards advancing social and economic equality'.[4] In 1977–1978, Bihar Chief

---

[1] Niraja Jayal Gopal, *Representing India: Ethnic Divers and the Governance of Public Institution* (London: Palgrave, 2006), 191.

[2] Sunanda K. Dutta Ray, 'Darkness at Noon: Implications of Student Riots', *The Statesman*, Calcutta, 30 September 1990.

[3] Rosalind O'Hanlon, *Caste, Conflict and Ideology: Mahatma Jotirao Phule and Low Caste Protest in Nineteenth Century Western India* (Cambridge: Cambridge University Press, 1985).

[4] Andre Beteille, 'Caste and Politics: Subversion of Public Institutions', *The Times of India*, Lucknow, 12 September 1990.

Minister, Karpoori Thakur, introduced 26 per cent reservation for OBCs. The formula[5] which took into account the economic backwardness as a criterion for reservation provoked a violent outburst in which 118 people were reported to have been killed. Madhya Pradesh government raised reservation from 28 per cent to 32 per cent in 1985 which sparked off violent riots and arson. So widespread and alarming was the trouble that the government was forced to revoke its decision. Gujarat shared the same fate in 1985 when the Madhav Singh Solanki government fell following the introduction of reservation in promotions of posts in medical colleges. These illustrations draw out the fact that North India has not had a consensus evident in the South'.[6] This probably explains why in North India 'the acceptance of the Mandal Commission Report has resulted in condemnation verging on hysteria'.[7]

Mandal II: Reservation for Social Justice or Appropriation by the Creamy Layer?

Reservation in educational institutions is referred to as Mandal II. In August 2005, the Supreme Court abolished all caste-based reservations in unaided private colleges. On 21 December 2005, the Lok Sabha passed the 93rd Constitutional Amendment Act, 2005, rolling back the Supreme Court judgment by introducing a new clause into Article 15 to allow for reservations for SCs and STs as well as OBCs in private unaided educational institutions other than minority institutions. In 2006, the UPA government

---

[5] Karpoori Thakur formula is as follows: statutory reservation to the SCs and STs, Notification Nos 755, 756, 757 of 10 November 1979, Government of Bihar, 12 per cent reservation for the extremely backward class, 8 per cent reservation for the backward class, 3 per cent reservation for the women of all castes, 3 per cent reservation for the extremely backward upper castes.

[6] V. N. Srinivas, 'The Mandal Formula: Backwardness—Caste vs. Individuals', *The Times of India*, Lucknow, 18 September 1990.

[7] Mihir Desai, 'The Need for Reservation: A Reply to Shourie and Others', *Lokayan Bulletin* 8, no. 4 (July–October 1990): 54.

agreed to introduce 27 per cent reservations for OBCs in central government funded higher education institutions such as Indian Institute of Management, Indian Institute of Technology, All India Institute of Medical Sciences and central universities. In other words, the proposed design is meant to introduce 27 per cent 'quota' to all institutions of higher learning. This blanket guarantee for reservations stands in contradiction with the 1992 Supreme Court judgment in the case of *Indira Sawhney v. Union of India* delivered on 16 November 1992, which upheld 27 per cent reservations subject to the exclusion of socially advanced persons/sections (creamy layer) from among OBCs. The Court also directed the government to evolve criteria for identification of this creamy layer. In response to the Court directives, the government appointed a committee which suggested that rules of exclusion apply to children of persons holding different con-stitutional positions, Class I officers and defence personnel who hold the rank of colonel and above. Children of persons with annual income greater than ₹100,000 were also to be excluded. The limit was later revised to ₹250,000 in 2004. The recom-mendations were accepted and circulated among all ministries/ departments of union and state governments in September 1993, allowing reservations to come into force.[8]

Viewed in a long-term perspective, Mandal II is a logical corollary of Mandal I. It takes forward 'the process of transfer of social and political power to majority communities'.[9] In the context of Mandal II, V. P. Singh, thus, characterized Mandal as 'a macro-process that has acquired its own dynamics. [Hence] no matter which party forms a government, it has to take the process further'.[10] It would not be an exaggeration if one thus argues that the centre of gravity in Indian politics is now defined by 'quota politics'.[11] Whatever the implications,

[8] Drawn from *The Times of India*, 10 April 2006.

[9] Yogendra Yadav and Satish Deshpande, 'Wrong Route, Right Direction: Reservation Policy Needs to Be Fine-tuned', *The Times of India*, 31 May 2006.

[10] V. P. Singh's press interview, *The Hindu*, 14 June 2006.

[11] Jaffrelot, *India's Silent Revolution*, 493.

reservation through quota translates 'protective discrimination' into reality. In contrast with 'affirmative action' that is practised in the USA, it is the combination of quotas and lower eligibility criteria that defines protective discrimination in India.

The Mandal II Arguments

The state can adopt discriminatory measures[12] to favour one group of people against another in a multicultural society. In order to neutralize inequality, the state must provide resources to the underprivileged 'on non-market principles—free education, assured income, nutritious food and health'.[13] The idea of 'recognition' is, thus, clearly political because it is justified keeping in mind a specific type of power relationship. Can 'reservation' be, thus, an appropriate scheme to accord 'recognition' to the disadvantaged due to historical reasons? Perhaps, yes. A politically 'liberal' society, however, does not endorse social discrimination because citizenship, conceptually speaking, is 'universal'. Hence 'ascribed' identities are completely disregarded while defining citizens. One may perhaps theoretically defend this position. But given the peculiar evolution of societies in various socio-economic and political contexts, this position may not appear tenable simply because 'identical' rights for all are inadequate for protecting cultural minorities. What we, therefore, require are 'special' rights for minorities who are identified as 'disadvantaged' groups. The argument that justifies discriminatory laws draws on the idea that since citizens are 'differentiated' and, thus, are 'unequal', for obvious reasons, different communities should have different rights as citizens. Based on this logic, theorists of multiculturalism articulate the notion of 'differentiated citizenship'. There are two significant implications of this conceptualization: (a) in contrast with universal citizenship of liberal variety,

[12] Bhagwan Das, 'Moments in a History of Reservations', *Economic & Political Weekly* 35, no. 43–44 (28 October 2000): 3891–3834.

[13] Neera Chandhoke, 'Three Myths about Reservations', *Economic & Political Weekly* XLI, no. 3 (10 June 2006): 2289.

differentiated citizenship clearly argues for discrimination in favour of cultural minorities as 'justified' and (b) by taking into account 'the cultural distinctiveness' as a denominator, those championing differentiated citizenship challenge the ideologically charged attempts at 'homogenizing' communities with clear sociocultural differences.

There is a historical dimension too. Different communities undergo different social churning processes. Hence, some are 'privileged' and some are 'marginalized'. A society that rejects 'differentiated citizenship' and appreciates 'universal citizenship' seeks to insist that the latter gives up its identity and submerges with the majority. This is how a society flourishes. From the multicultural point of view, this position smacks of 'cultural imperialism' because the prism through which a society is uniformly viewed insists on treating unequals equally. This is clearly a case of cultural imperialism because norms and values of the privileged majority acquire salience given their well-entrenched nature and, therefore, any opposition to them provokes consternation among those who tend to belittle the importance of historical processes in dividing mankind.

There are, thus, strong arguments in favour of reservation in a multicultural country like India. But difficulty arises the moment groups or communities that deserve reservation are identified on the basis of ascribed identity, namely caste. Besides the 1931 Census of India, caste was never a criterion in classifying Indian population. So if caste is a defining category, the 1931 index remains critical. This is hardly persuasive because the 1931 Census was guided by imperial priorities and may not have reflected India's actual demographic profile. Furthermore, since the criterion of 'backwardness' is historically conditioned, it is doubtful whether it remains valid even in the 21st century. Similarly, reservation in higher education seems to be an empty slogan in the light of the fact that seats for SCs and STs remain vacant for lack of applicants. Even after more than half a century of reservation for these communities, the number of beneficiaries is abysmally low. The reasons are not difficult to seek. As evident in the latest educational statistics, released by the union Ministry of Human Resource Development, while 73 per cent of the SC students quit school before taking Class X final examination, the figures for the ST students (79%) are worse. Interestingly, the dropout rates are not so high among the children within the Classes I–IV. Only 37 per cent of the SC students discontinue, while 59 per cent of the ST students fall under this category. If contrasted with prevalent high gross enrolment ratio, which is 83 per cent for SCs and 86 per cent for STs, the dropout rates reveal the unfavourable socio-economic circumstances in which they are forced to take up odd jobs for mere survival. Since majority of SC and ST population draws on agriculture for livelihood, these children are roped in for farming once they reach 10–12 years of age.

Given this reality, reservation in higher education makes no sense so long as dropout rates in schools are alarmingly high. In order to translate the scheme into practice, what is, thus, required is to pursue 'the literacy mission' seriously, especially among the downtrodden by creating conditions in which benefits for going to school outweigh the forced alternative of working in the field for mere survival. Otherwise, the benefits of reservation continue to be 'uneven' among those who can avail them. The well-placed group of the backward section would be better off with such reservation. It would help only the creamy layer to grab the advantages. Thus, the social justice agenda will always remain a distant goal.

It is difficult to suggest a convincing scheme to get out of the imbroglio relating to the reservation issue. In order to arrive at a solution, one may begin by taking into account most seriously the creamy layer judgment of the Supreme Court. Unless one reviews whether it is appropriate to extend reservation to the creamy layer generations after generations, it makes no sense if the children of the IAS officers, for instance, enjoy reservation simply because of their ascribed social status, even though they, despite their caste identity, are socio-economically better placed than their upper-caste counterparts. As the argument goes, 'to allow the undeserving to benefit from reservation is to deny protection to those who deserve to be protected'.[14] So is the cause of social justice served well if reservation is confined to first generation learners or further? Differentiated citizenship is a powerful device to achieve social justice. But it causes serious social distortion unless it is conceptualized in the affirmative action mould rather than extending a blanket licence to those differentiated merely by virtue of birth.

Rise of Identity Politics

The rise of identity politics could be traced from the turn of events just before the announcement of the 10th general election. That way, the elections to form the 10th Lok Sabha could be said to be one of the most complex general elections in India where the shape of things to come was just beyond the speculation and forecasting. The turn of events leading to the declaration of the 10th general elections had been full of such intriguing moves and malicious countermoves that they could not have led to any other scenario but the primordialization of the democratic processes in the country. The announcement of V. P. Singh government's decision to implement the Mandal Commission recommendations with regard to the reservation of 27.5 per cent of seats for the candidates belonging to the social and educationally OBCs had a revolutionizing impact on the majority middle-rung classes of the Indian society. This announcement apparently re-energized the political stakes of the people belonging to these intermediary castes to such an extent that clamoured to corner the prime place in the electoral democracy of the country. In order to counter this artful dodging of V. P. Singh, the BJP also raised the bogey of Ram temple in Ayodhya as its main electoral plank in the ensuing general elections. The resultant social and political landscape of the country became so complex that the fragmentation of the

[14] Zoya Hasan, 'Countering Social Discrimination', *The Hindu*, 2 June 2006.

democratic process in the country on the lines of the primordial affinities became a distinct reality.[15]

Exploitation of the social issues and concerns of the people for sheer political benefits took the alarming proportions since the times of the Janata Dal government headed by V. P. Singh. There could not be denying the fact that the reservations for the socially and educationally backward classes of the Indian society have been visualized in the Indian Constitution and the same should have been implemented in the due course of time. Moreover, the reservations for SCs and STs have already been implemented right since the adoption of the Constitution and the scheme has been working successfully since then. But such constitutional stipulations were ingrained in the Constitution as sacrosanct ideals of the Constitution that should not be exploited for selfish and motivated gains for a particular individual or political party. Such a silent spirit of the constitutional provisions was blatantly sought to be shattered during this period of time in such a way that the politics of that time turned out to be competitive moves and countermoves among the different stakeholders to gain greater political or electoral mileage than their adversaries. Since then, the circumstantial dynamics of the political process in the country turned vicious with all sorts of manoeuvring becoming acceptable towards securing votes during the elections.

The ruling period of Prime Minister V. P. Singh was undoubtedly full of ups and downs from the very beginning. Although he tried to ride on the wave of anti-Congressism by raking up the cases of corruption and maladministration of the Rajiv Gandhi government, he could not secure as strong mandate from the people as he had expected. Moreover, since his political base had traditionally been rooted in the core constituencies of the Congress Party, he could simply not go beyond that traditional voter base once he left the government and the

[15] Bidyut Chakrabarty and Rajendra Kumar Pandey, *Reconceptualising Indian Democracy: The Changing Electorate* (New Delhi: SAGE Publications, 2020), 173.

Congress to create a distinct political space for himself. His Jana Morcha virtually consisted of the former Congressmen who also were dissatisfied with the working of the Rajiv Gandhi government. So what V. P. Singh had to depend on was the disparate groups of the former Janata Party that were also looking for some sort of sheet anchor which could help them expand their electoral base beyond their select pockets of influence. Thus, the party they formed in the name of Janata Dal was nothing but a conglomerate of disparate politicians having their own pocket parties seeking to attain certain degree of formidability in the political landscape of the country which would never have been possible on their own.

So when the Janata Dal government was formed under the stewardship of V. P. Singh, the disparate political groups had been anxious from day one to secure as much political space in the government as possible. Well aware of such latent desires and aspirations of different leaders and their parties, the prime minister himself tried to accommodate as much of these leaders as possible in the key positions of the government. For instance, in recognition of the key role played by the Haryana stalwart, Devi Lal, he was made the deputy prime minister. But the major hurdle in the smooth running of the government was probably the hidden desire of a number of leaders of the Janata Dal to become the prime minister in place of the incumbent prime minister. As a result, they could not tolerate the smooth running of the government and tried to create such hurdles that would unseat the incumbent prime minister and would allow them to take his place. The first of such attempt was made by Devi Lal through a massive rally to be organized in his pocket borough of Jind in Haryana. Such a political manoeuvring of Devi Lal was sought to be countered by the prime minister through his misuse of constitutional mandate for political gains by declaring his government's decision of implementing the Mandal Commission recommendations straightaway.[16]

[16] M. P. Singh, 'Whither Indian Party System? The Electoral and Legislative Dimensions', *Indian Social Science Review* 3, no. 1 (2001): 85.

The decision of the government naturally took all the political parties off guard as they were not prepared to face such a potentially stirring decision on the part of the government. The decision immediately started polarizing the mass of Indian society into two distinct groups of those supporting and opposing the decision. But the tricky fact in this regard was that no political party or individual could openly challenge the veracity or need for implementing the constitutional provisions envisaging reservations for the socially and educationally backward classes in government jobs. But at the same time, they also could not take the situation as it is because that could have spelled political doom for them. It was in this context, therefore, that the different political parties started their own creative investigations into the primordial cleavages of the Indian society that could have been exploited to gain political mileage in both short and long terms. The decision was taken enthusiastically by the forces of social justice who took it as their overdue that the previous governments denied them. So in the celebratory mood for securing their long-drawn desire to have reservations in the government jobs, these forces started galvanizing the beneficiaries of the OBC reservation so that they could be used as a solid vote bank in the elections. But the other parties, particularly the BJP, could also not be left behind in rivalling with the forces of social justice and started sharpening its Hindutva agenda to put before the masses an alternative vision of politics where the vision of Hindutva would prevail over all other considerations of the people.

The 10th general elections would have turned into the greatest fight between the proponents of Mandal and Mandir but for the tragic assassination of the Congress leader. The emotive appeal of the non-Congress parties in the name of Mandal and Mandir had really impacted the voting behaviour of a large number of people voting in the first phase of these elections. But the tide of their appeal became bloated in the aftermath of the death of Rajiv Gandhi. The subsequent voting in different parts of the country had gone in favour of the Congress Party in a substantive manner. As a result, the party which was considered to have been pushed to a corner by the forces seeking votes in the name of the emotive issues of caste and religion bounced back magnificently. In the final reckoning, the party was able to improve its seat tally to the tune of 244 in comparison to the seats of the other parties that had remained way behind the tally of the Congress. Yet the party was short of a clear majority staring at the scenario of a minority government at the centre with support of other parties.

Apart from the Congress, the party that had improved its seat tally in the Lok Sabha in the aftermath of the 10th general elections had been the BJP. The onward march of the BJP in the electoral arena of the country had quite significantly been propelled by the spade work done for the party by its parental organization, the RSS. At the same time, the party had positioned its emotional appeal to the people in such a way that the upper-caste voters did not find any other avenue to go than the BJP. In other words, the increasing stridency of the middle castes along with the open appeal of the Janata Dal to these castes even at the cost of the upper-caste voters, in fact, pushed the non-OBC voters to the fold of the BJP. These voters, who had traditionally been the vote bank of the Congress, had presumably shifted their loyalty to the BJP in the wake of the discrediting of the Congress government headed by Rajiv Gandhi. Since then, the turn of events in the country had been so that they could not find any other alternative than to vote for the BJP as the saviour of the interests of the Hindus.

Identity Politics and Political Instability

Democratic processes in the country during the four tumultuous years from 1996 to 1999 took such curious turns that a number of unconventional tendencies appeared to become the defining features of Indian democracy. For instance, the economic backwardness of the country at the time of Independence had tended to make the economic and developmental issues as the core concerns of different political parties in the succeeding elections for a long period of time. Even the ideological skirmishes between the competing ideologies during that period of time revolved around the issues of the economic policies of the country apart from the policies and programmes that could be visualized to ameliorate the social and economic conditions of the toiling masses of the country. Sectarian and primordial affinities of the people were considered by the mainstream parties as some sort of taboos that need not be raked up lest that might create social cleavages and magnify the divisive tendencies in the society. Even if the opposition parties were to raise the issues of the public concern, these basically related to the issues such as price rise, cases of corruption and non-availability of the basic goods for the people which were considered as the failure of the government for which it needed to be voted out at the time of the elections.

But this decade witnessed the radical transformation in the democratic discourse in the country that also impacted the electoral politics in a big way.[17] As Congress Party's position in the democratic politics of the country weakened, the rise of opposition parties was the obvious outcome. But what turned out to be the astonishing feature of the political discourse of the time was that the opposition parties could not secure a foothold among the psyche of the general public on the basis of common concerns and issues of governance and economic development. Their long-drawn discomfitures in the electoral politics of the country had virtually compelled them to opt for certain unconventional methods of political or democratic discourse that might help them to attract the attention of the common people and provide them the much-desired space in the electoral arena. However, such space could not have been provided by the conventional tools of political mobilization and, therefore, certain emotive issues and concerns of the people had to be invented so as to strike an emotional chord with them to arouse their affinity with a particular party. Thus, politics during this period turned out to be the theatre of invention of catchy emotional

[17] Sudha Pai, 'Transformation of the Indian Party System: The 1996 Lok Sabha Elections', *Asian Survey* 33, no. 12 (December 1997): 1178.

issues and raking up the controversial subject that would earn greater political dividends for a party. These resulted in widening of the electoral participation of the different sections of society.[18]

The electoral outcomes of the two general elections held in quick succession with each other might be reckoned as marker of the political uncertainties prevailing in the country. Moreover, the deepening of the democracy in the country had been taking such curious turns that the established norms and conventions of the democratic system of India were getting shattered one by one. The situation has further been complicated with the arrival of a number of actors and competing claims on the votes of the similar groups of people. In the place of the developmental and governmental issues and promises, the transformed democratic discourse in the country had been underlined by overt appeal to the people of distinct castes and religions to vote for their so-called custodians. Along with these, the ideological and programmatic rivalries as well as animosities among the different parties had been increasing so much that certain parties had turned out to be pyrrhic in the political spectrum. In such a complex scenario, the outcomes of the two general elections presented a very interesting picture that cast a distinct impact on the process of the formation of government as well as the longevity of the government. India, during this period, was thrown in the vortex of extreme instability not seen before in the political history of the country.

Amidst the social and political churning that had become the hallmark of this phase of electoral politics of India, the most significant gainer in terms of seats had definitely been the BJP. In fact, this phase might be seen as the reinvention of the BJP from being a fringe element of the Indian politics to become the nucleus of the political system. However, two significant pointers of the time could be seen as the important terms of discourse of BJP's rise to the top of the system. With the appeal of the cultural nationalism cutting ice with different social groups, particularly the upper-caste people, who once constituted the

[18] Yadav, 'Electoral Politics in the Time of Change'.

core support base of the Congress, the party had consistently been improving its tally of seats in the Lok Sabha. Thus, the party could improve its seat tally from 161 in 1996 to 182 in the 1998 general elections. But the growing acceptability of the BJP on the part of the people did not go well with the other political parties who stood in clear competition with the BJP in cornering the benefits arising out of the social and political churning in the country. For instance, in the beginning, the parties that came into open alliance with the BJP had been just a few except its traditional ally, Shiv Sena. The social justice based parties tried to portray the BJP as some sort of untouchable but the electors of the country had something else in mind.

Changing Fortunes of Identity Politics

The 11th and 12th general elections were held in the period of extreme political instability in the country. With the production of the hung Parliament in both the elections, no party stood the chance of forming a government that could last long. Thus, these elections introduced the element of sustained instability in the political system of the country. Such a state of things in the country could be understood as an aberration given the long track record of the country for having stable and strong governments.[19] But the circumstances prevailing after the 11th and 12th general elections, in fact, did not permit the formation of strong and stable governments for two distinct reasons. One, the politicking during this period had reached its peak in the country. All of the parties were busy in undermining the position of the other in such a way that they become the culprit in the public perception for making the government unstable. Two, the selfish interests of a number of leaders had become so pronounced during this time that they had started exploring the possibilities of occupying the chair of the prime minister. In such situations, nobody was ready to help the other in becoming the prime minister unless the reciprocal gesture

[19] Chandan Mitra, 'Unholy Alliances', *Seminar* 454 (June 1996): 17.

was also offered to them. In the absence of such reciprocity, the government formation remained a very difficult proposition with the major contenders of power remaining outside the power games to buy time for entering the poll arena once again.

The role of the Congress during this period had been quite unstable and aimed at taking advantage of the situation in order to maintain its hold over the government. Right from the declaration of the results after both the elections, an anxious BJP did try its luck in forming the government. But given the political scenario and the party position in the Lok Sabha, it was sure from the very beginning that the party would not be able to form a stable government. Yet when the party failed to understand the writings on the wall, the rest of the things were done by the regional parties on whose support the BJP was banking to prove the majority in the Lok Sabha. But once the BJP was out of the scene, the scenario was quite open for the regional parties as well as the Congress to evolve their concerted strategies on the formation of the government. However, in these situations, the Congress was in the dilemma of staking its own claim to form the government or to go for supporting the leaders of the regional parties. Eventually, the Congress arrived at the conclusion of desisting from forming government on its own and extending outside support to the other parties. But such experiments of the party could not last long as the desperation of the party with the governments that it was supporting grew sooner than expected. As a result, the party did not shy away from pulling the governments down. Thus, the Congress machination to enjoy the power without being held accountable to the Parliament and the people did not continue for long and the bluff of such a strategy was called very soon.

Contemporaneously, the surge of identity politics has decisively been halted by the meteoric rise of the BJP in almost all parts of India. The result of the 17th general election expanded the reach of the party even to those areas and states where the party was groping in the dark in the past. In this regard, the states of West Bengal and Odisha have been quite indicative. In West Bengal, Mamata Banerjee led TMC has suffered the most serious erosion in its support base with a large section of electorate switching their loyalty to the BJP. In fact, the rise of the BJP to take pole position in the politics of the state may be considered to be one of the most unexpected outcomes whose implications would not be felt only in the state but in the whole country in the times to come. In Odisha, though Naveen Patnaik led BJD has been able to return to power in the state, the rapid pace with which the BJP has increased its areas of influence in the state need to ring warning bells for the regional party sooner or later. In the north-eastern states, majority of the regional parties have been able to hold on to their citadels despite earnest efforts on the part of the BJP to make inroads in as many north-eastern states as possible with the strategy of alliances and coalition governments in different states.

The most miserable conditions have, however, been of the caste-based parties of UP, Bihar and Jharkhand whose ambitions of reasserting the supremacy of caste as the cardinal factor in tilting the scales of electoral politics have decisively been demolished in these elections. In anticipation of wiping out the BJP by forging powerful caste combinations, the two important regional parties of the state, the SP and the BSP, along with Ajit Singh led Rashtriya Lok Dal (RLD) foisted the Mahagathbandhan (grand alliance) in the state. But in Modi wave, their ambitions were forcefully dashed leading to wash out for the RLD and confinement of the SP to its previous tally of just five. Mayawati led BSP has indeed improved its performance in these elections by raising its tally from 0 to 10. Incidentally, the most important losers in these elections have been Lalu Prasad Yadav led RJD in Bihar and Shibu Soren led JMM in Jharkhand. At one point of time, these regional parties were the epicentre of politics in their respective states. Once hailed as the most formidable mascot of social justice in Bihar, Lalu Prasad Yadav and his clan have surely now gone into political wilderness after drawing blank in his erstwhile bastion.[20] This is an indication, a persuasive

[20] Navin Upadhdyay, 'Lalu in the Wilderness', *The Pioneer*, 30 May 2019, 9.

indication indeed, of the decline of the identity politics even in areas where it remained most effective in political mobilization till the 2014 national poll.

Concluding Observations

The historicity of identity politics remains an important factor in the electoral politics of the country. However, this factor has acted as a value-neutral element whose usage could well be manipulated by the shrewdest of the political players. While in the past a number of caste-based parties had played this card to great success, the scene seemed to have gone in favour of the BJP for the last two general elections. Moreover, the general elections 2019 have altered the landscape of identity-based regional parties in the country. While well-entrenched regional parties based on the solid ideologies and working for the general welfare of their people have indeed been able to retain their clout in their respective states, the parties based on sectarian considerations and banking upon the support base of people belonging to particular castes have suffered heavily as people have found the ideology of Hindutva more attractive than their primordial affinities. Moreover, even the parties that have somehow been able to defend their turfs seem to be put on tenterhooks by the voters to mend their ways lest they might be shown the doors in the forthcoming assembly elections. In many cases, the national parties, particularly the BJP has made earnest efforts to reach political understanding with them for electoral purposes if they were not willing to get assimilated with the BJP in the first place. Prospectively, these elections have probably rung the alarm bells for the identity-based regional parties in the sense that the electoral juggernaut of the BJP might roll over them sooner or later unless they are able to solidify their hard-earned clout in their respective states.

What is unique here is the point that there is hardly a definite conceptual parameter to explain the relative importance or otherwise of one's socio-economic identity in one's electoral responses. The situation appears to have been further complicated with the rise of Hindutva as a vote-catching device. Hindutva is a wider category in which many socio-economic identities are submerged which makes the task far more difficult since it contributes to the formation and consolidation (as the outcome of the 2014 and 2019 Lok Sabha polls suggest) of a sum total of identities, especially during the election. Implied here are two conceptual points: on the one hand, it is suggested that Hindutva, despite being a marker of identity vis-à-vis non-Hindu communities, evolves into a widely accepted political platform to garner electoral support; notwithstanding its capability of cementing a bond among a specific socio-economic groups, Hindutva is also an ideological voice that, on the other, alienates (rather permanently) a section of the population presumably because of the widely accepted conceptualization that it is instinctively divisive. Nonetheless, the voters appear to have been swayed by the BJP and its star campaigner, Narendra Modi, which was reflected in both the 2014 and 2019 general elections in India. This further confirms that Hindutva, which is not just a marker of socio-economic identity but also a way of life that, despite being organically linked with the rise of India as a polity, lost its significance due to the blind imitation of the post-colonial leadership of the politico-ideological views, bequeathed by the colonial authority. Hindutva is, in this sense, not merely an indigenous source of identity but also an endeavour to re-articulate Indian identity with reference to those sociocultural influences which did not receive, so far, the importance that they deserved. A new era has, thus, ushered in when the narrow vision of identity disappears with the consolidation of macro identity around Hindutva and other concomitant value preferences.

10

Political Choice amidst Anti-incumbency Sentiments/ Preferences

Anti-incumbency sentiments seem critical in determining the poll outcome, as the past elections show. In other words, the assessment by the voters is an important criterion insofar as voting behaviour is concerned. The chapter, therefore, seeks to understand how anti-incumbency sentiments influence voting behaviour in India which also does not preclude the possibility of pro-incumbency tilt of the voters. Implicit here are two points: on the one hand, elections in India are governed by anti-incumbency passion that gains momentum especially during the election campaign since that is the time when political parties interact with the voters; this is, however, not to ignore the pro-incumbency opinion which ensures, on the other, the continuity of the government in power presumably because the voters are favourably disposed to those in harness. The chapter is, therefore, an elaboration of the argument that anti-incumbency sentiments are as decisive in elections as pro-incumbency feelings.

Spectacular Performances of UPA

Although the factor of anti-incumbency was there in the times of Jawaharlal Nehru as well, the stridency of that factor as a major determinant of the electoral outcomes in the second and third general elections could never had been beyond a certain point given the nationalistic fervour with which the electoral politics was conducted during the Nehruvian period of Indian political history. After the departure of Nehru from the political scene, the anti-incumbency factor has seen to have played a critical role in ensuring the ouster of the ruling parties from the seat of power. Hence, the unconventional political choice of the people in the wake of anti-incumbency was remarkably seen for the first time during the 14th and 15th general elections during which the UPA government under the leadership of Dr Manmohan Singh was swept back to power.

The outcomes of the 2004 general elections had been momentous for a number of reasons (Table 10.1). First, the hopes of the BJP that had been riding on the wave of the

TABLE 10.1	Performance of Major Parties and Groups in 2004 General Elections	
Parties	**Seats**	**Vote Share (%)**
Congress	145	26.53
BJP	138	22.16
Regional parties	174	32.86
Others	86	18.45
Total	543	100.00

Source: Computed from the *Statistical Report on 2004 General Elections* (New Delhi: Election Commission of India, 2004), available at https://eci.gov.in/statistical-report/statistical-reports/ (accessed on 1 July 2020).

'shining India' to return to power with even a better or independent majority had decisively been dashed as the party was reduced to the tally of seats that was well behind the Congress. In fact, the aspirations and the convictions of the party had been so high that it had decided in favour of advancing the elections taking the prevailing situation as quite opportune for the party to go to the electorate to get their mandate for governance of the country for a term of five more years renewed. However, that had not to be the case as the electorate of the country had something else in their mind which the BJP surely could not read well before deciding in the favour of advancing the general elections by a few months.

Next, the loss of the BJP had unmistakably been the gain of the Congress. Ever since the departure of the government of P. V. Narasimha Rao, the Congress Party appeared to be in doldrums in the absence of the party leadership by a scion of the Nehru–Gandhi family. The reclusive stand of Sonia Gandhi in the wake of the assassination of her husband presumably in order to keep her children as well as herself safe from the hazards of political animosity had left the party in the hands of the non-Nehru–Gandhi member of the party. But for whatsoever reasons, such a stewardship of the party could not prove to be a beneficial step for the party. As a result, the party kept on sliding down the ladder of its importance in the national politics in such a way that people had started writing off the party from the political reckoning of the country. It was during such a delicate juncture that she decided to take up leadership of the party into her own hands and readied the party machinery for the electoral battle likely to ensue very soon. In these elections, the acceptance of her leadership of the party had very well been taken by the general electorate of the country and the Congress was indeed able to beat the BJP in the battle of ballots.[1] This revived the political fortunes of the party in such a way that it eventually turned out to be the ruling party of the country for the next 10 years.

[1] Yogendra Yadav, 'The Elusive Mandate', *Economic & Political Weekly* 39, no. 51 (18 December 2004): 5385.

The winning streak of the Congress continued even during the 2009 general elections with even improved tally of seats. A number of factors might be discerned that had contributed to the rise in the electoral fortunes of the party. As for the case of the 2004 general elections, the party leadership resting in the hands of a member of the Nehru–Gandhi family had reassured the cadres and leaders of the party that the party was now well on track and they needed to work hard to make the electoral performance better than the previous one. This was accompanied by the sacrificial image of the party president, Sonia Gandhi, who earlier had refused to take charge of the government as the prime minister and appointed a seasoned Congressman, Dr Manmohan Singh, as the prime minister. This master stroke of the party president had indeed been able to establish an image of sacrifice and integrity in the minds of common people with regard to the personality of Sonia Gandhi. Most of all, what seemed to have gone in favour of the party had been the clientele approach that the government had adopted as the basic strategy of governance as well as underlying principle through which the government wanted to take care of the well-being of the people. Such an approach had helped in the creation of a dedicated vote bank for the party that had credit their economic upliftment to the policies and programmes of the UPA government. As a result, the Congress score in the 2009 general elections had soared dramatically to cross the 200 mark and stood at 206 (Table 10.2).[2]

In comparison to the upward movement of the Congress tally in the 2009 general elections, the BJP suffered the loss of substantive number of seats as well as percentage of votes. The party's electoral performance during this election took a backward march to reach the levels of the early 1990s when the party was looking helpless in the face of the formidable performances by the parties standing for social justice. The

[2] See Paul Wallace and Ramashroy Roy, eds, *India's 2009 Elections: Coalition Politics, Party Competition and Congress Continuity* (New Delhi: SAGE Publications, 2011).

TABLE 10.2	Performance of Major Parties and Groups in 2009 General Elections	
Parties	**Seats**	**Vote Share (%)**
Congress	206	28.55
BJP	116	18.80
Regional parties	159	31.01
Others	62	21.6
Total	543	100.00

Source: Computed from the *Statistical Report on 2009 General Elections* (New Delhi: Election Commission of India, 2009), available at https://eci. gov.in/statistical-report/statistical-reports/ (accessed on 10 July 2020).

loss of the BJP in these elections could be explained with reference to two interrelated factors. One, as the clientele-based approach of the UPA government had created a wider base of supporters and sympathizers for the party, the BJP could not find much leg space among such groups of people to expand its base and augment the number of seats. Second, the BJP had been able to reach at the centre stage of electoral politics in the country, thanks to its emotive appeal to the people in the name of cultural nationalism and Hindutva. For instance, the party had steadfastly called for the construction of Ram temple which could never be done despite the party remaining in power for almost full term of office. So the general electorate of the country had by now understood the hollowness of such emotive issues and, therefore, did not get motivated by the renewed appeal of the BJP to vote for it in the name of its ideological baggage.

Although the onward march of the Congress in these general elections had acted to stem the tide of the rise of regional and other national parties as important players in the national politics on the strength of their position in the Lok Sabha, these parties, in fact, continued with good performances they had been showing for a number of years. The basic reason for them to put up good shows in these elections had been their deep penetration among the distinct social groups nurtured by them as their core vote bank. Such a turnaround in the electoral dynamics of the country had undoubtedly been brought about by the deepening of democracy in the wake of unleashing of the forces of social justice since the early 1990s. Moreover, a number of regional and national parties had also been able to create particular spheres of influence in different states on the strength of which they were successful in reaping good electoral harvest year after year. Yet the electoral performance of the communist parties had seen drastic dip in the 2009 general elections on account of the TMC emerging as a powerful challenge to the communist monopoly over the Lok Sabha seats from West Bengal. Similar dip could also be seen in the number of seats of the regional parties coming from UP and Bihar. The non-Congress, non-BJP parties had, therefore, a reduced number of seats in the Lok Sabha in the wake of the changed political scenario in different states.

A comparative study of the outcomes of the two general elections reveals a number of interesting trends with regard to the democratic process of the country. The Congress which had been looked upon as the worn-out force in the Indian politics had made a remarkable comeback riding on the back of the re-energized party under the leadership of Sonia Gandhi. Thanks to the governmental policy thrust on clientelism as the hallmark of the public policy, the party was able to make a deep impact on the lives of the poor and marginalized sections of society that readily became the supporter of the party. It was probably on the support of these voters that the party could substantially improve its tally in the Lok Sabha in the 2009 general elections. The electoral fortunes of the BJP had gone down in the two general elections making the party realize that only emotive issues are not able to win the votes consistently. The party was, therefore, shattered out of its complacency to relook at its electoral strategy if it had to return to power at the centre in the near future. In these two elections, the major gainers had been the regional and other national parties, well entrenched in their islands of support. The inculcation of a core support base had helped these parties to maintain their winning streak in both the general elections and remained the key players in the national politics.[3]

The two general elections held in 2004 and 2009, respectively, had brought about a number of fundamental transformations in the democratic polity of the country. They proved the dynamic nature of Indian democracy by showing that the electoral fortunes of a party could never be written despite the successive discomfitures of the party over a long period of time. Otherwise, during the past many years, the continuous dismal performances of the Congress Party would have reduced the party to existential issues. But the way the party was able to make a dramatic comeback in the political arena of the country had been quite striking. The continuous losses of the party could not dent the enthusiasm of the core cadre of the party to work hard for the victory of the party in the general elections. Moreover, the traditional vote bank of the party had also come to its rescue when they could foresee that the party had overcome the hiccups of the previous years and was poised for a comeback. Thus, the political landscape of the country had experienced a subtle turnaround with the emergence of the Congress from the doldrums to take charge of the government at the centre. The dramatic comeback of the party had been accompanied by such turn of events in the later years that after a very long time, the party was able to repeat its spectacular performance in the two general elections back-to-back and run the government at the centre for full two terms of office.

Notwithstanding the return of the Congress to the centre stage of the democratic process in the country, a number of important pointers could be discerned about the party from its electoral performances over the years. For example, the

[3] Ajay K. Mehra, 'India's Fifteenth General Election: Realities, Implications and Prospects' (working paper no. 56, Heidelberg Papers in South Asia and Comparative Politics, South Asia Institute, Heidelberg University, Heidelberg, 2010), 39.

changing electoral fortunes of the party over the years had amply proved the perception that the party had moulded itself into a pocket borough of the Nehru–Gandhi family. In the absence of any member of the family at the helm of affairs, it would be almost impossible for the party to remain a formidable force in the democratic process of the country. As could be seen, after the assassination of Rajiv Gandhi when the family had decided against getting involved in politics, the fortunes of the party had started dipping like anything. Although the party was able to form the government after the assassination of Rajiv Gandhi, the electoral turnaround in the fortunes of the party could well be credited to the death of its leader that ultimately created a sort of sympathy wave for the party and it was able to win a sizeable number of seats in the remaining phases of the elections. But after that, the party could never recover from the handicap that it suffered due to the absence of family members to guide and encourage the workers to work for the party in a tireless manner. The bad run of the party could be reversed only after arrival of Sonia Gandhi as the party president.

Arrival of the coalition system of government in the lexicon of the Congress could also be taken as the important contribution of the two general elections. While the BJP had from day one accepted the fact that its inability to reach the different parts of the country could be compensated by entering into strategic alliances with a number of regional parties so as to not only augment its tally of seats in the Lok Sabha but also create an environment of positivity for the party in the hitherto unreached areas of the country. For the Congress such a state of things appeared improbable, given the habit of the party to run the governments enjoying comfortable majorities in the Lok Sabha. As a result, as late as in 1999, the party was averse to the idea of forging any kind of alliance with any party. Its electoral alliance with the regional parties in Kerala could be taken as an exception, given the coalitional nature of politics in the state. The coalitional inhibitions of the party could be warded off only after the arrival of Sonia Gandhi at the helm of affairs of the party. But once the party accepted the possibility of forming and running the government in coalition with the likeminded parties, it indeed was able to not only become the lynchpin of the UPA but was also credited with running two consecutive coalition governments despite various kinds of pushes and pulls from the coalition partners and other allies.[4]

The repetitive nature of Indian politics could also be seen in the wake of the two general elections. There have been phases in the Indian politics when anti-Congressism emerged as the defining feature of democratic politics in the country. During such times, parties of all hues and ideologies cutting across all sort of differences, divergences and variations in their perspectives on different aspects of public life in the country did join hands together to keep the Congress away from power at the centre. During the two general elections, the same story was repeated in the Indian politics. The only difference was that this time in the place of the Congress, it was the BJP. In other words, anti-BJPism had also become the prominent trait of the Indian politics during the 11th and 12th general elections. Interestingly, during these elections, a number of parties could put up formidable electoral shows in different parts of the country. As a result, neither the BJP nor the Congress could secure sufficient number of seats to form the government. But on both the occasions, the disparate parties and leaders did not waste even a minute in declaring their intention of aligning with the UPA to help it form the government at the centre. Such kinds of untouchable parties or ideologies could be seen as an old feature of Indian politics and its repetitive character is likely to be experienced in the democratic processes of the country from time to time.

[4] For an analytical overview of the coalitional complexities in India, see K. K. Kailash, 'The Emerging Politics of Cohabitation: New Challenges', in Emerging Trends in Indian Politics: The 15the General Election, ed. Ajay K. Mehra (New Delhi: Routledge, 2010), 86–113.

The Case of NDA

While the electoral performance of the UPA government had indeed set a new trend in beating anti-incumbency against the ruling party, the streak has been repeated by the NDA through its impressive performances during the 16th and 17th general elections. The arrival of Narendra Modi on national level as BJP's prime ministerial candidate in 2014 had introduced an element of freshness in the electoral foray of the party during the 16th general election. Moreover, the long-drawn voting schedule has resulted in torturous election campaigns in different parts of the country with varying stakeholders and differing moods of the voters. It has always, therefore, been anybody's guess to visualize what could have been the outcome of these polls. The BJP being the only pan-India formidable stakeholder with the probable exceptions of the southern-most states of Kerala and Tamil Nadu (though the party has played its cards well by entering into an electoral alliance with the AIADMK in Tamil Nadu), throughout all the seven phases of polls, never lowered its guard and kept its tempo of campaign in full throttle. The Congress-led UPA, therefore, fell under the weight of anti-incumbency with the BJP-led NDA emerging as the new ruling dispensation of the country with the group securing a comfortable majority in the Lok Sabha (Table 10.3).

TABLE 10.3	Performance of Various Parties/Coalitions in 2014 General Election	
Parties/Coalitions	**Seats Contested**	**Seats Won**
NDA	542	336
UPA	539	58
Others	6,806	132

Source: Computed from the *Statistical Report on 2014 General Elections* (New Delhi: Election Commission of India, 2014), available at https://eci.gov.in/statistical-report/statistical-reports/ (accessed on 11 February 2020).

In the wake of the 17th general election, the factor of anti-incumbency seemed to be weighing heavily against the BJP. But the party kept its fingers crossed and entered the poll arena with full preparedness. Given the vigour and campaign strategy of the party, it was expected that the party was likely to emerge as the single largest party even if it fails to secure a clear majority in the Lok Sabha. Conjectures were also put forward by certain analysts and activists that these polls would result in the non-BJP, non-Congress parties nearing majority in the house in which case there would be clear probability of the BJP getting unseated from power in Delhi. The most reluctant participant in these elections appeared to be the Congress whose aging top leadership had almost bestowed the responsibility of steering the party's electoral engine on the shoulders of its president, Rahul Gandhi.

The declaration of results came as a shock for the political pundits who were foreseeing the prospects of either a hung Lok Sabha or a working majority for the Third Front parties drawn from various states. The poll outcomes indicated a clear wave sweeping across the country in the name of Prime Minister Narendra Modi catapulting his party at the top of all.[5] As Modi himself has said in his post-victory speech that his chemistry with the common people of the country has decisively trumped the mathematics of poll pundits.[6] What appeared unique in the case of BJP's electoral fortunes has been that Modi's charisma has adequately been matched by the moves of master strategist Amit Shah as party president. As a matter of fact, on the issues of entering into electoral alliances as well as identifying the states and seats where his party stood in an advantageous position in comparison to the other parties, Shah's calculations hit almost cent per cent mark.[7] On the contrary, in gauging

[5] Venkitesh Ramakrishnan, 'Right on Top', *Frontline*, 7 June 2019, 6.
[6] Sanjay Singh, 'Its Victory of Chemistry over Arithmetic: Modi', *The Economic Times*, 28 May 2019, 2.
[7] Shishir Gupta, 'Shah of Strategy Has Emerged as Leader of Masses', *The Hindustan Times*, 24 May 2019, 4.

TABLE 10.4	*Party Position in 17th Lok Sabha*
Alliances	**No. of Seats Won**
NDA	354
UPA	91
Others	97

Source: Computed from the *Statistical Report on 2019 General Elections* (New Delhi: Election Commission of India, 2019), available at https://eci. gov.in/statistical-report/statistical-reports/ (accessed on 21 June 2020).

the public mood, the seasoned politicians like N. Chandrababu Naidu also failed to arrive at right conclusion even if one ignores the calculations of political novices such as Akhilesh Yadav in UP and Tejashwi Yadav in Bihar.

A clear landslide for the BJP and its NDA allies sweeping across the country was visible in this election. By winning 354 seats out of 542, the NDA has proved to be the most formidable political alliance ever made at the national level in the country (Table 10.4). In fact, right from the days of the Janata Party, the electoral alliances in India have never been able to secure such a landslide victory. In the previous elections, electoral alliances had just been able to secure a workable, or on occasions, only comfortable majorities that allowed them to complete the full terms of the government. Moreover, in the past, partners in an alliance were powerful players in their respective states or areas of influence and did not owe their good electoral performances to the dominant partner or the charisma of its leader. But in the case of the position of the NDA in the 17th Lok Sabha, the things would not have been same had the alliance partners would have to contest the polls on their own.

In the run up to the elections, as usual, there came a time when some sort of alliance swapping appeared on the scene. Given the five years of iron-handed rule of Modi, certain degree of apprehensions was natural in the minds of some of the NDA partners who either thought of striking hard bargain with the

BJP in the seat sharing parleys or decided to leave the alliance altogether. In such a scenario, while the long-term allies such as the Shiv Sena and the Janata Dal (United) bargained hard with their dominant partners to extract as many seats in their respective states as possible, a suspicious ally like the Rashtriya Lok Samta Party led by Upendra Kushwaha, a minister of state in the Modi government, decided to leave the alliance in the hope of reaping rich dividends out of anti-incumbency against the central government. Naturally, he joined the Mahagathbandhan (grand alliance) in Bihar to contest the polls. But to his great surprise, the result of his move proved counterproductive and his party lost all the seats it contested including his own.

What is, therefore, been argued here is that the Modi wave that clearly swept these elections proved very advantageous for the allies as well apart from the BJP. Indeed, barring a few states where the Modi wave was stymied by regional factors or leaders, the NDA allies in different states were able to defy any kind of anti-incumbency presumably on account of Modi wave only. As a result, while most, if not all, of the seats contested by alliance partners in different states were won by them, in certain cases, a few alliance partners dramatically improved their kitty of seats riding on the Modi wave. A clear example in this regard is that of the Loktantrik Janshakti Party led by seasoned politician and a cabinet minister in Modi government, Ram Vilas Paswan. His party which had just two members in the 16th Lok Sabha trebled its tally by winning all the six seats it had been allotted under the seat sharing formula in Bihar. Thus, the outcome of these elections proved to be landslide not only for the BJP but also for most of its allies that made NDA win historic mandate in these elections. Comparatively, when one looks at the performance of alliance partners of the UPA, the story is just opposite to that of the NDA.

BJP's Landslide

The most spectacular outcome of the 17th general elections may be considered to be the historic landslide for the BJP that has moved it to the centre of Indian politics.[8] Such a landslide was probably not expected even by the leaders of the party themselves though in their public addresses as well as media interviews, they claimed that the party would be able to return to power again with absolute majority. Given the enormous hue and cry raised by the elements opposed to the BJP government over the policies and programmes of the government including certain untoward incidents such as cow vigilantism, lynching of certain individuals, path-breaking economic measures like demonetization, and likewise, it appeared even in the general perception that the party was going to face a very tough challenge in the ensuing polls. The situation was further made challenging for the party with coming together of even sworn enemies in the critical states like UP just for the purpose of checking BJP's return to power again at the centre. In such scenarios, though the party leadership could definitely visualize the enormity of the situation and made earnest efforts to initiate appropriate public posturing including concerted publicity and propaganda to browbeat opposition's moves, the situation, nevertheless, did not permit any space for complacency in the party cadres as well as top leadership.[9]

When the results of the polls started pouring in on 23 May 2019, the deep penetration of Modi wave even into the unchartered territories of the country began to get exhibited. In the place of mandatory 272 seats required to secure a working majority in the Lok Sabha, the party's individual seat tally swelled to cross the magical 300 marks and landed at as much as 303. When one looks at the contributions of different states and union territories in such a landslide for the party, three categories of states and union territories could be discerned in accordance with the performance of the party in these regions. At the top of all come the traditional strongholds of the party

[8] Sanjay Baru, 'Right Moves Closer to Centre', *The Economic Times*, 27 May 2019, 16.

[9] Sunita Aron, 'How the Saffron Party Overcame the Opposition in UP', *The Hindustan Times*, 26 May 2019, 10.

where it could land up monopolizing the seats leaving no scope for any other contender to even open their account. Interestingly, the sweep of such states did not remain confined to any particular region and spanned to different parts of the country as shown in Table 10.4. For instance, if the landslide was most visible in the Hindi heartland of Rajasthan, Haryana, Himachal Pradesh and Uttarakhand, it was also witnessed in the western part of the country like Gujarat.[10] Similarly, apart from the capital city of Delhi, BJP's juggernaut also rolled out fantastically in the north-eastern states of Tripura and Arunachal Pradesh.[11]

Although other parties could also manage to secure a few seats, the overwhelming majority of seats in these states also went in favour of the BJP in alliance with its coalition partners. Such a situation prevailed not only in the most critical states such as UP and Bihar but also in many of the states where even the party did not expect such a landslide. The caste-ridden politics of Hindi heartland, especially UP and Bihar, was trumped by Modi's lucrative economic and emotive security measures.[12] For instance, while the party was able to defy all sorts of doomsayers to establish its dominance of the political scenarios in UP, Bihar, Jharkhand and Maharashtra, it apparently bounced back in the states such as Madhya Pradesh and Chhattisgarh where it had just lost the State Assembly elections a few months back. Most importantly, the Modi wave really helped out the party to reach even to hitherto unchartered territories of eastern, north-eastern and southern parts of the country and secured handsome, if not overwhelming, number of seats in the states such as West Bengal, Odisha, Assam and Karnataka. Of these, the party's stunning performance in West

[10] Nilanjan Mukhopadhyay, 'Clean Sweep', *The Economic Times Magazine*, 26 May 2019, 10.

[11] Vivek Chhetri, 'Triumphant BJP Takes All in Hills', *Telegraph*, 24 May 2019, 8.

[12] Kunal Singh, 'How Modi Conquered Caste in 2019', *The Hindustan Times*, 30 May 2019, 16.

Bengal has probably signalled the ouster of the regional parties from the state.[13]

In spite of riding on the Modi wave, the BJP could not breach certain isolated citadels of the regional parties or states where the Congress or other regional parties showed resilience to withstand BJP's sweep to win majority, if not all, of the seats as presented in Table 10.4. Of such states, the rudest shock for the party apparently came from the southern states of Kerala, Tamil Nadu and Andhra Pradesh. Rather, it could be argued that these states somewhat witnessed a kind of anti-Modi wave which formidably prevented the party from opening its account in these states despite all kinds of long-term efforts such as supporting Sabarimala agitation in Kerala and entering into an electoral alliance with the AIADMK in Tamil Nadu. At the same time, the party was also restrained from expanding its landslides in states such as Punjab, Telangana and Meghalaya where the opposition parties solidly remained in the saddle. In these states, either the BJP has traditionally been absent from the scene or has not remained as formidable as it has been in the states of Hindi heartland. Certain states like Punjab really defied the Modi wave to keep the Congress flag flying high in the state.

Ideational Continuity

The anti-incumbency as a factor in determining the electoral outcomes for the ruling party has probably never been a formidable factor in the country so long as the nationalist euphoria governed the voters' choice. As shown in Chapter 3, the Congress Party appeared to have been invincible in elections in the first four national polls presumably because the voters were favourably inclined towards its leaders who sacrificed worldly comforts by being involved in the struggle

[13] Kanchan Gupta, 'Bengal's Green Fort falls', *Business Standard*, 24 May 2019, 4.

for freedom. It was primarily pro-Congress sentiments that acted decisively in its favour in elections after elections till the 1971 national poll. Initially, the Congress Party can be said to have been rewarded by the voters for its relentless battle for India's political freedom in adverse circumstances. By 1967, the scene had undergone a radical metamorphosis once the voters, born after Independence, became critical to elections. Voters endorsed the claimants for power once they were persuaded to do so on the basis of their assessment of the government that they led. Although the Congress Party succeeded in capturing power at the centre, it lost miserably in many provinces presumably because electorates did not seem happy with the governance there. The result was obvious. The Congress lost power to the coalition of political parties that drew on anti-Congress sentiments. It was Ram Manohar Lohia[14] who was the main priest of this radical political change that resulted in the displacement of the Congress Party in the 1967 State Assembly elections.

The Congress victory in 1971 general election was attributed to Indira Gandhi's leadership in eradicating poverty from India. Here too, her role as the supreme commander of governance between 1969 and 1971, just before the election, acted as a determinant of voting behaviour. The near decimation of the opposition was possible presumably because the voters held the Congress leader as capable of delivering what she promised. The storyline did not change much in the sense that voters' opinions or sentiments remained most significant in shaping

[14] Born in 1910, Ram Manohar Lohia was a member of JP-constituted Congress Socialist Party that came into being in 1934. By creatively blending Gandhian ideas with those of Karl Marx, Lohia evolved a mode of conceptualizing Indian nationalism. Because of his participation in the 1942 Quit India campaign, he was incarcerated in 1942 and was released in 1946. Critical of Jawaharlal Nehru, he always felt that an undiluted socialist regime was the only panacea for India's poverty. Twice elected to the Lok Sabha (in 1963 and 1967), Lohia remained committed to his ideas of socialism till his demise in 1967.

voting behaviour. As the poll results of 1977 general elections reveal, the Congress was severely punished by the voters for the excesses that the Indira Gandhi led Congress government committed during the 1975–1977 Emergency. In a similar vein, the Janata Party government was also dislodged in 1980 for its failure to provide stability in governance. The 1984 national poll was held in uncertain circumstances that had emerged in the wake of the assassination of incumbent prime minister, Indira Gandhi, which acted decisively in securing a thumping majority in the Lok Sabha for the Congress Party. A perusal of the 1989 electoral outcome suggests that many financial irregularities in which the Congress Party leaders, including Prime Minister Rajiv Gandhi, were involved created an opportunity for the opposition to strengthen its claim for power on the basis of voters' anti-incumbency sentiments. With the return of the Congress Party to power in 1991, it was a reiteration of the same point. The voters' anti-incumbency passion was translated into votes in favour of the Congress Party. Given the political doldrums between 1996 and 1999, neither of the pan-Indian political parties was willing to shoulder the responsibility of governing India. The situation seemed little calm and in 1999 election, the BJP and its partners in the NDA formed the government and finished its term in 2004.

That anti-incumbency factor shaped the voting behaviour in the 14th national election (held in 2004) does not require an elaboration. Like the BJP, the Congress Party also realized the importance of a coalition of likeminded political parties which led to the formation of the UPA. By choosing the Congress Party and its partners in the UPA in 2004 election, the voters again substantiated the claim that anti-incumbency views mattered in electoral choice. Despite endeavours towards winning voters' confidence in the 2009 general poll, the BJP and its NDA partners failed to muster adequate support to form the government. The UPA was returned to power which again justifies the contention that pro-incumbency clamour ensured the poll victory. In five years, the popular mood had changed:

the image of the UPA, especially of the prime minister being an indecisive person, is said to have created a space for the BJP and the NDA. That the UPA government was neither well equipped to rule out corruption nor was able to sustain the pace of economic growth of the yesteryears contributed to its electoral downfall. By projecting a strong leader and by exposing the inadequacies of the policies that reportedly protected the socio-economic interests of specific minorities at the cost of the majority, the NDA built a strong support base which led to its success in the 2014 general election. The charge of the NDA that the UPA, especially its leading partner, the Congress, resorted to 'minority appeasement' gained credence in view of the 2013 communal riots in Muzaffarnagar in UP in which the Muslims were reported to have been responsible in the skirmishes between the Hindus and the Muslims. As the studies show, the voters were unhappy with the overall functioning of the UPA government and the Muzaffarnagar riots just before the poll were reportedly the final nail in the coffin. So it is not just anti-incumbency sentiments of the voters that decided the UPA fate, the Muzaffarnagar riots had also played an equally critical role in garnering support for the Narendra Modi led NDA in the 2014 Lok Sabha poll.

That voters reposed faith in the NDA government which was evident with its impressive victory in the 2014 national election. It was undoubtedly a scintillating win, especially for the BJP, since in comparison with the tally of 282 parliamentary seats in 2014 poll, it had won in 303 Lok Sabha constituencies in the 17th national poll which is illustrative of a strong pro-incumbency wave in its favour for a complex set of reasons. Prominent among them was surely the image of the incumbent prime minister as capable of meaningfully addressing many of India's age-old socio-economic ills. That India rose as a strong player in the international arena during the NDA regime also acted decisively in bringing many of the fence sitters in its favour in the 2014 parliamentary election. On the whole, it can be argued that voters' pro-government opinion was based on their assessment of NDA's performance in its first term of office.

It is also argued here that it was not possible for the opposition to firmly establish its claim for office presumably because of its failure to emerge as a united force around a leader; the failure of the UPA and anti-NDA political forces to effectively counter the ruling conglomeration of parties was also cited as a plausible reason for the assumption of power by the Modi-led coalition for two consecutive terms.

There are three complementary points that deserve attention here: the first obvious and simple point relates to the critical importance of anti- or pro-incumbency passion in shaping voting behaviour. A casual view of the election results confirms the contention. The second point, which is little complex, concerns the view that sentiments either for or against the incumbent ruling party remain significant though they may not be sufficiently plausible to conclusively explain the electoral outcome as the 2014 Lok Sabha poll illustrates. There is no denying the critical importance of the 2013 Muzaffarnagar riots which instantaneously generated a favourable wave for the BJP and the NDA for being supportive of the cause of the majority. Whether it was morally right or wrong does not seem to be relevant since election is a battle for victory, and the contesting political parties leave no stone unturned for bringing voters in their favour. Similarly, there was, no doubt, a positive opinion for the NDA government that was evident once the election campaign had kicked off. Besides being an endorsement of an effective authority, the electoral support for the NDA by the voters was consolidated with the successful attack on the secret terrorist camps in Balakot in Pakistan just before the elections in most of the constituencies after the completion of the first two phases. Here, the Balakot strike along with the pro-incumbency stance of the voters appeared to have made the NDA electorally invincible in the 2019 national poll. Furthermore, as argued above, the confused and divided leadership of the UPA and those opposed to the NDA did not enable, for obvious reasons, the opponents to really effectively challenge the Modi juggernaut in the 17th parliamentary election.

Concluding Observations

Right from the times of Nehru through the rules of the UPA and the NDA, the ruling parties or combinations have comfortably been able to retain power. Contemporaneously, the 17th Lok Sabha polls produced a scenario in which the BJP not only returned to power at the centre by registering a landslide victory but also got sustenance to emerge as a truly pan-India political party that could register its presence in most, if not all, of the states in India. The strategic penetration of the party into the hitherto unclaimed territories like West Bengal has really been a battle handsomely won. Party's amazing performance in its traditional strongholds need not overshadow its more far-reaching and long-term gains of spreading its wings to such areas that have remained, more or less, out of reach for the party. In fact, it should not be undermined that at least the party could get electoral partners in the states like Tamil Nadu and ambitiously tried to open its account in the states like Kerala that have remained inaccessible bastions for the party. Undeniably, in the coming times, the party would surely extend the depth of its reach in the twin states of Telangana and Andhra Pradesh along with consolidating its gains in West Bengal. That way, these elections have not only helped the party beat the factor of anti-incumbency but have also opened new vistas for the party to dominate the political firmament of India.

The discussion on whether anti or pro-incumbency sentiments of the voters plausibly account for the victory or otherwise of political parties seeking office can never be conclusive for obvious reasons. Prominent among them is the critical role of certain triggering events or issues in shaping the electoral outcome. For instance, the Twenty-sixth Amendment to the Constitution of India, 1971, created an image of the ruling Congress Party and Prime Minister Indira Gandhi of being pro-poor. The Amendment was justified as an effective step towards establishing equal rights for all citizens and the need to reduce the government's revenue deficit. In other words, not only did it build an image of Indira Gandhi being a messiah of the poor, but it also generated adequate support for the ruling party that was reported to have been seriously trying to address revenue deficit as well. The favourable image that this decision had purportedly created did not last long as the 1977 Lok Sabha poll outcome shows. The excesses of the 1975–1977 Emergency seemed to have bulldozed the good will of the voters that the ruling party had created by adopting many policy designs that seemingly justified its pro-people image. Contrarily, the organized campaign by the opponents against the BJP and the other constituents of the NDA for being supportive of majoritarianism did not work neither in the 2014 election nor in the 2019 poll. Whether the renewal of the NDA government in the 2019 election reconfirms the contention that the demographically preponderant Hindu en masse support the incumbent political authority does not seem to be persuasive given the fact that the conglomeration secured approximately 39 per cent of popular votes which means that the majority of the voters did not endorse the ruling combination. The argument is vacuous because given the first-past-the-post system of voting in parliamentary democracies, it does not seem logical to argue for proportional representation. This is the universally accepted rule of the game and political parties seeking office are guided by this formula. Nonetheless, the fact that the incumbent ruling parties returned to power by securing less than half of the popular votes also adds substance to the argument that a united opposition was likely to halt the Modi juggernaut in the 17th Lok Sabha poll. As evident in the 1977 and 1989 national elections, a combined opposition led to the defeat of the ruling party on both the occasions. The storyline was not different in the 16th and the 17th Lok Sabha poll. It was easier for the NDA to ensure its electoral victory because (a) the voters' pro-incumbency sentiments acted in its favour and (b) the failure of anti-NDA political forces to challenge the ruling coalition in unison sealed their fate.

Instead of suggesting that election results can be persuasively explained in terms of a neatly designed model, the chapter argues that it is also improbable, given the complex nature of elections and their outcomes, especially in a socioculturally diverse society like India. The argument couched in monochromatic explanation can, thus, never be convincing for its obvious limitations. What is, thus, required is to comprehend the election results both in terms of the mindset that evolves over the period of governance by a ruling party or a combination of parties and the immediate triggering factor, as the 2019 Balakot incident evinced. By insisting on a nuanced understanding of the electoral behaviour, the chapter not only provides meaningful inputs but also will help us develop a meaningful explanatory framework.

Conclusion

I

Choosing the political representatives by the electorates is integral to democracy since it evolves a mechanism through which the voters are involved in the processes of selecting those in governance. In other words, election is a system whereby the fact that *demos* are critical to democracy is firmly established. Following this logic, one is persuaded to argue that democratic governance epitomizes an ideological response in specific socio-economic and political circumstances. As history has shown, India has witnessed change of political guards at regular intervals in accordance with voters' preferences. Nonetheless, what is common to all the political actors is to accept the 1950 Constitution as the sole guide while preparing the road map for the future. One of the most striking examples is the gradual transformation of the Indian economy from the Licence Raj system of control to a relatively open economy which is not averse to the investment by the foreign companies, of course, within the stipulations that the Government of India has set out for foreign investment. By electing a government in favour of opening up of the economy, the Indian voters have demonstrated their inclination for such an economy. The idea is crystal clear: the electorates remain paramount in representative democracy in the Westminster mould. Critics, however, point out that the mere casting of vote for candidates may not always be an exact articulation of how the voters vote. The argument has substance as recent examples of how Indian voters voted in recently national and state polls reveal. There are many reports confirming that the electorates may not always have chosen the candidates on the basis of specific rational priorities but were governed by non-rational criteria. For instance, in the past few national elections, the issue of Ram temple in Ayodhya in UP had influenced a significant number of voters. With the 2020 Supreme Court judgment in favour of the construction of the Ram temple, the voters felt that the present union government (2019–2024) with Narendra Modi at the helm of affairs and the prevalent BJP government in UP have fulfilled what they had assured to them during the elections. Whether this will continue to remain effective in garnering votes in the next election is a matter of conjecture at this point of time though the argument substantiates the claim that the fulfilment of voters' demands pay dividends to the political competitors in elections.

Elections also endorse the view that voters always remain supreme in electoral democracy. In theory, this is correct since once the voter goes inside the polling booth, she/he is sovereign because nobody else has any mechanism to know his/her choice unless it is made public by the voter himself/herself. In other words, so long as the *vox populi* (voice of the people) is of paramount importance, the voters shall remain critical to the processes of election. This is one of the foundational ideas on which the idea of representative democracy rests. There are two serious implications of this concept-driven assumption: on the one hand, with the recognition of voters as primary to the election, the argument that they are pertinent to representative democracy is established beyond doubt. Voters are, in other words, indispensable insofar as representative democracy is concerned. Along with defending the voters' supremacy, this conceptual idea reinforces, on the other, the point that bereft of voters' free choice, the claim that representative democracy ensures a government of the people, for the people and by the people shall be futile. Significant here is also the idea that the voters play a critical role in sustaining democratic governance. This also justifies the argument that while changing the political guards, voters exercise their views not whimsically but on the basis of well-though-out plans and programmes. It is a matter of common knowledge that the outcome of the 2019 national poll was not just a statement in favour of Ram Mandir, or strong leadership or support for Hindutva, the election results were reflection of a combination of views based probably on these issues. There is no doubt that BJP's victory in 18th Lok Sabha constituencies in West Bengal (and 22 parliamentary seats for the ruling TMC) is also a reflection of voters' disillusionment with the existent state administration, as many studies have shown. There are, therefore, reasons to make the argument that voters also respond to the contextual difficulties which they confront under a particular regime. In view of the ideological traditions that West Bengal has witnessed, it will be simplistic to pursue the point that the West Bengal voters were persuaded by Hindutva as the detractors tend to argue; this is simplistic also because in view of the atrocities committed by the Trinamool activists, especially in the villages, the voters voted against the Trinamool candidates to teach them a lesson. Furthermore, the visible affluence of the party activists reinforced the charges against those belonging to the ruling party of having squandered the amount sanctioned by the union government for developmental work in the villages. Complaints to the police against the perpetrators are invariably ignored. It will not be an exaggeration to suggest that those responsible for maintenance of law and order appear to have been clearly partisan and driven by the party in power by almost losing their independence in what they are expected to do. Fundamental here is the claim that the 2019 Lok Sabha poll is a testimony of how the voters reacted to establish their sovereignty during the election by contributing to the defeat of the ruling party's candidates and victory to their opponents.

It is now evident that there is hardly a formula to explain the electoral behaviour in clear terms because the phenomenon itself is far complex than it appears on the surface. There are many unstated assumptions which are contextually made and justified. Each election is fought in unique circumstances and the results are accordingly conditioned, if not governed, to a large extent. An analytical scan of Indian elections, held so far, reveals that voters are hardly swayed by wider ideological concerns; they decide on the basis of their assessment of the socio-economic context and political situations in which they are placed at a particular point of time. Moreover, in the first-past-the-post, it is also difficult to persuasively argue that the winning candidates represent the majority of the voters since a candidate by garnering maximum votes in comparison with those in the fray is declared a winner. Nonetheless, it cannot be disputed that the voters have always a critical role in elections because unless they participate in the processes of choosing a candidate of their choice, elections as mechanisms for ascertaining the voters' choice shall be futile. In other words, by reinforcing the critical importance of voters in polls, representative democracy can be said to have privileged their role in constituting a government.

As the results of some of the past national polls show, the electoral outcome may not always be decisive which also helps us build the argument that voters, with their diverse assessment of the contemporary realities, express their choice in a fashion justifying the fractured mandate. For example, the outcome of the 1977 Lok Sabha poll in which the Janata Party led coalition formed the government in Delhi reflected voters' resentment against the incumbent Congress government which imposed 26-month national Emergency (supported by Article 356 of the 1950 Constitution of India) which led to the rise and consolidation of constitutional authoritarianism at the aegis of Prime Minister Indira Gandhi. The 1989 poll outcome was also voters' comments on the corrupt government that Rajiv Gandhi formed after having won a thumping majority in the 1984 national poll following the assassination of his mother, the then incumbent prime minister. There are many studies showing that on both these occasions, the voters' appear to have made up their mind to dislodge the governments in power since they were deviant and undertook activities which were not only endeavours towards destroying the constitutional governance in India but also sought to undermine the *demos* by striving to create a set of oligarchs who were solely driven by partisan interests. That voters change the course of history was evident when the Janata Party government which was hailed as a saviour of democracy in India was immediately dislodged for its failure to provide a stable government largely due to internecine feud among the coalition partners. The history of what followed with the installation of the Janata Dal government in 1989 is little different because with its fall in 1991, again due to internal squabbles, India witnessed a long phase of instability in governance since no government was able to complete the full term of five years presumably because of their failure to muster a majority in the Parliament. Despite having seen political instability, the period also witnessed an era of Third Front governments which meant that besides the government led by the two pan-Indian political parties, the Indian National Congress and the BJP, there were other parties which, by being ideologically different from both the Congress and the BJP, had support to form the government in Delhi. The story of the Third Front government is dismal; nonetheless, it was a unique political experiment which also reaffirms the critical role that the voters discharge in shaping India's political future in accordance with their ideological priorities. In other words, by dissociating themselves from both the national political parties, the Congress and the BJP, the voters had again proved how important they were in elections. Here too, the argument made above is reinforced by reiterating that in representative democracy, voters shall have the last say and, thus, their voice can neither be ignored nor muzzled. Fundamental here is the view that the importance of *vox populi* can never be undermined except to the detriment of the democratic system that draws its sustenance from the critical role that the voters play in its protection and consolidation.

II

Election is a mode of ensuring political democracy by insisting on universal adult suffrage though it is required to be complemented by economic democracy to contribute to the growth and consolidation of a stable democratic polity. A perusal of the history of making of the 1950 Constitution reveals that the founding fathers had expressed uncertainties on the continuity of the democratic system that the Constitution stipulated. Based on his apprehension about the future of India's democratic constitution, he further elaborated that 'on the 26th of January, 1950, India would be a democratic country in the sense that India from that day would have a government of the people, by the people and for the people' which was a matter of joy 'for the framers of the constitution' though he was not sure whether India 'will ... be able to maintain it or will she lose it again'. This was the thought which made him 'anxious'.[1] Being trained by John Dewey at Columbia University, USA, Ambedkar was persuaded to believe that regardless of whether representatives were elected by the voters, the future of democracy might not be as bright as it appeared on the surface. He defended his argument by saying, in the spirit in which his academic mentor, Dewey, couched his point, that democracy was not

'just a form of government ... it was essentially a form of society [which was drawn on] two things: the first is the attitude of mind, an attitude of respect and equality towards their fellows [and] the second is social organization free from rigid social barriers'.[2]

What is striking is the point that the establishment of mere mechanisms of democracy will not ensure its survival; according

[1] B. R. Ambedkar's speech on 25 November 1949 in the Constituent Assembly, *Constituent Assembly Debates*, Book No. 5, 978.

[2] B. R. Ambedkar, 'Ranade, Gandhi and Jinnah' reproduced in Vasant Moon (compiled), *Dr. Babasaheb Ambedkar Writings and Speeches*, vol. 1, reprint (New Delhi: Dr. Ambedkar Foundation, 2014), 222.

to him, what is required is a mindset immune from prejudices against those who always remain socio-economically marginalized merely by the accident of birth. Emphasizing that the trio of liberty, equality and fraternity were critical to democracy, Babasaheb, as Ambedkar was popularly known, now argued that it would be difficult to establish and sustain democracy in India because these values were completely alien to the Indian psyche. A mere surface understanding of India's social reality revealed that equality was, as he argued, an anathema to the majority community, the Hindus. The most glaring example of social inequality was the careful nurturing of the principle of graded inequality which meant 'elevation for some and degradation for others; similarly, on the economic plane [India] is a society in which there are some who have immense wealth as against many who live in abject poverty'.[3] The most perceptive point he offered while expanding his argument by exhorting that

> on the 26th of January, 1950, we are going to enter into a life of contradiction: in politics, we will have equality and in social and economic life we have inequality. In politics, we will be recognizing the principle of one man one vote one value. In our social and economic life, we shall, by reason of our social and economic structure, continue to deny the principle of one man one value.[4]

Implicit in the above statement are two fundamental points about the nature of democracy that was likely to evolve in India following decolonization. Babasaheb was not at ease with the adoption of universal adult suffrage because he believed that participation in election was not, at all, an effective shield against the socio-economic atrocities that the poor, especially the Dalits suffered. This is a reiteration of the point which he mentioned while identifying the weaknesses of the proposed Constitution. Just by adopting political democracy the newly

[3] B. R. Ambedkar's speech on 25 November 1949 in the Constituent Assembly, *Constituent Assembly Debates*, Book No. 5, 979.
[4] Ibid.

independent India was not likely to be a real democratic country. This was evident when he perceptively commented,

> if you wish to preserve the Constitution in which we have sought to enshrine the principle of Government of the people and by the people let us resolve not to be tardy in the recognition of the evils that lie across our paths and which induce people to prefer Government for the people to Government by the people, nor to be weak in our initiative to remove them. This is the only way to serve the country.[5]

The above assessment of India's socio-economic reality helps us conceptualize whether election is an effective mode for democratic governance. At the surface level, the answer is affirmative because universal adult suffrage ensures equality though, at a much deeper level, the argument is deceptive since political democracy without economic equality shall merely be a system without much substance. The idea is hardly debatable and there are many instances to show that citizens' voice is severely constrained due to the fact that those who are economically better off are also well equipped to control governance to a significant extent. So election is invariably a design to sustain the hegemonic importance of a section of the demography over the rest which, by implications, means that political democracy can never be an effective means for democracy in the real sense of the term.

There is another constraint which does not seem to be peculiar to India alone; the Western democracy is not immune from this, namely the importance and continuity of the dynasts in contemporary politics. Based on the simplistic argument that politicians' offspring have a legitimate reason to join politics since it does not seem odd to find the latter following the former. The argument is made and defended by stating that 'the primary objective of dynastic politics in a modern democracy is that it introduces a form of exclusion among elected representatives that is antithetical to democracy; it is not exclusion

[5] Ibid., 980.

per se but birth-based exclusion'.[6] By being born in a family of politicians, the dynasts have both locational and social advantages in comparison with those who gradually reach the higher echelon of politics by dint of their hard work. In other words, these dynasts, because of the accident of birth, are always politically better placed vis-à-vis their competitors as they are provided with a platform which others have to create for themselves. There are two intertwined aspects that deserve notice here: on the one hand, the newcomers in politics do not get things in a platter which is not the case for the dynasts simply because they join the race with obvious sociopolitical advantages. The political journey of the dynasts does not seem to be, on the other, as hazardous as of the non-dynasts for the former have always mentors at their side and are most likely to receive support and help from their counterparts presumably because they are compatible in class terms and are likely from the families with more or less identical socio-economic priorities. The present leadership of the Congress Party is illustrative here: not only the Gandhi scions, there are many Congressmen who, by following in their fathers' or grandfathers' or mothers' or grandmothers' footsteps, are enthusiastically included in the Congress leadership than many of those who devoted all their lives for sustaining and strengthening the party over the decades. In the contemporary scenario, the trend is clearly universal. Hence, it is not surprising when the former chief ministers, Lalu Yadav in Bihar and Mulayam Singh Yadav in UP, were devoted wholeheartedly to project their sons and daughters as their heir in politics. Examples can easily be multiplied. These examples support the contention that dynastic politics is hardly an exception in India. How does it affect election? In two major ways, the dynasts generally accrue advantages: first, they do not have to toil hard to prepare constituencies of support which their mentors have already created for them. The endeavour of the RJD leader, Lalu Yadav, towards projecting his younger son as the leader of the party and the effort of Ram Vilas Paswan in Bihar to place his son as his political

[6] Chandra, ed. *Democratic Dynasties.*

heir are illustrative here. Second, this is undoubtedly a source of strength for them because not only will this justify their claim that they will carry forward the legacy of the 'great leaders' but will also automatically draw specific constituencies of supporters nurtured by their respective mentors. In such circumstances, the voters do not appear to cast their votes on the basis of rational calculations, but on the basis of their emotional attachment with the candidates' mentors. Contrary to the assumption that electorates choose by being true to their politico-ideological preferences, dynastic politics introduces a new dimension which could neither be democratic nor be strictly logical since the choice is based probably on sentimental affinity with the patriarchs. If dynasts hegemonize the politics, it is most likely that democracy shall be a casualty as they hardly undergo the drill that the commoners cannot avoid. Given the fact that 'the dynasts are wealthier and have stronger local organizational capacity than other politicians', it follows that 'they have natural advantages over their competitors ... while battling for political ascendency'.[7] This argument does not require elaboration as the above examples demonstrate that being sons of politically established fathers, many dynasts have successfully established their claims as true heirs to the legacy that the former has established by dint of their sustained struggle for creating a definite political space for themselves.

The above narrative remains incomplete without dwelling on how India's democratic governance was reduced to a mere form with no substance at all during the 1975–1977 Emergency which led to the complete usurpation of constitutional democracy in India. Here too, the devastating role of a dynast who hardly had believed in any of the foundational values of democracy accounts for a serious distortion in India's polity. Averse to elections, Sanjay Gandhi, the youngest son of the Congress supremo, Indira Gandhi,

> cast a large shadow over the nation. He held no official position, yet he wielded immense power. Ministers, ambitious

[7] Ibid., 264.

Congress *Party* politicians and businessmen, administrators and police officials competed to win his favour. Nobody had dared to challenge his command and he exercised his influence, second to the Prime Minister, Indira Gandhi, to execute the decisions that he preferred.[8]

The outcome of Emergency is too well known to deserve a full-length discussion.[9] Suffice it to say here that the 1975–1977 declaration of Emergency by the Congress government was both a warning for and a reconfirmation of the resilience of Indian democracy. The Emergency had shown that Article 356 in Part XVIII (dealing with the Emergency provisions) of the Indian Constitution was a potential threat to Indian democracy since it was embedded with authority to create constitutional authoritarianism. As argued by an analyst, 'the Emergency turned what was a power struggle into a constitutional crisis'[10] by executing atrocious policies to establish the hegemonic control of a Sanjay Gandhi steered caucus in governance. With the declaration of 1977 national election, the draconian Emergency had also put before us that it was difficult to uproot democracy in India so easily since it was a well-entrenched value that flourished over generations. In other words, democracy was not just procedures but a value, a daily exercise of equality of human beings challenging endeavours towards undermining, if not crippling, voice against those supporting divisive mindsets. Democracy as it evolved in India out of the nationalist struggle and its aftermath is a grand design to generate bonhomie among the Indians regardless of class, caste and ethnicity. Although the classical theorists of democracy, particularly J. S. Mill, were sceptical of the success of democracy in India as the country was socioculturally highly diverse, the survival of universal suffrage and elections at regular intervals

[8] Gyan Prakash, *Emergency Chronicles: Indira Gandhi Democracy's Turning Point* (New Delhi: Penguin, 2018), 205.

[9] Bidyut Chakrabarty has dealt with the nature and outcome of the 1975–1977 Emergency in India in his *Ethics in Governance* (New York, NY: Routledge, 2016).

[10] Prakash, *Emergency Chronicles*, 345.

has proved them wrong. The Indian democratic experiment is, therefore, innovative not only in terms of articulation but also in substance. Political institutions holding the spirit of democracy are regularly being restructured in view of the constantly changing socio-economic milieu, giving it distinctive localized characteristics within the larger universal paradigm of liberal democracy.

It is true that elections are a moment to capture, to borrow a vocabulary from the media, 'the dance of democracy'. With their zealous participation in polls, the argument supportive of voters' engagement in the electoral processes is established beyond doubt. One has to add a caveat here since the proportion of the electorates who do not cast votes is not negligible; on an average, almost 30 per cent of voters seem to be reluctant to exercise franchise. Nonetheless, it is a matter of great excitement that the number of voters participating in elections is gradually increasing since the first national election, held in 1952. Also, the nature of the issues that govern the voters' choice has also undergone a sea change over the years. Nonetheless, elections have always been espoused as perhaps a time-tested mechanism for the voters to articulate their politico-ideological priorities. There are two complementary reasons that can be offered in support of this contention: on the one hand, for the voters, elections provide them with an opportunity to take part in the processes of selecting the future rulers which they do by casting their votes; elections are also the occasions, on the other, when, by being the sovereign, the electorates decide the fate of the political parties in the fray by casting votes either in their favour or against them.

III

As mentioned above, elections are a litmus test for the political parties to prove which one of them is fit to rule. Besides campaign for votes once the election dates are announced, political parties are involved in various other campaigns in order to remain in the reckoning of the voters. This means that for the political parties, elections are either an endorsement or rejection of what stands for in socio-ideological terms. There are three points that deserve attention here. First, it is true that the future of the political parties is decided supposedly by their activities round the year which means that they should be engaged in activities supportive of the voters' cause. Second, it is also true that during the election, political parties focus on some of the major issues that appeared to have drawn the attention of the voters. For instance, the 2012 death of brutally sexually assaulted Jyoti Singh (also known as Nirbhaya) shall always be raised by the political parties if that gives them political dividends. In the 2014 Lok Sabha poll, the BJP-led NDA included this case as part of its campaign strategy. Third, as the history of Indian elections show, there are some issues that trigger voters' attention to an extent which is unexpected, and the political parties endeavour hard to translate this into votes. There are many examples to substantiate the claim. Hence, it is argued that elections in India are fought on immediate issues since public memory is said to be poor and the voters do not remember the issues of the past (despite their veracity) while casting votes in specific elections. In other words, as public memory is claimed to be poor, those in electoral fray tend to draw on the immediate issues affecting their socio-economic interests.

Before we proceed further, two remarks seem pertinent: on the one hand, elections during this period were fought on the basis of issues that the political parties upheld. As the evidence shows, voters usually made up their mind before 2014 Lok Sabha poll, with the exception of 1971 poll, on the basis of their assessment of both local and national issues. Voters' choice was generally a response to how they reacted to the prevalent issues which they confronted as citizens. In the last two polls, held in 2014 and 2019, respectively, the nature of leadership also mattered to a significant extent in shaping the voters' choice as it happened in the 1970 Lok Sabha poll. A careful study of these elections suggests that the projection of Narendra Modi (the incumbent prime minister) acted favourably for the BJP and its NDA constituents helped a lot in garnering votes in their favour. The image of Modi as a strong leader seems to have convinced majority of the voters to cast votes for the coalition. This was also the case in the 1971 election when the rise of Indira Gandhi as an invincible leader of the country ensured victory for most of the Congress candidates then. That the nature of the leadership is important cannot thus be ruled out. There should be a caveat here. In the first-past-the-post system of voting, winning of the political parties does not necessarily mean winning of the majority of votes. As the proportion of votes for the candidates who had won (and consequently the political parties) clearly shows that the victorious candidates had obtained maximum number of votes in comparison with their competitors, but never had majority of the votes in their favour. To prove this point, one may draw one's attention to the fact that only in 1984 Lok Sabha poll (which was held following the assassination of the incumbent prime minister, Indira Gandhi), Rajiv Gandhi, the son of the slain leader, garnered a record number of seats in the Parliament with approximately 44 per cent of popular votes which is the highest proportion of votes that a political party had amassed. In the last Lok Sabha poll that took place in 2019, the BJP of the ruling NDA coalition received only 33 per cent of total number of votes cast in the election though the leading partner had, in collaboration with its constituents, succeeded in winning almost 60 per cent of parliamentary seats.

So far, 17 national polls have been held. Except the first four elections, between 1952 and 1967, when the Congress Party was returned to power, the rest of the 13 general elections saw new trends. What is striking about the first four elections was the continuity of the Congress Party with Jawaharlal Nehru at its helm, which is attributed to the critical role that the Congress activists had in winning India's independence in 1947. The members of the Congress Party were hailed by the people for their sustained battle for freedom despite adverse consequences which was reflected in their uncritical support to them when they fought in elections. It was, in other words, an expression of gratitude to the Congress activists by the voters, especially to its leader, Jawaharlal Nehru, who was also held in high esteem for his contribution to India's rise as a self-reliant nation by following the Western model. This was widely accepted and so long as Nehru reigned as leader, the Congress Party had comfortably won the national polls. In other words, being viewed as a party that successfully fought the battle for India's political freedom, the Congress Party continued to attract the voters across the length and breadth of the country. For the analysts, the uninterrupted Congress rule was attributed to this sentiment that appeared to have prevailed in India.

The fifth national poll, held in 1971, presented a different scenario in which election to the lower house of Parliament was organized. What mattered most then was Indira Gandhi's slogan of *garibi hatao* for socio-economic improvement of the ordinary Indians. She had won 352 seats out of 441 constituencies in which the Congress Party contested. This was a remarkable achievement for the party that she led especially in the post-Nehru era. The 1971 poll was different from the past election for two complementary reasons: on the one hand, the voters made their preferences for the Congress Party since its leaders assured of removal of poverty of people regardless of region, religion and class which means, on the other, that this was an election in which voters seem to have shifted their concern for their caste identity to hardcore economic gains. The voters' choice was based on what they were likely to gain in the new regime which also created a solid base for the Congress Party and its leader, Indira Gandhi, in India.

The last phase of the Indira Gandhi regime is a history by itself because in 1975, the Congress government imposed Emergency by resorting to Article 356 of the Constitution of India which led to the consolidation of constitutional authoritarianism at the behest of Indira Gandhi and her son with unconditional support of his cohorts. The sixth general election, held in 1977, was a response of the voters against the authoritarian rule that unfolded with the adoption of the Emergency. For the first time, the Congress was ousted, a trend that had begun with the winning of power by the non-Congress political parties in the constituent provinces in the 1967 State Assembly elections. The Janata Party, which was a coalition of the political parties opposed to the Congress, captured power in Delhi. This was a short-lived government; because of the internecine feud among the coalition partners, the Janata Party government collapsed in 1980. What seems to have mobilized the voters against the Congress Party was the excesses of Emergency rule which led to the establishment of an authoritarian regime. So the votes that went in favour of Indira Gandhi did not seem to be, as some of the writers underline, a positive vote for the Janata Party and its constituents, but negative votes for the incumbent government.[11]

There was a reversal in the story; with the disintegration of the Janata Party conglomeration, the government that it led crumbled which necessitated a fresh election in 1980. The Congress Party in its new name Congress (Indira) formed the government in Delhi after having won the election. For her, it was a victory in a platter since the voters did not want political instability which was the case earlier since the government of the Janata Party conglomeration was almost crippled because the constituents had differed from one another on almost all the major policy decisions. So the voters' decision to bring back the Congress Party was governed by their urge for political stability which, they expected, the Congress Party, steered by a strong leader like Indira Gandhi, could easily provide. So the reason was highly pragmatic which resulted in the return of the Congress (Indira) to power in 1980 national poll. Before the completion of the full tenure of five years, Indira was assassinated in 1984 and a fresh election was announced. The 1984 national poll was fought on a sentimental issue, namely the murder of the incumbent prime minister which created a support base for the Congress Party, led by Indira Gandhi's son, Rajiv Gandhi. By securing almost 44 per cent of popular

[11] Ibid.

votes and having won a record number of parliamentary seats (414 out of 533 Lok Sabha constituencies), the Rajiv Gandhi led Congress Party assumed power. The 1980 and 1984 Lok Sabha polls were different in two specific ways: while in 1980, the voters chose the Congress Party since they opted for an alternative which was capable of providing political stability in India. As the Janata Party government failed, the Congress Party emerged as the only messiah for the voters. The 1984 situation was radically different since the election took place following the brutal murder of the prime minister by her security guards. It was a sentiment-driven election which gave enormous dividend to the Congress Party and its leader, Rajiv Gandhi, who was 'a reluctant entrant' to politics as per the media. Nonetheless, under his leadership, the Congress Party not only expanded its sphere of influence but also captured a record of seats in the lower house of the Parliament.

Indian political scene had undergone a sea change in the 1989 national election. For the first time, there were signs that the Nehru–Gandhi dynasty was on the wane. The failure of the Congress to muster a majority led to the rise of the Janata Dal under the leadership of V. P. Singh who held the portfolio of finance during the last Congress regime (1984–1989). Not only did Congress's share of popular votes declined, but it had lost a large number of parliamentary seats. The Janata Dal cobbled up a majority and formed the ministry which had the weaknesses of a collation of ideologically incompatible partners. The prime minister was always busy in sorting out differences among his colleagues who constituted the Janata Dal conglomeration. Instead of devising far-reaching developmental works, the government was busy in examining the Bofors scandal in which the former prime minister, Rajiv Gandhi, was reported to have been involved. Soon, the sordid internal feud that almost completely paralyzed the government came to the surface which led to the resignation of the V. P. Singh led Janata Dal government. Similar to the 1977–1979 non-Congress Janata Party coalition, the Janata Dal government did not survive largely due to the failure of its constituents to sustain the bond among the partners. As a result, what was inevitable had happened and the government resigned which created another occasion for another national poll soon.

The 10th national election ushered in a new era in Indian politics; with the transformation of the language of politics, it was realized that a coalition era appears to have unfolded following the failure of the pan-Indian political parties to muster a majority in the Parliament. In other words, just like West European situation, India also witnessed a new political scene in which neither of the principal political parties succeeded in winning parliamentary seats to cobble up a majority on the floor of Parliament.[12] Much like the 1984 Lok Sabha poll, the 1991 election was also fought under the cloud of an assassination: the killing of Rajiv Gandhi on a campaign train in Sriperumbudur, Tamil Nadu. Although Congress Party's election campaign couched around the sacrifice of the late leader of the party, it did not appear to have swayed the voters in its favour to the extent it had happened in 1984 when the dastardly killing of Indira Gandhi created an unprecedented wave in favour of the Congress and its leader, Rajiv Gandhi. With the winning of Congress candidates in 232 constituencies, the Congress Party was the single largest party in Parliament. P. V. Narasimha Rao (who decided to stay away from politics) emerged as an acceptable leader which led him to be the prime minister when a coalition was forged with the like-minded political parties following the 1991 Lok Sabha poll. The period, 1991–1996, shall be remembered for two important reasons: first, Hindutva rose as an important ideological trend in Indian politics, especially with the demolition of the controversial Babri Masjid in Ayodhya in UP on 6 December 1992; second, this was the period when the Mandal Commission recommendations of 27 per cent reservation for OBCs (accepted in 1989) were implemented leading to mass protest across India. From then, Indian political voices were articulated in the languages of Hindutva and Mandal (that ensured reservation of the majority

[12] Bidyut Chakrabarty has elaborated this theme in his *Forging Power*.

of the population, particularly in public employment and other public benefits).

Following the completion of the tenure of the Narasimha Rao government in 1996, there were four national polls (11th, 12th, 13th and 14th) during the period between 1996 and 2004 in which the non-Congress political parties formed the union government in India. This was also the period which saw the ascendancy of non-Congressism which connotes the coming together of political parties opposed to the Congress for forging a collectivity despite being disparate ideologically. Pragmatism seems to have prevailed over ideological chasms. Before the 2004 national election was held, there were experiments of coalition formation which, however, did not last long; in this phase of experimentation, there had also emerged a conceptual notion of Third Front which refers to a combination of parties bereft of the two pan-Indian political parties, the Congress and its bête noire, the BJP. Although the experiment of the Third Front failed, it was a new endeavour with the idea that without the two major parties, government formation was not impossible. Despite severe public critique of Hindutva, in the 1999 election, it was the BJP and its partners in the NDA which had the majority to form the national government; it was a real coalition government that not only completed its full term of five years but also confirmed the claim that Congress no longer remained as critical to government formation as it was in the past. It lost power in 2004 and another coalition, led by the Congress, known as the UPA, came to power. The Congress-steered government finished its term in 2009 and put its claim for re-election in the 15th Lok Sabha poll, held in 2009.

For the Congress Party and its partners in the UPA, the 2009 election was a cakewalk; the coalition formed the government again. Whether it was a reward for the seemingly pro-people work of the last UPA government is debatable though it will not be an exaggeration to suggest that the voters hardly had a meaningful alternative presumably in view of the fact that the BJP failed to project before them that it was capable of forming a stable government in Delhi. The situation, however, had undergone a sea change following the public exposure of the many scams involving the ministers belonging to the Congress and other UPA partners which made a severe dent in UPA's support base across India. It was manifested with the massive victory of the BJP and its NDA constituents in the 2014 Lok Sabha poll. The government that came into being in 2014 was a coalition government since the leading partner of the NDA, the BJP, did not have a majority on its own which resulted in its dependence on the NDA partners for its survival and continuity.

The 16th Lok Sabha poll, with the victory of the NDA, set in motion processes according a legitimate space to Hindutva which, so far, remained ideologically peripheral, if not hated. Nonetheless, by accepting the 1950 Constitution as supreme and accepting that it was their obligation to sustain the system of constitutional democracy, the BJP government was just an alternative drawing on different ideological predilections. This is not a place to dwell on the nature of Hindutva as an alternative ideological priority.[13] In a nutshell, Hindutva is a politico-ideological viewpoint in which India's indigenous sociopolitical ideas have received adequate importance in shaping the polity which was sadly missing in the past. That BJP's ideological preferences remained effective in sustaining BJP's support base was evident in its victory in a record number of constituencies (323 out 545 Lok Sabha constituencies) in 2019. One must add a caveat here. Although the BJP captured almost 60 per cent of Lok Sabha seats, the party received only 33 per cent of popular votes. The reason needs to be located in the first-past-the-post system of voting in India. Nonetheless, there is no denying the fact that in comparison with those parties (including the Congress Party) opposed to the BJP and the NDA coalition partners, the incumbent political party (namely the BJP) appeared to be invincible in the 17th Lok Sabha poll, held in 2019, presumably because of its positive ideological penetration among

[13] Bidyut Chakrabarty has dealt with this phenomenon in detail in his *Politics, Ideology and Nationalism: Jinnah, Savarkar and Ambedkar versus Gandhi* (New Delhi: SAGE Publications, 2020).

the voters at large and the failure of the opposition to stand united while challenging the ruling coalition.

The above long intellectual journey from the first national poll in 1952 and the 17th Lok Sabha election is an endeavour to show how elections in India are fought and decided. The electoral outcome is the combination of many factors and processes which one needs to take into account to provide a plausible explanation. Above all, the effort should be directed to understand the public mood which swings in accordance with the voters' assessment of the role of the party in power or any of the triggering factors supportive of one of the major contentions that the contestants uphold. For instance, the 2019 surgical strike in Balakot (in Pakistan) terrorist camps by the Indian Air Force instantaneously created a space for the ruling party among those voters who characterized this as India's superior capability over Pakistan and helped the BJP cement a bond with those wavering voters who, so far, remained non-committal. Core here is the point that a contextual analysis is perhaps most plausible though one cannot ignore the importance of the ideology in sustaining a support base for the political parties in the electoral fray regardless of whether it remains in power or in opposition.

IV

The above narrative is a historical account of how elections have unfolded in India since the beginning of her journey as a parliamentary democracy. Apart from providing a seamless commentary, the above discussion also helps us understand the conceptual parameters of electoral democracy that flourished in India following decolonization in 1947. For instance, what is most intriguing is the fact that how does India continue to remain a democratic country where elections act effectively in changing (also retaining) the party in power at regular intervals. Prominent here are two issues: how does one explain the continuity of democracy in India which runs counter of J. S. Mill's proposition that democracy is 'next to impossible' in multi-ethnic societies and completely impossible in linguistically divided countries. This is, therefore, 'a puzzle'[14] for the analysts since democracy is not only a well-entrenched phenomenon in India, it is gaining strength day by day. B. R. Ambedkar, the chairman of the Constitution Drafting Committee, also expressed his apprehension on the continuity, if not success, of democracy in India. According to him, a serious impediment towards establishing democracy was the absence of fraternity which means 'a sense of common brotherhood to all Indians, or, the idea of Indians being one people, an idea which gives unity and solidarity to social life'.[15] It was not possible for India, he argued further, since the divisive caste order was so well entrenched, fraternity was neither instinctive to the Indians nor organic to their psyche. So as long as caste remained, the point about inculcation of a sense of being one as a community seems fruitless. On this basis of this conceptualization, Ambedkar made a very perceptive theoretical formulation which was useful to comprehend Indian socio-economic reality. Since caste was a segregating device, it was 'anti-national [because] in the first place [it] bring about separation in social life and [secondly] because [it] also generates jealousy and antipathy between caste and caste'.[16] Being an obstacle to the building of a sense of fraternity or belongingness, caste was required to be immediately discarded to create and consolidate the sense of brotherhood, lack of which, the fundamental principles of democracy—liberty, equality and fraternity—would be 'no deeper than coats of paint'.[17] Core to his belief was the idea that democratization involved sharing of power among the *demos* regardless of their social and economic locations, besides their political viewpoints. While Ambedkar

[14] Arend Liphart, 'The Puzzle of Indian Democracy: A Constitutional Interpretation', *American Political Science Review* 90, no. 2 (1996): 258–268.

[15] B. R. Ambedkar's speech in the Constituent Assembly on 25 November 1949, *Constituent Assembly Debates*, Book No. 5, 979.

[16] Ibid., 980.

[17] Ibid.

sought to evolve a model of togetherness by striving to erase caste distinctions, his nationalist colleagues, M. A. Jinnah and V. D. Savarkar, deployed precisely the liberal argument supporting the view that a unitary nationhood was necessary for a democratic polity. India was divided and Jinnah's two-nation theory drawing on Muslim's distinctive sociocultural identity justified the creation of Pakistan after India was dismembered.[18] In fact, by justifying the claim for Pakistan for the fear of Muslims not being adequately represented in government, Jinnah defended his argument by drawing on a familiar liberal predisposition, namely representation should not, at all, be restricted on grounds of caste, clan and ethnicity which were essentially constructed forms of identity. Savarkar's Hindutva was less exclusive than what Jinnah proposed for he explained his model of Hindutva in terms genealogical and territorial terms. Here, Hinduism was not conceptualized as a design for narrow identities of those in its fold; instead, it was, as per his conceptualization, a model of togetherness of people appreciative of being in one geographical compact with specific genealogical roots. In other words, the oft-quoted argument that Savarkar's viewpoint is exclusionary does not seem to be plausible given the emphasis that Hindutva remains a blanket and all-pervasive model of being accommodative of communities within a specific geographical space known as Hindustan. Furthermore, there is a need to highlight the contextual roots of this conceptualization; Hindutva was articulated as an antidote to Jinnah's two-nation theory. Savarkar might have highlighted the exclusionary character of Hindutva to gain political mileage at a particular point in India's recent historical past though there exists, at the core of this conceptualization, an endeavour towards building togetherness or brotherhood cutting across social, economic and political barriers. Savarkar's

[18] Hector Bolitho in his *Jinnah: Creator of Pakistan*, reprint (Karachi: Oxford University Press, 2006) and Ayesha Jalal in her *The Sole Spokesman: Jinnah, the Muslim League and the Demand for Pakistan* (Cambridge: Cambridge University Press, 1985) elaborated the processes that finally culminated in the rise of Pakistan as an independent polity.

clear articulated distinction between *pitribhumi* (fatherland) and *punyabhumi* (holy land) is a reiteration of the point that Hindutva is basically a conceptually valid accommodative template since it is about an effort to bring together socioculturally diverse people of Hindustan. It was primarily a meaningful alternative that he designed in specific circumstances when the mainstream nationalism appeared to lose its steam with the consolidation of the Muslims by the Muslim League.

In the Westminster form of democracy that India has adopted after Independence in 1947, election is critical to the formation of the government. Implied here are two important conceptual points: on the one hand, election was accepted by the framers of the 1950 Constitution of India as perhaps the most effective mode of choosing representatives in socioculturally extremely diverse India. With the introduction of universal adult suffrage, the argument that the *demos* would have a chance to express their preferences was most persuasively addressed. From the point of view of the voters, election was, on the other, a device for empowering them and the realization of the argument that ultimately they remained supreme in democracy. Election, thus, created a level playing field where the voters, irrespective of class, clan and ethnicity, could finally meaningfully choose their own representatives. Being a means ensuring democracy to strike roots in India, election is thus characterized as indispensable for democratic governance. That election became very important for the founding fathers was based on their belief that 'the superimposition of democracy ... [was meant] to dissolve other ascriptive identities and create in their stead the new overarching identity of the Indian citizen, equal before the law and equal in political voice'.[19] It was easier said than done given the well-entrenched sociocultural prejudices segregating one section of India's demography from another. By drawing attention of the framers of the Constitution to socially nurtured discriminatory practices, B. R. Ambedkar was also

[19] Niraja Gopal Jayal, ed., 'Introduction' in *Democracy in India* (New Delhi: Oxford University Press, 2001), 24.

terribly perturbed because he knew that mere promulgation of laws against them was hardly effective in bringing about radical socio-economic changes unless it was complemented by endeavours towards transforming the well-entrenched mindset in their favour. A perusal of India's recent political history and how elections were generally fought reveals that the mindset supportive of socio-economic discrimination continued to play a decisive role even today. The contestants generally did not ask for votes by approaching the voters by reference to their caste identities though they usually couched their appeal by intelligently linking the economic backwardness of specific groups of people with their ascriptive status. Although the process was very subtle, it was most effective in cementing a bond among the deprived section of the people belonging mostly to the socio-economically marginalized groups. It has been confirmed by various studies that drew on empirical analysis of how the voters and candidates worked in tandem for ascertaining victory of candidates from specific caste groups. An analyst has, thus, argued that a specific kind of electoral outcome in recent election symbolizes 'a silent revolution' at the grassroots when the hitherto marginalized OBCs exercise a determining influence in shaping the poll results.[20] India's political scene has also undergone a sea change with the shifting of power from the upper-caste Hindus to OBCs which is irreversible since the latter is demographically preponderant in comparison with the former. What is critical here is the idea that without adult franchise and acceptance of democratic election, it would not have been possible for the majority of the population to effectively determine the poll outcome. Significant here is also the point that election is indispensable for democracy to strike roots in Indian polity notwithstanding the apprehension of the classical theorists of liberal democracy, particularly J. S. Mill and his cohorts, that being a multi-ethnic society, India was completely 'unfit' in this regard. Not only has the deep rootedness of India's democracy (despite odds) defied the widely accepted conceptual formulations, the sustenance and consolidation of democracy

[20] Jaffrelot, *India's Silent Revolution*.

in India since the first national election in 1952 provide newer inputs to build conceptually innovative theoretical models of democracy which were inconceivable so long as the ideas of the classical theorists were considered to be axiomatic. So the Indian experiment is a step forward to reconceptualize theories of democracy in the post-colonial perspective in which election is not merely an occasion for casting vote by the voters, but it is also an opportunity for articulating a voice that has hardly received the attention that it deserves.

As argued above, election is a game-changer device in the sense that it also brings about changes in the political guards of a state. Nonetheless, it will be conceptually erroneous to comprehend Indian election with reference to the 'one-size-fits-all' formula since it has clear contextual roots. Implicit here are certain fundamental points that need elaboration: on the one hand, unlike the Western societies, what has evolved in India is 'patronage democracy' in which the fate of candidates is decided not by the ideological appeal of the political party to which they belong but by their ability to accrue benefits for their voters. Next, by implication, it means that the success of the candidates needs to be understood by their ability to patronize the electorates by allowing them access to those benefits that the state provides. It will, therefore, not be possible to understand the voting behaviour, as the argument goes, without reference to this aspect showing how the ability of individual candidates in securing benefits for their voters determine the poll outcome.[21] Reiterating the argument, Jennifer Bussell also underlines the fact that 'constituency service' acts positively in determining how the voters behave while casting their votes in Indian elections. On the basis of her extensive empirical study of voting behaviour in India, she further adumbrates that 'building and maintaining a personal support base is a key underlying incentive for politicians to provide assistance to individual

[21] Kanchan Chandra in her *Why Ethnic Parties Succeed: Patronage and Ethnic Head Counts in India* (Cambridge: Cambridge University Press, 2004) provides a detailed analysis of this theme.

constituents'.[22] A politician's reputation as a responsive representative, she further argues, depends on his/her ability to secure for the voters benefits which the state is expected to extend. In view of unusual bureaucratic entanglement, the voters do not get those benefits easily which allows the politicians to intervene and once they succeed, they invariably refer to this when they come for their votes. It works because the image of a politician of being helpful and attentive to the local needs is generally effective in garnering votes in elections. This appears to be one of the most effective means in generating support for the politicians seeking votes. As Bussell's study shows, the politicians value 'constituency service ... because it allows them to increase their personal vote ... [and] also create valuable opportunities for them to reach persuadable voters directly through individualized assistance'.[23] Implicit is also the argument that although the election decides the fate of the politicians, there are reasons to believe that the poll outcome is also illustrative of their meaningful (or otherwise) roles in extending community services and distributing benefits to the voters which they would not have had access to so easily. It is, therefore, surprising that the politicians in India devote a great deal of effort to providing assistance that their voters have reasons to value; through this, they build their reputation of being responsive which also boosts their electoral chances. Election is, therefore, an occasion which serves as 'an important tool for citizens to hold their representatives to account and [also] for the politicians to establish their claim as responsive representatives'.[24] It is, therefore, a double-edged sword since it allows the voters to judge whether the contestants have fulfilled their expectations or not and it also gives an opportunity to the politicians to establish their claims as most voter friendly in comparison with their competitors in the same constituency.

[22] Jennifer Bussell, *Clients and Constituents: Political Responsiveness in Patronage Democracies* (New Delhi: Oxford University Press, 2019), 228.

[23] Ibid., 226.

[24] Ibid., 333.

Besides election being integral to procedural democracy, it is also a device for assessment by the voters of the politicians. A unique achievement by itself, the sustenance of procedural democracy in India is a distinctive contribution to the theories of democracy. It is now established beyond doubt that democracy in India is firmly rooted which cannot be persuasively explained in the received wisdom of democratic theory. The 1975–1977 Emergency is usually cited as an organized attempt by the ruling party, the Congress, to destroy democracy in India though the 1977 election and the acceptance of defeat by the incumbent ruling party confirm that democracy is integral to Indian polity. B. R. Ambedkar's apprehension notwithstanding, democracy survived the Emergency and continues to remain vibrant even today. Also, the fact that elections are held at regular intervals justifies the contention that democracy in India is momentum day by day. It was a difficult task indeed when the founding fathers opted for democracy presumably because the very idea of the *demos* being sovereign was alien to the Indian psyche. In his assessment of the situation, Babasaheb while attributing the natural unfolding of democracy in India to the absence of equality and fraternity, thus, argued that democracy was unlikely to flourish in a caste-driven hierarchical society because of what Ambedkar characterized as 'the graded inequality'[25] which is a deterrent to the unfolding of democracy in its true spirit and form. Nonetheless, unlike India's neighbours that had the same colonial past, India retains democracy and the ruling authority is changed regularly by the voters by zealously participating in the regularly held elections. This is not a mean achievement. Reasons are plenty.[26] One of the reasons is certainly the consolidation of a mindset among the Indians in support of democracy as perhaps the most effective means of sustaining a polity which is socioculturally highly diverse. That

[25] B. R. Ambedkar's speech in the Constituent Assembly on 25 November 1949, *Constituent Assembly Debates*, Book No. 5, 979.
[26] Ayesha Jalal attempts an explanation in her *Democracy and Authoritarianism in South Asia: A Comparative and Historical Perspective* (Cambridge: Cambridge University Press, 2004).

it is so is evident by the fact that elections take place at regular intervals since India became politically independent in 1947 and people's mandate is acceptable to all parties involved. In other words, the endorsement of election as a definite device to change political party in power is reflective of Indians' socio-psychological inclinations in its favour, as the history of last 17 Lok Sabha polls and many State Assembly elections amply prove.

V

Electoral Dynamism of Indian Politics: Deciphering the Enigma is an analytical statement on the changing nature of national polls held so far. The transformation is visible not only in voters' profile but also in the election campaigns that the contesting political parties undertook to garner votes. The fact that the number of both the candidates and political parties had increased manifold in recent elections as compared with those held in the first four national elections (1952–1967) also substantiates the claim that elections became a widely accepted mode of expressing the voters' choice. Held in 1971, the fifth election was watershed in Indian politics since, for the first time, what appeared to have governed the voters' preferences was the economic agenda of the parties seeking office. As shown above, the Congress supremo, Indira Gandhi's call for removal of poverty struck an emotional chord with the electorates and she had won in 352 constituencies out of the 441 seats that the Congress contested in the 1971 election. This election was also strikingly different in another respect, namely none of the political parties involved in the poll had hardly referred to their contribution to the nationalist struggle which culminated in India's independence in 1947 which means that the nationalist legacy that acted decisively in favour of the Congress no longer remained a meaningful agenda in soliciting votes. The reason is perhaps located in the metamorphosed complexion of voters who did not appear to have been enamoured by what the Congress did to wrest political freedom from the British rule; they had a completely different vision for the country, a country free from poverty, hunger and frustration on account of the spiralling rise of unemployment which Indira Gandhi's slogan for *garibi hatao* (remove poverty) not only captured but also devised a design for inclusive development. Furthermore, the 1971 poll outcome also highlighted the importance of a strong leadership in shaping the voters' choice. There is no doubt that the image of Indira Gandhi being a strong leader acted decisively in securing votes for the Congress faction that she led. It is, therefore, fair to argue that the fifth Lok Sabha poll had ushered in a new era in India's parliamentary democracy. The trend was visible in the 2014 Lok Sabha poll in which the BJP and its NDA partners triumphed. This impressive victory is also attributed to the role that BJP's prime ministerial candidate, Narendra Modi, played in creating an instantaneous support for the conglomeration seeking office. It has, thus, been argued that

> the rise of Narendra Modi as the central figure, around whom the BJP's campaign revolved, made the election something of a plebiscite on the leader rather than a choice of either candidates in constituencies or a new set of political elite. The 'presidential turn' gave a sudden fillip to the to the BJP by infusing new life in the party and enthusing the activists of the party that otherwise looked drifting and listless a year ago.[27]

Just like the fifth Lok Sabha poll, held in 1971, the 2014 national poll had elements of a plebiscite in the sense that voters' preferences were governed by their assessment of the leader who was hailed for being strong and capable of guiding the nation towards its well-being. These two elections were also different, as argued above, because they were apparently fought by the candidates for their leaders who also represented specific ideological priorities that appeared to them to be useful for the

[27] Suhas Palshikar and K. C. Suri, 'Epilogue: Critical Shifts in 2014 Election', in *Electoral Politics in India: Resurgence of the Bharatiya Janata Party*, eds Suhas Palshikar, Sanjay Kumar, and Sanjay Lodha (Oxford: Routledge, 2017), 282.

country at large. What is, however, strikingly similar in these elections was the importance vote banks which are usually conceptualized as groups with specific identity markers. For instance, one of the critical factors that seemed to have swayed the voters in favour of the BJP-led conglomeration in 2014 and 2019 was the claim that the erstwhile political regimes by depending, to a significant extent, on the identity-based vote banks sustained sociocultural schism in India. Furthermore, by providing a persuasive critique of secularism that evolved in India, the Modi-steered NDA characterized this constitutional principle as nothing but 'pseudo secularism' and was a planned design to 'appease' the minority at the cost of the majority. With this argument in place, one is now equipped to suggest that the last two national polls (held in 2014 and 2019) were, besides being plebiscites, an electoral battle in which political parties in the fray couched their campaign strategies around specific ideological priorities as well.

To conclude, India's parliamentary elections are multifaceted since their texture differs from one election to another which means that it is difficult to capture their intricate nature in a single conceptual axis. *Electoral Dynamism of Indian Politics: Deciphering the Enigma* is an endeavour to theoretically comprehend the phenomenon with reference to the contextual peculiarities in which elections in India take place. There are two core points that need elaboration here: on the one hand, it is argued that election is a text, a meaningful text, which articulates how it unfolds in specific historical circumstances while also keeping in mind its roots in the colonial effort. What was introduced in the 1882 Local Self Government Resolution as a design of accommodating the Indians in rural governance through election became gradually acceptable as history has shown. It will not, therefore, be an exaggeration to suggest that election was also a strategy for the Raj to defuse opinions challenging its continuity for it created a group of supporters for the alien rule given their integration with the prevalent system of administration. Notwithstanding its colonial roots, election became, on the other, perhaps the most effective device to dislodge a party in power since it provides the electorates with the authority to choose their representatives in accordance with what they deem appropriate. As the present study has shown, elections are an empowering tool as far as the voters are concerned. Examples can easily be multiplied. Suffice is to say here that being sovereign, the electorates shape the poll outcome in a fashion which also catches the pollsters by surprise. The defeat of Indira Gandhi's Congress in 1977 and BJP's massive victory in 2019 Lok Sabha poll are illustrative of how critical the role of the voters was in determining the poll results which also confirms that democracy has deeper roots in India.

Instead of making a tall claim, this monograph is just a seriously pursued analytical endeavour to fathom the complex nature of India's democracy by reference to 17 national elections held so far. The aim here is to understand how democracy evolved and became integral to India as a polity notwithstanding the fact that it did not even survive in none of her neighbouring countries. That democracy in India is neither magical nor coincidental, but an outcome of complex socio-economic churning which also resulted in the consolidation of a mindset supportive of the *demos'* legitimate role in choosing their rulers by being respectful to their carefully nurtured ideological priorities. Fundamental here are two points which need to be conceptualized at two levels: at the level of the political parties and their leaders, elections are thus a testing time since they are an occasion when those seeking office through democratic means of election publicize what they prefer to do and how if they win. Elections are, in other words, an opportunity for the contestants to present before the voters their preferred set of socio-economic packages for them. At the level of voters, elections provide the electorates with a chance to assess the trustworthiness of the candidates in a situation when many of them are in the fray. It will, therefore, be also an occasion for the voters to comparatively judge the bona fides of the claims that each of the candidates makes to win their confidence. Especially in a multi-party electoral contest, as is the case in India, voters always remain supreme since they determine the fate of the contesting candidates by supporting one as against another.

Elections are, metaphorically speaking, a battle in which political parties are engaged in an organized fight to solicit voters' favour. Because elections are a legitimate device to replace or retain the political guards, they are indispensable for democracy to survive and flourish. Regularly held elections are also indicative of the strength (and otherwise) of the democratic will that surfaces during the elections. As the history of 17 national poll demonstrates, elections continue to remain critical to India's existence as a democratic polity which is unlikely to be reversed given their growing acceptance both by the voters and the political parties as the most effective means for choosing the rulers in accordance with the sociopolitical priorities. Here lies the justification of the claim that elections are a dance of democracy in which both the electorates and those fighting for victory happily participate.

Annexure

The 2021 West Bengal State Assembly Election—Stability versus Change

The high-octane campaign by the contenders in the 2021 West Bengal Legislative Assembly election ended with the resounding victory of the All Indian Trinamool Congress (AITC, hereafter) by almost completely trouncing its immediate rival, the BJP. Besides privileging one political party over the another, this poll also disproves the conceptual validity of the contention of B. R. Ambedkar that electoral democracy in India is 'a top-dressing on an Indian soil which is essentially undemocratic'.[1] The argument appears to have been invalidated with the fact that the voters continue to have unalloyed faith in electoral or political democracy despite the claim that it is not adequate to ensure economic democracy.

[1] B. R. Ambedkar's speech in the Constituent Assembly on 4 November 1948, *Constituent Assembly Debates*, Book No. 2, reprint (New Delhi: Lok Sabha Secretariat, 2009), 38.

Perhaps with this idea in mind, Babasaheb expressed his doubt regarding the success of democracy in India.[2] A scan of earlier Lok Sabha polls and Vidhan Sabha polls reveals that the viewpoints that Ambedkar held appear to have lost their viability given the zealous participation of voters in choosing their rulers after regular intervals. The latest State Assembly election in West Bengal, held in April–May 2021, is, therefore, a continuity of similar behaviour on the part of the electorates despite the fact that economic democracy remains elusive in India even after being politically independent for more than seven decades.

It is easier for a post-mortem analysis of why the AITC had a landslide victory while its bête noire, the BJP, miserably failed. Nonetheless, the outcome helps us understand the reasons that put the AITC ahead of its rival. Before we go into the probable factors explaining the AITC victory in more than 200 constituencies, let us highlight some of the major significant features of this election. First, for the first time in West Bengal's political history, neither the Left Front nor the Congress succeeded in winning a single seat; so the West Bengal State Assembly shall have no representative from both these political outfits. This is also surprising because in the past, both the Left Front and the Congress ruled the state: while the former continued its administration uninterruptedly for 34 years, the latter had reigned supreme almost till 1977 with an interruption of 2 years between 1967 and 1969. The washout of the Left Front and the Congress is attributed to their failure to sense 'the devastating impact of the spread of the BJP's ideological influence [which accounted for] their indifferent attitude to the battle that the [AITC] launched against those championing Hindutva'.[3] Characterizing this miscalculation as 'a historic

---

[2] B. R. Ambedkar, 'Prospects of Democracy in India', reproduced in Vasant Moon, comp., *Dr. Babasaheb Ambedkar Writings and Speeches*, vol. 17, pt. 3 (New Delhi: Dr. Ambedkar Foundation, 2014).

[3] Dipankar Bhattacharya who heads the Communist Party of India (Marxist–Leninist) unit in India wrote this in his newspaper essay entitled 'Another Historical Blunder', *The Telegraph*, Kolkata, 6 May 2021.

blunder',[4] it is further argued that sooner the intensity of BJP's ideological impact is clearly understood, it will be better for the progressive forces seeking to build a genuine democratic polity in India. Implicitly, the argument pursued by the hardcore radical Left is also an attempt to suggest that under the present circumstances, the support to the AITC is needed to halt the far more dangerous BJP. Second, for the first time, the entire national leadership of the BJP was involved in the poll campaign in West Bengal; not only did Prime Minister Narendra Modi, Home Minister Amit Shah and some of the chief ministers from the BJP-ruled provinces take part in the campaign, the BJP national president, J. P. Nadda, also devoted his energy for mobilizing voters by addressing many election rallies and organizing many roadshows in various parts of the state. This is a rare phenomenon since as history shows, the state elections are usually managed by the state units of the political party, especially of the pan-Indian parties. Third, the highly impressive win of the AITC candidates also confirms that in West Bengal, the party has a base in rural areas which did not appear to have dissipated due to the sustained campaign of the opposition parties, including the BJP. Although the victorious party gained enormously in Kolkata and semi-urban towns, its performance in the villages is equally scintillating. Fourth, the claim that the RSS developed organic linkages with the villagers in West Bengal did not seem to have succeeded in translating support to the Sangh into votes. What it also suggests is the claim that the RSS organizational network may not have been as widespread or well entrenched as is assumed. In its place, the role of the grassroots workers of the AITC was far more effective in garnering votes for the party than their counterparts in other contending political forces. Finally, the poll results also substantiate an age-old dictum that what matters are the appeal of the contextual issues and the familiar faces seeking votes for specific parties. In other words, it is difficult to persuade a voter in West Bengal by reference to those issues which

[4] Ibid.

are useful in creating a base for a contestant in, for instance, the Hindi heartland or in the south of India. The issues are required to be context driven and contextually meaningful. For instance, the slogan 'Jai Shri Ram' may be adequate to generate electoral support for an organization in UP or Bihar, but it will have no or very little impact among the voters in West Bengal presumably because the idea of Ram has hardly an emotional connect with the Bengalis at large as compared to North India. Furthermore, the failure of the BJP to project a possible candidate as the chief minister was also a weakness; during the campaign, despite repeated queries by the media, the BJP avoided responding in this regard which meant that the party fought the election with Narendra Modi as its face. This is likely to succeed at the national level but at the state level, it is remotely possible. In West Bengal, by being the chief minister who is fondly addressed as *Didi* (elder sister), Mamata Banerjee created a space for herself as one who will fight for the Bengalis against any odd. Hence, a slogan was coined, 'Bengal wants her daughter, Mamata', which worked favourably in defending the claim that with her as the chief minister, the state shall have a competent head of government. In this respect, the BJP lagged behind; furthermore, with the BJP preferring candidates from outside West Bengal in a large number of constituencies, the AITC claim that the outsiders would rule the province if the BJP is elected gained ground. For majority of the voters, it amounted to the demeaning of Bengali dignity and the charge that the BJP was parachuting candidates from outside West Bengal was readily accepted as creditable. One is tempted to draw a parallel with what the erstwhile prime minister, Indira Gandhi, did which finally destroyed the organic connection that the party leadership had with the grassroots workers in the bygone days. By selecting chief ministers according to her choice, she annoyed many Congressmen in the organization and activists at the grassroots. For instance, the Congress decision to retain Siddhartha Shankar Ray as the Congress leader in the 1977 assembly poll was largely responsible for its dismal electoral performance in the election.

As the available proportion of the share of popular votes shows, after the Sitalkuchi death because of the firing by the paramilitary forces, BJP's popularity considerably waned: in the sixth, seventh and the last phase, the share of votes for the AITC and the BJP was 47.8 per cent and 38.4 per cent, 52.1 per cent and 32.8 per cent, and 52.2 per cent and 32.3 per cent, respectively. What it confirms is that difference in the share of votes between the BJP and the AITC was 9.4 per cent, 19.2 per cent and 19.9 per cent in the sixth, seventh and eighth phase, respectively. This was reflected in the massive dwindling in the number of assembly seats for these two principal contenders. There are, therefore, reasons to believe that this incident was one of the principal reasons for a clear vote swing away from the BJP to the AITC. The astounding victory of the AITC in most of the constituencies where election took place after the fourth phase is a testimony to this claim.

What is attempted here is not a clinical analysis of the election outcome but a conceptual evaluation of voting behaviour with reference to the probable factors that shaped the voters' decision to choose one party against another. There is no doubt that because of their acceptability to the voters, the AITC candidates won rather comfortably which, in fact, was not expected by the candidates themselves. Broadly speaking, the charge of the BJP being an outsider and, thus, a threat to West Bengal's distinct sociocultural characteristics seems to have created a support base for BJP's rival, the AITC; besides, the grievance of BJP's local workers that they were marginalized by the candidates and their minions was not persuasively addressed by the top leadership. There were some of the major reasons for BJP's disappointing performance. In contrast, AITC's endeavour at involving even the booth-level workers gave electoral dividends; in some of the constituencies in North Bengal, the RSS, by spreading its tentacles in remote villages, laid an organizational network which helped the BJP candidates win the election although this was not possible throughout the state presumably because of paucity of time in creating a base for the politico-ideological views that the BJP represented in comparison with its main rival.

| | **TABLE A.1** | *Poll Performance of the Contending Political Parties in 2021 and 2016* | |

Party	Seats Won in 2021 Election	Seats Won in 2016 Election[a]
AITC	213 (47.9%)	209 (44.9%)
BJP	77 (38.1%)	3 (10.1%)
Independent	1 (0.09%)	
Rashtriya Secular Majlis Party (RSMP)	1 (0.10%)	
Total	292[b]	

Sources: For the figures of 2016 State Assembly election, see *The Times of India*, Kolkata, 5 May 2021.

For the figures of 2021 election, see https://results.eci.gov.in/Result2021/partywiseresult-S25.htm?st=S25 (accessed on 25 May 2021).

Notes: [a]The Left Front obtained 32 seats, while the Congress won in 44 constituencies in the 2016 State Assembly election.

[b] Voting for two seats remained suspended due to the death of the candidates.

Figures in parenthesis show the share of votes.

As Table A.1 shows, the BJP is nowhere near the AITC though it has increased its tally from just 3 assembly seats in 2016 to 77 in the 2021 assembly election. It was not a mean achievement given the fact that West Bengal has always been a citadel of non-BJP political parties. The outcome also underlines that in terms of share of popular votes, the AITC is far ahead with an increase from 44.9 per cent (in 2016) to 47.9 per cent in 2021; in terms of seats, the party has added two more seats in 2021 than what it had obtained in 2016. Despite not having succeeded in winning the magic number of seats, the BJP has not only increased its tally of seats from just 3 to 77 in this election, but it has made an impressive gain in its share of popular votes: from just 10.1 per cent of popular votes in 2016, the BJP is now widely spread out by winning 38.1 per cent of popular votes. What is striking is also to note that despite having constituted more than half of the total voters in the state, there are only 40 women members in the newly formed State Assembly which is just 14 per cent of the total of assembly seats.

Analysis of the Poll Outcome

A post-mortem of election results does not seem to be difficult because the factors that appear to have swayed the voters can easily be identified. It is true that the anti-incumbency sentiments of the voters were believed to have alienated them from the AITC which was effectively addressed by the mechanism that the technical expert team, led by Prashant Kishore, devised. Two effective designs seem to have done miracle and brought the disgruntled voters, especially in rural West Bengal, to the AITC: one was *duare sarkar* (government at your footsteps) and the other was *Didike bolo* (inform Didi). These two creatively devised administrative designs generated a sense of being empowered which defused the anti-incumbency sentiments to a significant extent. These were micro-level interventions which had their macro-level manifestation in the regular visit of the chief minister to the districts along with the top administrators. This was a unique design of governance which worked well to sustain the image of the chief minister being close to the people in areas away from the state capital, Kolkata. The design worked in two complementary ways: on the one hand, those in districts had a chance to place before the administration the difficulties they underwent presumably because of the lackadaisical attitude of the district authorities; the endeavour gave, on the other, an opportunity to the chief minister and her team to get a first-hand report of the lacuna in governance there. These regular trips to the districts created and consolidated the view that this government meant business and the two later mechanisms—*duare sarkar* and *Didike bolo*—supported the chief minister's vision for radical administrative transformation in the province. As the poll results underline, the voters' confidence that the government was keen to meaningfully address their socio-economic concerns was evident when they voted the AITC back to power notwithstanding the all-out effort of its main contender, the BJP.

Some of the Distinctive Features

The 2021 Vidhan Sabha vote stands out because except in North Bengal, AITC's victory is the most impressive. In other words, while the BJP trailed the AITC by some distance in most parts of West Bengal, it did extremely well in North Bengal, winning comfortably in most of the constituencies. The Left Front and the Congress failed miserably there and in Bardhaman, Murshidabad and Malda regions where they had their best electoral performance in the 2016 election, as Table A.2 shows.

Not only did the AITC perform well in Kolkata and other towns, its tally of seats in rural West Bengal also surpassed in comparison with the number of seats that it had captured in the 2016 assembly poll. It was an all-out victory and the opposition, especially the BJP, was almost decimated in some of the rural constituencies, as Table A.3 demonstrates.

One of the major factors responsible for the AITC landslide victory is the massive support of the Muslim voters which means that they were persuaded to believe that the party was capable

TABLE A.2 *Performance of the Contending Political Parties in Selective Areas, 2021 Election*

Party	Bardhaman	Jangal Mahal	North Bengal	Greater Kolkata
AITC	46 (47.8%)	33 (46.1%)	05 (41.1%)	93 (49.9%)
BJP	08 (39.9%)	23 (43.7%)	21 (48.1%)	14 (34.9%)
Left Front	00 (0.9%)	00 (0.9%	00 (0.5%)	00 (0.7%)
Congress	00 (3.2%)	00 (3.1%)	00 (3.1%)	00 (2.8%)

Source: The Times of India, Kolkata, 5 May 2021.
Note: Figures in the parenthesis show the share of popular votes.

| | **TABLE A.3** | Performance of the Contending Parties in Rural West Bengal, 2021 | | |

Party/Alliance	Rural (156 Seats) Seats	Semi-urban (65 Seats) Seats	Urban (71 Seats) Seats
AITC	117 (48.9%)	45 (46.8%)	52 (48.2)
BJP	38 (38.1%)	20 (39.9%)	19 (37.2)
Left + Congress + ISF	1 (9.7%)	00 (.6%)	00 (11.1%)
Others	00 (3.5%)	00 (3.7%)	00 (3.5%)

Source: The Times of India, Kolkata, 5 May 2021.
Note: Figures in the parenthesis show the share of popular votes.

| | **TABLE A.4** | Performance of the Contending Parties in Muslim Pockets, 2021 |

Party/Alliance	Constituencies Where There Is a Sizeable Muslim Presence (141 Seats) Seats	Constituencies Where the Proportion of Muslim Voters Is Low (151 Seats) Seats
AITC	119 (50.7%)	95 (46.1%)
BJP	21 (35.1%)	56 (41.3)
Left + Congress + ISF	1 (11.1%)	00 (0.9%)
Others	00 (3.4%)	00 (3.7%)

Source: The Times of India, Kolkata, 5 May 2021.
Note: Figures in the parenthesis show the share of popular votes.

of defending their socio-economic and political interests despite the threat of the application of the Citizenship Amendment Act. There are constituencies where they en bloc cast their votes in favour of the candidates presumably because of AITC's success in generating confidence in them, as Table A.4 shows.

TABLE A.5 *Performance of the Contending Parties in Constituencies Where the SC and ST Voters Have Significant Presence, 2021*

Party/Alliance	General (208 Seats)	SC Constituencies (68 Seats)	ST Constituencies (16 Seats)
AITC	169 (49.2%)	36 (46.2%)	9 (45.2%)
BJP	38 (36.2%)	32 (42.8%)	7 (44.1%)
Left + Congress + ISF	1 (11.1%)	00 (7.8%)	00 (5.8%)
Others	00 (3.6%)	00 (3.1%)	00 (4.9%)

Source: *The Times of India*, Kolkata, 5 May 2021.
Note: Figures in the parenthesis show the share of popular votes.

The narrative, however, is little different in constituencies where a sizeable section of the population belongs to the SCs because here the BJP did relatively better. That the AITC did not succeed in mobilizing voters as it did elsewhere in West Bengal is evident if we draw our attention to the number of seats at its disposal, as Table A.5 underlines.

In comparison with the AITC success in SC constituencies, the BJP performed relatively better in the ST constituencies which is also a source of satisfaction for the workers who campaigned vigorously for the victory of their candidates. That hardly changed the overall scene because the BJP also lost ground in tribal-dominated districts, such as Jhargram, Bankura, Purulia and West Medinipur where it had performed better in the 2019 Lok Sabha poll.

A careful perusal of the above statistical figure justifies the argument that not only did the AITC enhance its tally of Vidhan Sabha seats, but it had also increased its share of popular votes in every segment of the demography. The AITC victory may not always have been the outcome of the performance of the government for the last one decade; it was also an off-shoot of anti-BJP sentiments that were carefully cultivated and translated into votes. As a result, the general exhortation, no vote to the BJP, worked favourably for the AITC candidates. It was thus easier for the AITC supremo to pursue the anti-BJP agenda and her mission of fighting the Modi–Shah machine was 'almost entirely due to the fact that she is the grassroots Rabindra Sangeet singing, *Chandipath* reciting Bengali leader and her roots in Bengal are deep [which further means that her] local connectedness ... gives her staying power against a formidable opponent'.[5] It was visible starkly when she visited a temple before filing her nomination for the Nandigram constituency. The idea is very clear: by being in a temple, she hit two birds with one stone; it firmly established her concern for being emotionally connected with the local people and it was also a powerful counter to BJP's charge that the AITC supremo had no inkling for Hindu sentiments. This was a new phenomenon because Mamata Banerjee undertook several steps to put across the views that her so-called policy of Muslim appeasement never stood against her commitment to the Hindus. Her visit to the famous Kali temple in Kolkata just before taking oath as the chief minister of West Bengal on 5 May 2021 is also another calculated move to reiterate that she is equally sensitive to the Hindu ethos. Here, one notices a pattern vis-à-vis elections in the provinces. In every state election, there is hyper-localization, even municipalization of issues and while championing the local needs, the local satraps are unleashing anti-Delhi rhetoric presumably to gain electoral dividends.

Explaining the Landslide Victory

AITC's landslide victory is attributed to a massive vote swing in its favour in a situation when the pan-Indian BJP plunged into the campaign with all its resources. With the publication of the poll results, one is now in a position to identify the constituencies of support for the AITC. *First*, one of the main factors

[5] Sagarika Ghose, 'Regional Boss as Challenger', *The Times of India*, 21 April 2021.

for the massive win of the AITC candidates was the support of the women voters. As per the available inputs, women voters for the AITC constituted almost 53 per cent, while their male counterparts had a share of 43 per cent.[6] The schemes such as Kanyashree and Rupashree granting funds for education and marriage, Sabooj Sathi giving cycles to the school-going female students and financial assistance to them generated a belief among them that the government was in their favour. To this was added Swasthya Sathi giving medical insurance to all irrespective of sex to the tune of ₹30 lakh (3 million). In order to extend more women-centric benefits, the 2021 AITC election manifesto also assures delivery of ration at the doorstep and monthly basic income of ₹500–₹1,000 to the families being run by the women. Undoubtedly, this was one of the reasons for retaining the women supporters to the AITC fold. It is, however, nothing new as history shows. In 2016 assembly election, 52 per cent of AITC voters were women; even in the 2019 Lok Sabha poll when the BJP wrested 19 out of 42 Lok Sabha seats, 51 per cent of the AITC voters were women. *Second*, the massive support of the Muslim voters also ensured the thumping majority for the AITC. With 30 per cent of the total West Bengal demography, Muslims constitute a significant section of the population. In more than one-third of total number of assembly seats of 294, located in the district of Kolkata, Murshidabad, Malda and North and South Dinajpur, the decisive importance of Muslim votes cannot be ignored. By winning most of the seats in these districts, the AITC again proved that the schemes that the erstwhile government devised for the Muslim acted favourably. By openly condemning the BJP as an anti-Muslim political party, the AITC, especially its supremo, Mamata Banerjee, generated confidence among the Muslims which was translated into votes when their opportunities came. It is evident in the vote share of the AITC in districts such as West Medinipur, Hooghly and Nadia where over 60 per cent of the population is Hindu. The incumbent ruling party's

[6] Data reproduced from *Ananda Bazar Patrika*, 5 May 2021.

TABLE A.6	Share of Votes (in Percentages) of the AITC and the BJP in Selective Districts (Where Muslims Constitute a Sizeable Section of the Population)

Districts	Kolkata	Murshidabad	Jhargram	North Dinajpur	Malda
AITC	60.4	53.4	53.1	52.8	52.5
BJP	29.9	23.8	37.1	37.1	32.5

Source: The *Telegraph*, Kolkata, 7 May 2021.

TABLE A.7	Share of Votes (in Percentages) of the AITC and the BJP in Selective Districts (Where Hindu Voters Are Preponderant)

Districts	Darjeeling	Cooch Behar	East Medinipur	Alipurduar	Jalpaiguri
AITC	28.1	44.4	46.7	42.2	43.1
BJP	49.1	49.1	46.8	46.9	46.1

Source: The *Telegraph*, Kolkata, 7 May 2021.

decisive victory in most of the districts is illustrative of Mamata Banerjee's promise of preserving the inclusive tradition of West Bengal, as Table A.6 shows.

The trend is identical in some of the other districts as well, such as East Bardhaman, North Dinajpur, South 24 Parganas, Birbhum and Howrah, where Muslims constitute 20 per cent of the total demography; the AITC bagged more than half of the vote share despite the high-octane campaign of its rival, the BJP.[7] The story, however, remains incomplete unless it is mentioned that the BJP also succeeded in persuading a majority of the voters in its favour in some of the districts where majority of the Hindus stood by the party. Table A.7 is illustrative of the same.

[7] *The Telegraph*, Kolkata, 7 May 2021.

As the figures show, BJP's electoral performance in these districts was relatively impressive though in the final tally of seats in the 2021 assembly poll, it lagged behind the magic number. This is also a justification for the argument that there are reasons to believe that the BJP retained its support base in the above-mentioned districts which helped retain the confidence of the grassroots workers who worked hard to bring about political transformation in the province. *Third*, BJP's hope of uniting SCs and STs also remained unrealized. The visit of the prime minister to Bangladesh, especially to Orakandi, the seat of the founder of Matua Mahasangha, also failed to woo the Muslim voters or the voters belonging to the Matuas, a SC community, who had considerable presence in North and South 24 Parganas and Nadia. *Fourth*, the firm belief that those who defected from the AITC would win also did not come true. Instead, they were condemned as opportunists. Out of a total 107 candidates (who joined the BJP from other parties, including the AITC), only 31 of them managed to win. Almost all the top-ranking former AITC leaders failed to sway the voters except Mihir Goswami from Natabari (Cooch Behar), Tanmoy Ghosh from Bishnupur (Bankura), Partha Sarathi Chatterjee of Ranaghat North-West (Nadia) and Suvendu Adhikari of Nandigram (Purba Medinipur). The excessive importance the BJP leadership paid to those who came from the AITC and other political parties alienated many of the BJP activists at the grassroots since they felt humiliated with this kind of strategy. Furthermore, the fielding of film stars as candidates in election also did not give dividends to the party presumably because they hardly had an organic connect with the grassroots people; their star value was of use to gather people in election meetings and rallies though it was not adequate to win a seat in the assembly. Despite the failure of the film stars to win for the BJP, the comfortable victory of their counterparts in the AITC also confirms that the Bengali voters chose them because they fought against the BJP which further means the failure of Hindutva to strike roots in West Bengal. *Fifth*, The sudden surge of the second wave of COVID-19 seem to have had a role in the massive loss of the BJP. It is believed that the election that had begun on 27 March witnessed aggressive campaign by both the BJP and the AITC in the first five phases which ended on 17 April. The BJP brought all the star campaigners, including Prime Minister Modi, Home Minister Amit Shah, Chief Minister Yogi Adityanath and many ministers of the union cabinet to solicit the voters' support. However, the second wave of the pandemic attack led to the cancellation of the open meeting that Modi and Shah were slated to address which probably gave the BJP a jolt since an opportunity was lost to the party to approach the voters with its most effective campaigners. It is true that the prime minister addressed the voters virtually; but that, for obvious reasons, had not had the effect of his personal appearance before the West Bengal voters. While the BJP had a disadvantage, by engaging the voters in many roadshows and public meetings, Mamata reaped the electoral dividends. In other words, the failure of the BJP to continue with the aggressive campaigns with their top and effective leaders sealed their fate in a large number of constituencies in the last three phases of the poll.

Sixth, it was believed that the Left–Congress and the Indian Secular Front (ISF) combine was likely to be a formidable opposition to the TMC and the BJP. It was also emphasized that the ISF, given its specific religious inclination, was certain to draw a large number of Muslim voters to its fold, while the Congress and the Left were believed to have had the capacity to draw the secular voters in the election. However, none of the assumptions came true. The decline of the Congress has a wider ramification. Now, there exists no pan-Indian party, which means that the BJP has effectively no national-level challenger with a pan-Indian presence. In future, one is likely to see a coalition of regional parties to challenge the BJP hegemony at the national level. But as experience shows, whether it will be a tangible alternative is a difficult question to respond. Finally, the 2021 West Bengal election also highlighted that the language used in the campaign had a significant effect on the voters' preferences. In three ways, it worked. *First*, the Bengalis did not appear to have endorsed BJP's national leadership to guide the campaign which supported the claim of the AITC of the BJP being outsider in the state. The provincial leaders remain decipher or, worse, merely the executioner of the order given by the central leadership. It was a source of irritation to many of the grassroots workers, especially among those belonging to the RSS. Their grudge was based on the fact that those who worked longer for the BJP had no place in the key decisions, while those who defected from the AITC received undue preferences. It is true that they did not completely withdraw from the campaign but they were suspected not to have devoted their energies for the campaign to the extent it was expected. So the internal dissatisfaction was one of the reasons why the BJP candidates did not receive support from the activists, especially in areas other than North Bengal. *Second*, the endeavour towards approaching one community against another did not auger well with the Bengali sensibilities despite the fact that Bengal suffered most, along with Punjab, as a result of the 1947 vivisection of British India. In other words, the appeal couched in Hindu–Muslim schism never became as effective as it was assumed by the central leadership of the BJP presumably because of its failure to comprehend the complex nature of the Bengali mindset. It is true that there may have been underlying differences between Hindus and Muslims or caste Hindus and the so-called untouchables, but it was never championed in the open as it was the case in northern and southern parts of the country. So BJP's campaign style was ill-equipped to address the concern that the Bengalis naturally evinced. During the campaign, an issue gained momentum. The decision of the UP government to ban Durga Puja in the province but to continue with the celebration of Ram Navami was cited frequently to put across the message that the BJP rule meant discontinuity of the main festival of the Bengalis, namely Durga Puja. That it worked can be proved because for the Bengalis, Durga Puja is less of a religious festival and more of a sociocultural event that brings them together during the celebration of the Puja. For the AITC, it was a powerful whip to take away many of the Hindu voters from the BJP fold. Despite having realized that this caused a severe dent to the Hindu voters, the BJP ideologues did not appear to have undertaken measures to scuttle the AITC campaign affecting adversely their support base. *Third*, there is no denying that the general sympathy of the voters helped Mamata Banerjee to create a strong support base for the AITC. In the first place, her image of being a lonely fighter against the forward march of the BJP juggernaut was enough to consolidate the anti-BJP voice in the election. She was appreciated, as the media report shows, for her courage to take on the aggressive campaign at the behest of BJP's star campaigners, such as the prime minister and home minister. Second, Mamata Banerjee's fractured leg helped her gain sympathy from the voters. She sustained leg injury on 10 March when she went to her constituency in Purba Medinipur, Nandigram, as the heavy door of her bulletproof car hit her before she could get inside the car; it was merely an accident that was caused because of the inadvertent failure of her security staff though the AITC claimed that it was a deep-rooted conspiracy of the BJP to kill the party's supremo. It was, however, proved later that the accusation was false as the doctors attending her certified that the ligament of leg was torn when the heavy door of the car hit her. Nonetheless, this was an incident which was magnified in the election speeches by the supremo and her colleagues. What was striking was her decision to participate in all the campaign meetings with plaster in her left leg which was likely to have created sympathy for her.

Sociocultural Factors

No analysis of the poll outcome supportive of AITC's landslide victory remains plausible unless one is drawn to the critical role of sociocultural factors in shaping the voting behaviour of the Bengalis. AITC's win is attributed to the fact that the Bengalis' dislike of the BJP ensured the astounding victory. It is well-elaborated by one of the erstwhile BJP ideologues, Sudheendra Kulkarni, who was associated with the former BJP prime minister, Atal Bihari Vajpayee. In an editorial piece in one of the leading Kolkata-based newspaper, *The Telegraph*, of 4 May 2021, Kulkarni defended the contention by drawing on his own experience of being in Kolkata during his two-month stay in the city during the eight phases of the 2021 election. In order to illustrate his point, he refers to his discussion with many non-party Bengali intellectuals and activists who 'dreaded the prospect of the BJP coming to power and tearing apart the secular fabric of Bengali society with its Hindu supremacist ideology'.[8] Hence, they devoted their energies 'to puncture the hubris of Modi and Shah'[9] since that was the only way to sustain the sociocultural milieu in which West Bengal as a unit of India flourished. The argument was defended further by suggesting that they were encouraged to mobilize votes for the AITC out of 'their deep-concern for Bengal's distinctive heritage which has been enriched by giants like Rabindranath Tagore, Nazrul Islam, Swami Vivekananda and Netaji Subhas Bose, to name a few [and] must not be allowed to be destroyed by the BJP's alien Hindutva invasion'.[10]

On a surface reading of the argument, one may be persuaded to believe that it was the secular image of the AITC in contrast with the BJP which helped build a solid vote bank for the winning outfit. Hence, the exhortation that no vote to the BJP created a strong base for the AITC since it was interpreted by the voters that a vote to any of the other contender was not going to make a difference. Furthermore, it was also believed that by casting vote in favour of the AITC, the voters also participated in a sociocultural mission of retaining West Bengal's distinctive existence in contrast with those provinces supportive of religious and caste polarization among the citizens. A deeper comprehension of the contention, however, reveals that the above argument is vacuous. It is true that the BJP succeeded in winning only 77 assembly seats, way behind the magic number of 148, it is also true that the AITC enhanced both seats in the Legislative Assembly and the share of popular votes. There is

[8] Sudheendra Kulkarni, 'Modi's Waterloo: Can Mamata Banerjee Become the First Bengali Prime Minister?', *The Telegraph*, Kolkata, 4 May 2021.
[9] Ibid.
[10] Ibid.

also the other side of the story: in comparison with BJP's tally of only 3 assembly seats with only 10.1 per cent of the popular votes in 2016 State Assembly poll, this pan-Indian political party has increased its seats by more than 25 times (77 seats) and almost 4 times of its vote share (39%). From this point of view, the increase of both seats and share of popular votes by the AITC is incremental (just 4%), while its rival has succeeded in augmenting its seat share and popular votes significantly. Moreover, in most of the constituencies, the margin of loss of the BJP candidates did not seem striking and the fact that they came second in these constituencies also helps make the argument that the BJP was rejected outrightly as some of the commentators seem to wrongly believe. What is most revealing is the fact that the Left conglomeration that had a share of 76 seats in the earlier Vidhan Sabha with 39 per cent of the popular votes disappeared from the scene. The Congress–Left–ISF combine had won only one seat that too belonged to the religious ISF. What does it mean? It is crystal clear that the BJP was accepted as a formidable alternative in West Bengal despite the widely hyped criticism that it was certain to severely damage the so-called secular fabric of the province. There is substance in the argument that the predominant role of BJP's central leadership may have adversely challenged the Bengali *ashmita* (pride, self-esteem) which failed to cement a bond among the voters searching for an alternative to the erstwhile AITC government that considerably lost its base presumably because of the emergence of the corrupt leaders and the failure of the top leadership to control the mafia within the party. Furthermore, BJP's impressive victory in a state where it was almost non-existent in the 2016 assembly poll is a testimony to the claim that it is no longer as socioculturally ostracized as it was felt when the campaign started. Hindutva is no longer an anathema to the Bengalis; even the AITC resorted to many Hindu symbols to strengthen its support base among the Hindus. For instance, the fact that the AITC supremo, Mamata Banerjee, recited the hymns from the Hindu religious text, *Chandi*, shows that she could not afford to ignore the Hindu sensibilities in this election. It is also to the credit of the BJP that Leftism no longer remains ideologically effective to draw the voters by itself; the Left Front was, thus, not hesitant to join hand with its arch-enemy, the Congress, and ideologically polar opposite, the ISF. So for the sake of winning assembly seats, it was not an impediment for the Left Front to hobnob with forces which were politico-ideologically contrary to what they espoused by being committed to Marxism. Even the coalition with a conglomeration of which the communal ISF was a constituent was readily accepted notwithstanding the murmur at the grassroots activists in rural Bengal. So for the Leftists, it was accepted because the strategy was expedient and was useful for capturing power. The AITC did not seem to be much different; for winning assembly seats, it also resorted to the steps that, despite being sectarian, were readily accepted due to political exigency. By agreeing to grant stipend to the Hindu priests, the AITC supremo can be said to have devised a means to draw the Hindus who were visibly upset with her many policy designs seeking to appease the Muslims.

The 2021 assembly election is thus a watershed in West Bengal recent political history in two ways: on the one hand, the poll outcome shows that the AITC devised strategies to counter the anti-incumbency sentiments despite genuine grievances of voters at large. With the decimation of the Left that ruled West Bengal for more than three decades, the BJP has successfully created, on the other, a support base by being true to Hindutva as an ideological priority. That the BJP with its commitment to Hindutva has carved a space in West Bengal is not a mean achievement in a situation where the muscle power and various kinds of sordid efforts were encouraged to completely liquidate the opposition. There are evidences to show that West Bengal has recently become a violence-prone state which, of course, is alien to her sociocultural fabric. The post-election vendetta, especially in rural areas in the state, is a cause of concern because, to quote the famous Gandhian warning, 'an eye for an eye will make the entire world blind'. The sooner it is understood, it is better for West Bengal that suffered first due to the 1947 dismemberment and later with the outbreak of the

Left-wing extremism leading to the innumerable loss of innocent human lives. Unless the self-defeating politico-ideological designs are effectively countered, the Bengali *ashmita* shall always remain a casualty so long as it is not internalized and concerted attempts are not made to translate it into practice not merely during the elections but also to make it integral to West Bengal's sociocultural milieu.

Concluding Observations

The 2021 West Bengal State Assembly election confirms that each of the provinces in federal India has its own socio-economic and politico-ideological dynamics that need to be understood to explain the poll outcomes. As the poll outcome demonstrates, BJP's effort at polarizing the Bengalis around the caste or religious axes did not work out in its favour. The situation would probably have been different in any of the provinces in the Hindi heartland. For instance, a perusal of the past election results establishes the argument that in UP or Bihar, neither the regional nor the pan-Indian political parties had ever stayed away from approaching the voters either in terms of their caste or religious identity. The activities of the SP in UP, the RJD and the Janata Dal (United) in Bihar during the elections are illustrative here. West Bengal cannot be said to be entirely free in this respect since along with the BJP, the AITC also adopted various steps to assuage the Hindu sentiments. Not only did the AITC supremo visited many Hindu temples during the campaign, but she also announced stipend to the Hindu priests just like what she agreed to provide monthly allowances to the imams and muezzins as the chief minister of the erstwhile AITC governments.

As the above analysis confirms, elections in West Bengal were between 'two big narratives: Hindu–Muslim versus West Bengal–Delhi'.[11] Through her successful poll management,

[11] Asim Ali, 'The Big National Takeaway', *The Times of India*, 3 May 2021.

Mamata Banerjee geared the electoral outcome in her favour; what explains AITC's astounding poll victory was the ability of the party ideologues to creatively amalgamate the politics of regional pride with the multiple welfare schemes that the government adopted to ameliorate the conditions of the majority of West Bengal's demography. In comparison with its earlier tally of just 3 seats in the last West Bengal Assembly, the BJP did exceedingly well though it failed to reach the magic figure of 148 seats in the Vidhan Sabha. The reasons are not difficult to identify: first, the expectation that the Left–Congress–ISF coalition caused a split in Muslim votes did not come true which meant that the Muslims voted en bloc for the AITC. So the failure of the conglomeration to divide the Muslim voters allowed the AITC to win in most of the constituencies where Muslim voters constituted a significant portion of the demography. Second, the alienation of the Muslim voters largely due to the abusive attack by the BJP leaders had also contributed to their consolidation for the AITC as an expression of protest. It was to the credit of the AITC supremo that the women voters cutting across class, caste and religion stayed with the party which was also the case in the 2016 assembly election. By adopting many pro-women policies, the government not only created but also consolidated support by implementing them in the true spirit. Finally, the endeavour of the BJP to win the Bengali voters exclusively by the ideological appeal of Hindutva clearly failed to generate support which means that what normally worked in the Hindi heartland would not be effective in West Bengal. It was also a failure to comprehend the complex Bengali mindset that generally privileged, at least, in the open, the so-called secular politico-ideological preferences. So the BJP poll managers were unable to comprehend, let alone meaningfully address, the specificities of the socio-economic and cultural priorities that were likely to help them develop a stable support base in West Bengal. Here too, the attempt to parachute a model from elsewhere which was hardly organically linked with the ground reality did not work. Hence, the ideological language that the BJP resorted to while mobilizing voters did not seem to have had any impact on them. The AITC rival performed relatively better in some of the districts in North Bengal bordering Bangladesh and being affected by the infiltration of people from across the border presumably because BJP's Hindutva narrative effectively garnered votes for the party; otherwise, it failed to breach the AITC fortress in the rest of West Bengal. The lesson from the 2021 West Bengal Vidhan Sabha election is that 'while Hindutva politics of BJP has mastered the politics of caste, it still hasn't cracked the code of beating the politics of regional-linguistic and cultural pride'.[12] In a nutshell, it can be argued that the import of models from elsewhere may not always be an effective tool in mobilizing voters unless they are adapted to the distinctive sociocultural milieu of the province. Hence, it has been argued that

a dissection of the poll results doesn't support the argument that the BJP's fundamental political approach is flawed. It indicates that the party needs to deepen its local roots and focus on internalizing a narrative that incorporates particularities. For the energy it demonstrated in the campaign, the BJP needs to acquire additional social depth in a state where political assumptions are being turned upside down.[13]

In other words, disregard of the Bengali *ashmita* by the BJP accounted for its defeat in most of the constituencies which also denotes that the AITC had also won because of the dislike that the voters expressed for the BJP by casting votes against their candidates.

With AITC's impressive victory, it is also evident that BJP's time-tested ideological design of pan-Indian Hindu consolidation by resorting largely to the politics of communal polarization cannot be universally valid. By winning more than 70 per cent of seats in an assembly of 294 members, Mamata Banerjee has proved that her commitment to Bengali *ashmita*

[12] Ibid.

[13] Swapan Dasgupta, 'Lessons Learnt: The Results of the West Bengal Assembly Elections Deserve a Close Analysis', *The Telegraph*, Kolkata, 13 May 2021.

was adequate to halt BJP's forward march in other states in India. Banerjee's simplicity in dress (wearing only white crumpled sari) and use of rubber slipper endears her to the ordinary citizens who feel easily connected with her that helps build her image as one of them. In elections, this image pays dividends to the party which also justifies the argument that when the voters vote for the AITC, they do not vote for the candidate, they support the candidates since they belong to the political party that Mamata Banerjee leads. In a democracy, a leader-centric party is likely to give rise to an authoritarian personality simply because there hardly remains a voice of opposition. Hence, B. R. Ambedkar warned in his speech in the Constituent Assembly that complete surrender to the Almighty leads one to realize salvation or *moksha*; but in politics, unconditional submission to the leaders creates conditions for the rise and consolidation of dictatorial ruler.[14] Nonetheless, a casual survey of the regional leaders reveals that in most of the Indian provinces where regional parties govern, the leader reigns supreme. This is certainly a deviation from the classical description of democracy, which, by discarding the hegemonic voice of the leaders, establishes a specific mode of governance with collective responsibility.

With the stopping of the BJP juggernaut by a regional party, many have started surmising that it was the beginning of the fall of the BJP and the rise and consolidation of political forces which are capable of devising a politico-ideological alternative at the national level. The surmise seems to be absurd as history suggests. The clamour for anti-Congressism in the 1967 assembly elections mainly in the Hindi heartland led to the growth of many political parties that were opposed to the Congress; later on, a national alternative was crystallized with the formation of the Janata Party government in 1977, followed by the Janata Dal government in 1989. The widely hyped Third

[14] B. R. Ambedkar's speech in the Constituent Assembly, 25 November 1949, *Constituent Assembly Debates*, (New Delhi: Lok Sabha Secretariat, 2004), 976.

Front experiment remained ephemeral. Only the BJP-led NDA that came to power in 1999 lasted full term; it was replaced by another coalition, the UPA, at the aegis of the pan-Indian Congress Party which also completed two terms of five years each. BJP's slogan of creating a Congress-*mukt* Bharat (India free from Congress) yielded results in 2014 and the BJP along with its NDA partners formed the union government which also comfortably won the 2019 parliamentary elections. The purpose of the above discussion is to argue that without a pan-Indian party in its fold, no coalition is likely to last, as history has shown. Despite the fact that AITC's success is scintillating, it is too early to suggest that the forces opposed to the BJP are likely to cobble up a successful coalition though the possibilities cannot be ruled out. Several over-enthusiastic media persons, thus, commented that an effective bond among the regional satraps is capable of successfully displacing a well-entrenched national player, like the BJP. Conceptually, it is conceivable provided another pan-Indian party, the Congress, gains enough strength to lead the conglomeration which does not seem possible now given the liquidation of the party in Kerala, Assam and West Bengal. Nonetheless, the Congress is still the one that has presence across the country though it is not adequate to rise as a formidable partner in immediate future due to many factors, including the issue of leadership and visible organizational weaknesses in many of the provinces where it has been in the saddles of authority. The punchline of the entire story is, thus, twofold: on the one hand, the West Bengal mandate has shattered the illusion of the invincibility of the BJP under the stewardship of the Modi–Shah duo. Along with this, it has also been persuasively established that the ideological appeal of Hindutva does not seem to be universal presumably because of the disparate socio-economic and cultural texture of India as a polity. On the other hand, the landslide victory of one regional party (the AITC) in one of the 29 constituent provinces of federal India is surely illustrative of the triumph of democracy in India although it is not a guarantee of the consolidation of an alternative ideological voice at the national level. Therefore, there are reasons to believe that the halting of an organized ideological force, with adequate support of the national leaders, by a well-entrenched regional political party is not a mean achievement in a country with just 70 years of experience of democratic governance. Conceptually, apart from discarding the one-size-fits-all theoretical format, the 2021 West Bengal Vidhan Sabha election adds to the democratic theory by emphasizing the criticality of the prevalent socio-economic context and politico-ideological preferences in comprehending the intricate nature of post-colonial democracies.

Bibliography

Bibliographical Note

Bibliography is integral to any academic monograph for two reasons: on the one hand, by listing some of the principal texts on the theme, it helps the future researchers to get acquainted with the available literature; it is, thus, a useful aid for further research. By allowing the researchers an easy access to the already published texts, a bibliography is, on the other, more than a mere list of books or other relevant academic tracks. Fundamental here is the point that a bibliography is unavoidable for any of the academic endeavours simply because it serves as a useful tool for research.

The following bibliography may not exactly be pertinent to the theme that the book dwells on, namely the conceptualization of the constantly changing texture and nature of democracy in India by focusing on the national elections, held so far. This is not exactly a study of the election per se, but one that seeks to understand democracy in India from the vantage point of elections. Basic here is the argument that elections are not mere battles for winning power, they are also indicative of the changing character of electoral politics since they were introduced in India in 1952. Keeping in mind the specific focus of this book, the list is prepared. Of course, there are texts dealing with the nature of democracy that has flourished in postcolonial India by defying the classical theorists' apprehension that it was unlikely to strike roots here given India's inherent sociocultural diversity.

Books and Published Articles

Adeney, Katharine, and Lawrence Saez. *Coalition Politics and Hindu Nationalism*. Oxford: Routledge, 2005.

Austin, Granville. *The Indian Constitution: The Cornerstone of a Nation*. New Delhi: Oxford University Press, 1966.

———. *Working a Democratic Constitution: A History of the Indian Experience*. New Delhi: Oxford University Press, 1999.

Bajpai, Rochana. 'Constituent Assembly Debates and Minority Rights.' *Economic & Political Weekly* 35, no. 21–22 (27 May 2000).

———. *Debating Difference: Group Rights and Liberal Democracy in India*. New Delhi: Oxford University Press, 2011.

Basrur, Rajesh M. ed. *Challenges to Democracy in India*. New Delhi: Oxford University Press, 2009.

Basu, D. D. *Introduction to the Constitution of India*. Gurgaon: LexisNexis, 2015.

Berlin, Isaiah. *Four Essays on Liberty*. New York, NY: Oxford University Press, 1969.

Bernstein, James. *Dawning of the Raj: The Life and Trials of Warren Hastings*. Chicago, IL: Ivan R. Dee, 2000.

Bhagwati, Jagdish, and Arvind Panagariya. *India's Tryst with Destiny: Debunking Myths That Undermine Progress and Addressing New Challenges*. Noida: Collins Business, 2012.

Bhargava, Rajeev, ed. *Politics and Ethics of the Indian Constitution*. New Delhi: Oxford University Press, 2008.

Bhatia, Gautam. *Offend, Shock or Disturb: Free Speech under the Indian Constitution*. New Delhi: Oxford University Press, 2016.

Bombwall, K. R. *Indian Constitution and Administration*. Ambala Cantt: Modern Publication, 1978.

Bose, Sumantra. *Transforming India: Challenges to the World's Largest Democracy*. New Delhi: Picador India, 2013.

Brass, Paul. Language, *Religion and Politics in North India*. Cambridge: Cambridge University Press, 1974.

———. *The Politics of India since Independence*. Cambridge: Cambridge University Press, 1994.

Bussell, Jennifer. *Clients and Constituents: Political Responsiveness in Patronage Democracies*. New Delhi: Oxford University Press, 2019.

Chakrabarty, Bidyut. 'BR Ambedkar and the History of Constitutionalizing India.' *Contemporary South Asia* 24, no. 2 (2016): 133–148.

———. 'BR Ambedkar: A "Rebel-Liberal" in the Gandhian Universe.' *Indian Historical Review* 23, no. 2 (2016): 289–315.

———. *India's Constitutional Identity: Ideological Beliefs and Preferences*. Oxford: Routledge, 2019.

Chakrabarty, Dipesh. *Provincializing Europe: Postcolonial Thought and Historical Difference*. New Delhi: Oxford University Press, 2000.

Chandhoke, Neera. *Rethinking, Pluralism, Secularism and Tolerance*. New Delhi: SAGE Publications, 2019.

Chandra, Kanchan, ed. *Democratic Dynasties: State, Party and Family in Contemporary Indian Politics*. Cambridge: Cambridge University Press, 2016.

Chatterjee, Angana P., Thomas Blom Hansen, and Christophe Jaffrelot, eds. *Majoritarian State: How Hindu Nationalism Is Changing India*. London: C Hurst & Co, 2019.

Chaube, Shibanikinkar. *Constituent Assembly of India: Springboard of Revolution*. New Delhi: Manohar, 2000.

Chaube, Shibanikinkar. *The Making and Working of the Indian Constitution*. New Delhi: National Book Trust, 2009.

Chiriyankandath, James. 'Creating a Secular State in a Religious Country: The Debate in the Indian Constituent Assembly.' *Commonwealth and Comparative Politics* 38, no. 2 (2000): 1–24.

Chopra, Pran, ed. *The Supreme Court versus the Constitution: A Challenge to Federalism*. New Delhi: SAGE Publications, 2006.

Chowdhury, Sujit, Madhav Khosla, and Pratap Bhanu Mehta, eds. *The Oxford Handbook of the Indian Constitution*. New Delhi: Oxford University Press, 2016.

Conniff, James. 'Burke and India: The Failure of the Theory of Trusteeship.' *Political Research Quarterly* 46, no. 1 (1993): 291–309.

Dalmia, V. *Nationalism of Hindu Traditions: Bharatendu Harishchandra and Nineteenth Century Benaras*. Delhi: Oxford University Press, 1997.

Dasgupta, Jyotirindra. *Language, Conflict and National Development.* Berkeley, CA: University of California Press, 1970.

Dasgupta, Sandipto. 'A Language which Is Foreign to Us: Continuities and Anxieties in the Making of the Indian Constitution.' *Comparative Studies of South Asia, Africa and the Middle East* 34, no. 2 (2014): 228–242.

Dasgupta, Swapan. *Awakening Bharat Mata: The Political Beliefs of the Indian Right.* Gurgaon: Penguin, 2019.

De, Rohit. *A People's Constitution: The Everyday Life of Law in the Indian Republic.* Princeton, NJ: Princeton University Press, 2018.

Devare, Aparna. *History and the Making of a Modern Hindu Self.* New Delhi: Routledge, 2011.

Dirks, Nicholas. *Castes of Mind: Colonialism and the Making of Modern India.* Princeton, NJ: Princeton University Press, 2001.

Doniger, Wendy, and Martha C. Nusbaum, eds. *Pluralism and Democracy in India: Debating the Hindu Right.* New York, NY: Oxford University Press, 2015.

Dworkin, R. *A Matter of Principle.* Cambridge, MA: Harvard University Press, 1986.

———. *Freedom's Law.* Cambridge, MA: Harvard University Press, 1986.

———. *Law's Empire.* Cambridge, MA: Harvard University Press, 1986.

———. *Taking Rights Seriously.* Delhi: Universal Law Publishing House, 1999.

Elangovan, Arvind. 'The Making of the Indian Constitution: A Case for a Non-nationalist Approach.' *History Compass* 12, no. 1 (2014): 1–10.

———. 'Constitutionalism, Political Exclusion, and Implications for Indian Constitutional History: The Case of Montague-Chelmsford Reforms (1919).' *South Asian History and Culture* 7, no. 3 (2016): 271–288.

———. 'Provincial Autonomy, Sir Benegal Narsing Rau, and an Improbable Imagination of Constitutionalism in India, 1935–38.' *Comparative Studies of South Asia, Africa and the Middle East* 36, no. 1 (2016): 66–82.

———. 'The Road Not Taken: Sir Benegal Narsing Rau and the Indian Constitution.' In *Decolonization and the Politics of Transition in South Asia,* edited by Sekhar Bandyopadhyay. New Delhi: Orient BlackSwan, 2016.

Gajendragadkar, P. B. *Law, Liberty and Social Justice.* Bombay: New Age Printing Press, 1965.

Galanter, Marc. 'Who Are the Backward Classes?' *Economic & Political Weekly* 13, no. 43–44 (28 October 1978).

Galanter, Marc. *Competing Equalities: Law and the Backward Classes in India*. New Delhi: Oxford University Press, 1984.

———. *Law and Society in Modern India*. New Delhi: Oxford University Press, 1997.

Government of India. *Indian Round Table Conference 12 November, 1930–19 January, 1931: Proceedings*. London: HM Stationary Office, 1931.

Gudavarthy, Ajay. *Maoism, Democracy and Globalization: Cross-currents in Indian Politics*. New Delhi: SAGE Publications, 2014.

Guha, Ranajit. *Dominance without Hegemony: History and Power in Colonial India*. Delhi: Oxford University Press, 1998.

Hansen, Thomas Blom. *The Saffron Wave: Democracy and Hindu Nationalism in Modern India*. New Delhi: Oxford University Press, 1999.

Hansen, Thomas Blom, and Christophe Jaffrelot, eds. *The BJP and the Compulsions of Politics in India*. Delhi: Oxford University Press, 1998.

Hasan, Zoya. *Politics of Inclusion: Castes, Minorities and Affirmative Action*. New Delhi: Oxford University Press, 2009.

Hasan, Zoya, E. Sridharan, and R. Sudarshan, eds. *India's Living Constitution: Ideas, Practices, Controversies*. Ranikhet: Permanent Black, 2002.

Hayek, F. A. *The Constitution of Liberty*. Chicago, IL: University of Chicago Press, 1978.

Jacobsohn, Garry. *The Wheel of Law: India's Secularism in Comparative and Constitutional Context*. New Delhi: Oxford University Press, 2003.

———. 'Constitutional Identity.' *The Review of Politics* 68, no. 3 (2006): 361–397.

Jaffrelot, Christophe. *The Hindu Nationalist Movement in India*. New Delhi: Viking, 1993.

———. *India's Silent Revolution: The Rise of the Low Castes in North Indian Politics*. Ranikhet: Permanent Black, 2003.

———. *Dr. Ambedkar and Untouchability: Analysing and Fighting Caste*. Ranikhet: Permanent Black, 2005.

Jayal, Niraja Gopal, ed. *Democracy in India*. New Delhi: Oxford University Press, 2001.

———. *Citizenship and Its Discontents: An Indian History*. Ranikhet: Permanent Black, 2013.

Jayal, Niraja Gopal, ed. *Reforming India: The Nation Today*. Gurgaon: Penguin, 2019.

Kalelkar Commission. *Report of the Backward Classes Commission*. New Delhi: Government of India, 1956.

Kashyap, Subhash C. *The Indian Constitution: Conflicts and Controversies*. New Delhi: Vitasta Publications, 2010.

———. *Our Constitution: An Introduction to India's Constitution and Constitutional Law*. New Delhi: National Book Trust, 2015.

Khilnani, Sunil. *The Idea of India*. London: Hamish Hamilton, 1997.

Khosla, Madhav. *The Indian Constitution*. New Delhi: Oxford University Press, 2012.

King, Robert D. *Nehru and the Language Politics of India*. New Delhi: Oxford University Press, 1997.

Komireddi, K. S. *Malevolent Republic: A Short History of India*. London: C Hurst & Co, 2019.

Krishnaswami, Sudhir. *Democracy and Constitutionalism in India: A Study of the Basic Structure Doctrine*. New Delhi: Oxford University Press, 2009.

Kumar, Aishwary. *Radical Equality: Ambedkar, Gandhi and the Risk of Democracy*. Stanford, CA: Stanford University Press, 2015.

Kumar, Ravinder. 'Gandhi, Ambedkar and Poona Pact, 1932.' *South Asia: Journal of South Asian Studies* 8, no. 1 (1985): 87–101.

Kymlicka, Will. *Multicultural Citizenship: A Liberal Theory of Minority Rights*. Oxford: Clarendon Press, 1995.

———. *Politics in the Vernacular*. Oxford: Oxford University Press, 2001.

Larson, Gerald. 'Mandal, Mandir, Masjid: The Citizen as an Endangered Species in Independent India.' In *Religion and Law in Independent India*, edited by Robert D. Baird. New Delhi: Manohar, 1993.

———. *Religion and Personal Law in Secular India: A Call to Judgment*. Bloomington, IN: Indiana University Press, 2001.

Legg, Stephen. 'Dyarchy: Democracy, Autocracy and the Scalar Sovereignty of Interwar India.' *Comparative Studies of South Asia, Africa and the Middle East* 36, no. 1 (2016): 44–65.

Ludden, David, ed. *Contesting the Nation: Religion, Community and the Politics of Democracy in India*. Philadelphia, PA: University of Pennsylvania Press, 1996.

Mahajan, Gurpreet. *Identities and Rights: Aspects of Liberal Politics in India*. New Delhi: Oxford University Press, 1998.

Maharaj, Ayon. *Infinite Paths to Infinite Reality: Sri Ramakrishna & Cross-cultural Philosophy of Religion*. New Delhi: Oxford University Press, 2018.

Mehrotra, S. R., and Dinyar Patel, eds. *Dadabhai Naoroji: Selected Private Papers*. New Delhi: Oxford University Press, 2016.

Mehta, Uday Singh. *Liberalism and Empire: India in British Liberal Thought*. New Delhi: Oxford University Press, 1999.

Metcalf, Thomas R. *Ideologies of the Raj*. Cambridge: Cambridge University Press, 1998.

Michelutti, Lucia. *The Vernacularization of Democracy: Politics, Caste and Religion in India*. New Delhi: Routledge, 2008.

Mukherjee, Mithi. 'Justice, War and Imperium: India and Britain in Edmund Burke's Prosecutorial Speeches in the Impeachment Trial of Warren Hastings.' *Law and History Review* 23, no. 3 (Fall 2005): 589–630.

Mukherjee, Ramkrishna. *The Rise and Fall of the East India Company*. New York, NY: Monthly Review Press, 1974.

Naoroji, Dadabhai. *Poverty and Un-British Rule in India*. London: S. Sonnenschein, 1901.

Nehru, Jawaharlal. *An Autobiography*. London: John Lane the Bodley Head, 1941.

———. *The Discovery of India*. Reprint, New Delhi: Oxford University Press, 1989.

Noorani, A. G. *Constitutional Questions in India: The President, Parliament and the States*. New Delhi: Oxford University Press, 2000.

Nussbaum, Martha C. *Political Emotions: Why Love Matters for Justice*. Cambridge, MA: The Belknap Press of Harvard University Press, 2013.

O'Hanlon, Rosalind. *Caste, Conflict and Ideology: Mahatma Jotirao Phule and Low Caste Protest in Nineteenth-century Western India*. Cambridge: Cambridge University Press, 1985.

Omvedt, Gail. *Cultural Revolt in a Colonial Society: The Non-Brahmin Movement in Western India, 1873–1930*. Bombay: Scientific Socialist Educational Trust, 1976.

———. *Dalits and the Democratic Revolution: Dr Ambedkar and Dalit Movement in Colonial India*. New Delhi: SAGE Publications, 1994.

Oommen, T. K. 'Religious Nationalism and Democratic Polity: The Indian Case.' *Sociology of Religion* 55, no. 4 (1994): 455–472.

Rau, Benegal Narsing. 'Outlines of a New Constitution, 1946.'
Reproduced in *The Framing of India's Constitution*, edited by
B. Shiva Rao, vol. 1. Delhi: Universal Law Publishing House,
1967.

Parekh, Bhikhu. *Debating India: Essays on Indian Political Discourse.*
New Delhi: Oxford University Press, 2015.

Petit, Philip. *Republicanism: A Theory of Freedom and Government.*
Oxford: Oxford University Press, 1999.

Philips, Anne. *The Politics of Presence*. Oxford: Clarendon Press,
1995.

Philips, C. H. *The East India Company, 1784–1834*. Manchester:
Manchester University Press, 1961.

Prakash, Gyan. *Emergency Chronicles: Indira Gandhi and Democracy's
Turning Point*. Gurgaon: Penguin, 2018.

Prasad, Ganesh. 'Whiggism in India.' *Political Science Quarterly* 86
(1966): 11–19.

Pylee, M. V. *Constitutional Government in India*. London: Asia
Publishing House, 1965.

Rajagopal, Arvind. *Politics after Television: Hindu Nationalism and
the Reshaping of the Public in India*. Cambridge: Cambridge
University Press, 2001.

Ramnath, Kalyani. 'We the People: Seamless Webs and Social
Revolution in India's Constituent Assembly Debates.' *South
Asia Research* 32, no. 1 (2012): 57–70.

Ram-Prasad, C. 'Hindutva Ideology: Extracting the Fundamentals.'
Contemporary South Asia 2, no. 3 (1993): 285–309.

Rao, Shiva. *The Framing of India's Constitution*. 5 vols. New Delhi:
Universal Law Publishing Company, 1968.

Rathore, Akash Singh. *Indian Political Theory: Laying the Ground
Work for Swaraj*. Oxford : Routledge, 2017.

Rege, Sharmila. *Against the Madness of Manu: BR Ambedkar's
Writings on Brahmanical Patriarchy*. New Delhi: Navayana
Publishing, 2013.

Roover, Jakob De. *Europe, India and the Limits of Secularism*. New
Delhi: Oxford University Press, 2015.

Rosenfeld, Michel. *Affirmative Action and Justice: A Philosophical
and Constitutional Enquiry*. New Haven, CT: Yale University
Press, 1991.

———. *Mapping Citizenship in India*. New Delhi: Oxford University
Press, 2010.

Roy, Anupama. *Citizenship in India*. New Delhi: Oxford University Press, 2016.

Roy, Srirupa. *Beyond Belief: India and the Politics of Postcolonial Nationalism*. Durham: Duke University Press, 2007.

Rudolph, Lloyd, and S. H. Rudolph. *The Realm of the Public Sphere: Identity and Policy*. New Delhi: Oxford University Press, 2008.

Saez, Lawrence. *Federalism with a Centre*. New Delhi: SAGE Publications, 2002.

Sampath, Vikram. *Savarkar: Echoes from a Forgotten Past, 1883–1924*. Gurgaon: Penguin, 2019.

Saxena, Rekha. *Situating Federalism: Mechanisms of Intergovernmental Relations in Canada and India*. New Delhi: Manohar, 2006.

Sen, Amartya. *Development as Freedom*. New Delhi: Oxford University Press, 1999.

———. *The Argumentative Indian: Writings on Indian History, Culture and Identity*. New York, NY: Picador, 2005.

———. *Identity and Violence: The Illusion of Destiny*. London: Allen Lane, 2006.

———. *The Idea of Justice*. New York, NY: Allen Lane, 2009.

———. *Collective Choice and Social Welfare*. Reprint, New Delhi: Penguin, 2017.

Sen, Mamta Chitnis. *Realpolitik: Exposing India's Political System*. New Delhi: SAGE Publications: 2020.

Sen, Sarbani. *The Constitution of India: Popular Sovereignty and Democratic Transformations*. New Delhi: Oxford University Press, 2007.

Seth, Sanjay. 'Rewriting Histories of Nationalism: The Politics of "Moderate Nationalism" in India, 1870–1905.' *American Historical Review* 104, no. 1 (February 1999): 95–116.

Sharma, Brij Kishore. *Introduction to the Constitution of India*. New Delhi: Prentice Hall of India, 2005.

Sharma, Jyotirmaya. *Hindutva: Exploring the Idea of Hindu Nationalism*. New Delhi: Penguin, 2003.

———. *Terrifying Vision: MS Golwalkar, the RSS and India*. New Delhi: Penguin, 2007.

Smith, D. E. *Nehru and Democracy: The Political Thought of an Asian Democrat*. Calcutta: Orient Longman, 1958.

Somanathan, Rohini. 'Assumptions and Arithmetic of Caste-based Reservations.' *Economic & Political Weekly* (17 June 2006).

Sowell, Thomas. *Affirmative Action around the World: An Empirical Study*. New Haven, CT: Yale University Press, 2004.

Stokes, Eric. *The English Utilitarians and India*. Cambridge: Cambridge University Press, 1959.

Sutherland, Lucy. *The East India Company in Eighteenth-century Politics*. Oxford: Clarendon Press, 1962.

Tilly, Charles. *Durable Inequality*. Berkeley, CA: California University Press, 2002.

Topdar, Sudipa. 'Duties of a "Good Citizen": Colonial Secondary School Textbook Policies in Late Nineteenth-century India.' *South Asian History and Culture* 6, no. 3 (2015): 417–439.

Tripathi, P. K. 'Free Speech in the Indian Constitution: Background and Prospect.' *Yale Law Journal* 67, no. 3 (1958): 384–400.

Upadhyaya, Prakash Chandra. 'The Politics of Indian Secularism.' *Modern Asian Studies* 26, no. 4 (1992): 815–853.

Vajpeyi, Ananya. *Righteous Republic: The Political Foundations of Modern India*. Cambridge: Harvard University Press, 2012.

Van der Veer, Peter. 'God Must Be Liberated! A Hindu Liberation Movement in Ayodhya.' *Modern Asian Studies* 21, no. 1 (1987): 283–301.

———. *Religious Nationalism: Hindus and Muslims in India*. Berkeley, CA: University of California Press, 1994.

Varshney, Ashutosh. 'Contested Meanings: India's National Identity, Hindu Nationalism and the Politics of Anxiety.' *Daedalus* 122, no. 3 (1993): 227–261.

———. *Ethnic Conflict and Civic Life: Hindus and Muslims in India*. New Haven, CT: Yale University Press, 2002.

Venkatesan. *Constitutional Conundrums: Challenges to India's Democratic Process*. Haryana: LexisNexis, 2014.

Verma, Vidhu. *Non-discrimination and Equality in India: Contesting Boundaries of Social Justice*. Oxford: Routledge, 2012.

Weiner, Myron. 'The Political Consequences of Preferential Policies: A Comparative Perspective.' *Comparative Politics* 16, no. 1 (1983): 35–52.

———. 'The Struggle for Equality: Caste in Indian Politics.' in *The Success of India's Democracy*, edited by Atul Kohli, 193–225. Cambridge: Cambridge University Press, 2001.

Williams, Melissa. *Votes, Trust and Memory: Marginalised Groups and the Failings of Liberal Representation*. Princeton, NJ: Princeton University Press, 1998.

Wilkinson, Steven. *Votes and Violence: Electoral Competition and Ethnic Riots in India*. Cambridge: Cambridge University Press, 2004.

Zachariah, Benjamin. *Developing India: An Intellectual and Social History, c. 1930–50*. New Delhi: Oxford University Press, 2005.

Zavos, John. *The Emergence of Hindu Nationalism in India*. New Delhi: Oxford University Press, 2000.

Zeillot, Eleanor. *From Untouchable to Dalit: Essays on the Ambedkar Movement*. New Delhi: Manohar, 1996.

Unpublished PhD Dissertations

Dasgupta, Sandipto. 'Localizing the Revolution.' Unpublished PhD diss., Columbia University, 2014.

Elangovan, Arvind. 'A Constitutional Imagination of India: Sir Benegal Narsing Rau amidst the Retreat of Liberal Idealism (1919–1950).' Unpublished PhD diss., University of Chicago, 2012.

About the Authors

Bidyut Chakrabarty is Vice-chancellor of Visva-Bharati, Santiniketan. He was a professor in the Department of Political Science, University of Delhi, until November 2018. He completed his PhD from London School of Economics and has been associated with teaching and research for more than three decades. He has taught in several prestigious educational institutions, such as the London School of Economics; Indian Institute of Management Calcutta; Monash University, Melbourne; National University of Singapore; and Hamburg University, Hamburg. He has authored several textbooks and academic books. Among his publications are *Sociopolitical Thought of Rabindranath Tagore* (SAGE, 2020), *Public Administration: From Government to Governance* (2017), *Winning the Mandate: The Indian Experience* (SAGE, 2016), *Communism in India: Events, Processes and Ideologies* (2014), *Indian Politics and Society since Independence: Events, Processes and Ideology* (2008) and *The Governance Discourse: A Reader* (2008).

Rajendra K. Pandey is Associate Professor, Department of Political Science, Chaudhary Charan Singh University, Meerut, Uttar Pradesh. Besides earning his masters, MPhil and doctorate degrees from the University of Delhi, he also holds the prestigious postgraduate diploma (with *summa cum laude*, excellent grade) in federalism, decentralization and conflict resolution from the Institute of Federalism, University of Fribourg, Switzerland. In the past, he taught graduate students at Delhi College of Arts and Commerce and Hindu College; both University of Delhi and Centre for Federal Studies, Jamia Hamdard University, New Delhi. His major publications, both authored and co-authored include: *Indian Government and Politics* (SAGE, 2008), *Modern Indian Political Thought: Text and Context* (SAGE, 2009) *Local Governance in India* (SAGE, 2019), *Reconceptualising Indian Democracy: The Changing Electorate* (SAGE, 2020) and *Disaster Management in India* (SAGE, 2020).

Index